Praise for Peter Kerasotis

"I've known Peter personally and professionally for most of my career. Dealing with media daily, I've never met a writer more prepared or thorough. He makes sure readers get the complete story! His passion for his story and writing are unparalleled."
  Bruce Bochy
  Manager San Francisco Giants
  2-Time World Series Champion

"After dealing with members of the media for the past 20-plus years, it's easy to say that Peter knows how to write a story so that the reader will understand it completely. Peter is the most gifted and talented guy I know, and it has been a pleasure knowing him both professionally and personally during the course of my career."
  Tim Wakefield
  Boston Red Sox
  2-Time World Series Champion

"Peter Kerasotis is a great author and writer. His style immediately draws you in and takes you on a wonderful journey. Whenever you see his byline, know that you're about to embark on something special."
  George Raveling
  Naismith Memorial and College Basketball Hall of Fame
  Director of International Basketball for Nike

"I look for Peter Kerasotis articles. He is tough but fair. He digs for details that complete the story. It is never about him, it is about the story. Enjoy, Peter is a rare breed today."
  Cris Collinsworth
  Former NFL star and 14-time Emmy Award winner

"When you read Peter Kerasotis, and have banked a solid depth of respect for his accuracy, experience, judgment and ability to recognize a quality story, you plunge into his words with confidence that this is going to be a feast for the eyes, the mind and the heart."
  Hubert Mizell
  8-time Florida Sportswriter of the Year
  National Columnist of the Year 1982

Praise for *Once a Coach, Always a Coach: The Life Journey of Thomas Errol Wasdin*

"A fascinating story that captures an incredible life. This book grabbed my attention from the first page and kept it there. I thought I knew Tom Wasdin, but this biography revealed him in ways that had me reading non-stop. A terrific job by a terrific writer about a terrific man."
Artis Gilmore
Naismith Memorial and College Basketball Halls of Fame

"Masterful writing from a masterful storyteller. In the hands of Peter Kerasotis, Tom Wasdin's life story is engaging, absorbing and entertaining. His reporting on the 1970 NCAA National Championship basketball game is alone worth the price of admission."
Pat Williams
Orlando Magic Co-Founder and Senior Vice President
Author of *Coach Wooden's Greatest Secret*

"Peter Kerasotis has written a richly detailed biography, which includes a thoroughly reported account of a very important time and place in the history of college basketball. I enjoyed this jaunt down memory lane, and I have no doubt any college basketball fan will enjoy it as well."
Seth Davis
Sports Illustrated Senior Writer
Author of *Wooden: A Coach's Life*

"This is a fascinating book, one that provides us with the opportunity to discover the backstory of collegiate basketball in the late '60s – the Elite Establishment, its disdain for unconventional teams, coaches, players and thinking. It's a journal of one man's look at the game from a player, coach and business perspective. Coach Wasdin's story, told in the hands of Peter Kerasotis, invites readers on an exciting journey of discovery of how basketball positively influenced his life. It's a story worth being told. It's a must-read."
George Raveling
Naismith Memorial and College Basketball Halls of Fame
Director of International Basketball for Nike

"The chapter of Tom Wasdin's recovery from 'The Beast' is a riveting, well-paced thriller. With his each spoken word, swallow of food or gentle touch to the face came devastating pain. His path to overcome it is an affirmation of faith over adversity. The story is spiced with Wasdin's dry wit that often emerges at his moments of greatest desperation. If you've ever had a twinge of pain and then another, then bargained for it to stop, read Tom Wasdin's story. What you learn from it may someday save a life."
   Jeffrey A. Brown, MD
   Neurological Surgeon

"A wonderful book about a wonderful man, mentor and coach. Peter Kerasotis did a masterful job capturing Tom Wasdin's life journey, as well as all the lives he touched, influenced and shaped. This is an inspiring biography about a man who continues to inspire others."
   Ron Sellers
   National College Football Hall of Fame

"Tom Wasdin was a cracker with swagger, a coach cooler than his hippest player, an irresistible salesman in all he did. His life is a story of a modernizing South and a still broken amateur athletic system."
   Steve Pajcic
   Attorney and former Florida State Legislator

"Tom Wasdin recruited awesome talent, and then he and Joe Williams unleashed it on an unsuspecting establishment. The result was a magical period of time in Jacksonville University's basketball history. This beautifully written biography is full of insight, warmth and truth. I couldn't put it down."
   Mike Patrick
   ESPN Broadcaster

"This is a life story that needed to be told, and now needs to be read. If you want to be inspired and engaged, then pick up this biography. But be prepared, because you won't be able to put it down."
   Cliff Ellis
   1999 Associated Press National Coach of the Year

Also By Peter Kerasotis

Stadium Stories: Florida Gators

ONCE A COACH ALWAYS A COACH

The Life Journey of Thomas Errol Wasdin

Peter Kerasotis

WingSpan Press

Copyright © 2014 by Peter Kerasotis

All rights reserved.

No part of this book may be reproduced or transmitted in any form or by any means, electronic or mechanical, including photocopying, recording or by any information storage and retrieval system, without written permission from the author, except for the inclusion of brief quotations in review.

Published in the United States and the United Kingdom
by WingSpan Press, Livermore, CA

The WingSpan name, logo and colophon are the trademarks of WingSpan Publishing.

ISBN 978-1-59594-524-2 (pbk.)
ISBN 978-1-59594-682-9 (hardcover)
ISBN 978-1-59594-863-2 (ebk.)

First edition 2014

Printed in the United States of America

www.wingspanpress.com

Library of Congress Control Number: 2014934714

1 2 3 4 5 6 7 8 9 10

DEDICATIONS

This book is for Susie, for her love, her assistance and for making my life happy and rewarding through all the ups and downs.
Tom Wasdin

For Shelley ... for everything.
Peter Kerasotis

Contents

Foreword: Once A Coach, Always A Coach iii
1. Is This The End? 3
2. Growing Up Waldo 8
3. A Boy Becomes A Man 20
4. Fifteen Miles To The Future 36
5. A Merging Of Magic 48
6. A New Opportunity Launches Along The Space Coast 67
7. A Big Role On The Big Stage 83
8. Twin Towers 99
9. Writing A Few Paragraphs On The Pages Of History 111
10. Answering The Question: JU Who? 139
11. This Time, Goliath Won ... With Some Help 146
12. The Spotlight And The Shadow Of Success 175
13. Life After Artis 200
14. A Last Hurrah And A Long Goodbye To Coaching 212
15. A Clean Break From Basketball And A Fast Break Into Business .. 226
16. Another Bend Along The Road Of Life 243
17. Remembering Old Roots While Establishing New Ones 254
18. In Battle With A Beast 268
19. Leaving Footprints Along The Space Coast 286
20. Public Service, Politics And People 294
21. The Personal Touch 313
22. The Long Sunset 319
Wasdinisms 329
Personal Testimonials 331
Acknowledgements 340

Foreword

ONCE A COACH, ALWAYS A COACH

In the 1990's, I was asked to be a speaker at Leadership Brevard, a leadership organization that trains future leaders for Brevard County, Florida. I was speaking to a class of college students that would be our future business leaders on "how to win friends and influence people" and "how to become a leader." Judge Frank Pound, who I had known for many years, introduced me and stayed to hear my presentation to the class. After the class, he said to me that he really enjoyed my talk and he asked if I had ever considered writing a book on the topic of my presentation and on my life. He said he thought my organized and common sense approach would be a very valuable tool for people. I didn't think much about it at the time. Years later, after the encouragement of my family and some of my friends, I decided to have someone write a book on my life. It was fortunate that we chose Peter Kerasotis to write my life story. This book is Peter's version of my life's journey.

As I look back on my life, I realize that I have learned so much from my family, my players and my friends. To those who have helped me, I will always be grateful. Most of the success I have had I owe it to them. The coaches I coached with and the players I coached probably had the most influence on me during the early part of my career as a coach and a businessman. The things we learned were the foundation on which I built my coaching and business philosophy.

This book is a reflection on how some of my business associates, my friends, my family, my players and I remember the past. I am sorry for one reason or another we did not get to interview more people. If this book offends anyone, I apologize. It was not our intent. In my life

I have made a lot of decisions, some good and some bad. When I made bad decisions, I have tried to learn from them and not make the same mistakes over again. If some of my mistakes have hurt anyone, I am sorry. I have not lived a perfect life, far from it.

I am under no false illusions on the importance of this book. The most important reason this book was written was so my family may learn about me and also learn something from my mistakes and successes. The second reason the book was written was so we could tell the Trigeminal Neuralgia (TN) story. Hopefully it will help others not give up in their search to find a cure for this awful disease. I have had some very difficult times in life dealing with the disease of TN. If this book can help one person find a cure and not have to experience what I did in finding a cure for TN, it's worth it. Because of my faith in God, even during my darkest moments, I never gave up in my search for a cure. I thank God I found relief.

I have really enjoyed reliving my life through the many interviews that were conducted in preparation for writing this book. I thank them for their time and patience.

I give thanks to:

Aunt Estelle and Uncle Wilbert Gunter for their everlasting love.

Joe Williams for hiring me at Jacksonville University and also being a lifelong friend.

Artis Gilmore and the others players for coming to Jacksonville University and putting us on the map.

Rick Stottler for what I learned from him and for giving me the opportunities in business.

Peter Kerasotis for his patience and many hours spent writing this book.

I give a very special thanks to my wonderful and talented wife, Susie, for playing such an important role in making my life very rewarding and happy.

Thomas Errol Wasdin
January 6, 2014

Once a Coach
Always a Coach

Chapter 1

IS THIS THE END?

"The world looks a lot different when you think you're going to die."
– *Tom Wasdin*

Some call it Suicide Pain. Others call it the Suicide Disease. Either way, the common denominator is suicide.

Tom Wasdin knew this academically, even intellectually ... but now his thoughts shifted to reality. His reality.

In his research into the disorder, the medical name of which is Trigeminal Neuralgia, or TN, Wasdin once read that it was the 16th century's leading cause of suicide. Of course, nobody knows for sure, since there is no way of documenting such things. Even today, nobody knows how many people suffer – and suffer is a mild word – from Trigeminal Neuralgia, much less how many people it drives to suicide.

Wasdin never thought he'd be one of them, but there he was one sunny spring day in 1998, just a couple of months after his 62nd birthday, driving from his Merritt Island high-rise condominium to his pastor's office in Suntree, where he found himself sitting next to Dr. Gary Spencer.

"What does the Bible say about suicide?" Wasdin asked.

Dr. Spencer's eyes flickered with surprise and then narrowed with obvious concern. He looked at Wasdin, looked at him in a way he'd never done before. This was more than a pastor-parishioner relationship. The two men played golf together, enjoyed social gatherings together. As he focused on Wasdin, Dr. Spencer saw something he'd not seen before.

"He was very somber. The tone in his voice, the look in his eyes, everything about him was serious. It wasn't Tom. Not the Tom that I knew. This was a man who was always upbeat, positive, jovial. I'd never seen him down. And now he's asking me about suicide."

As he measured Wasdin, Dr. Spencer gave him the only answer he knew.

"The Bible doesn't address suicide," he said as he searched his friend's face for further clues; a face pulled taut by the disorder that had taken control of Wasdin's life, and now threatened to take that life. "The Bible does say in the Ten Commandments that 'thou shall not kill.' It also says God values every person and cares for us, and he doesn't want anybody to suffer. But it doesn't address suicide."

Wasdin thought for a moment, absorbing the words.

"This pain," he finally said, before pausing again. "I'm telling you, this pain ... there are times if I had a gun I'd shoot myself. Sometimes it goes away for a couple of hours, sometimes a couple of minutes. Gary, I don't know if I can continue with this thing."

As Wasdin spoke, his mouth barely moved. In the 23 years he suffered from the Trigeminal Neuralgia, he'd gotten used to talking this way, and people had gotten used to seeing him this way. Everyone, that is, except his wife Susie, who hadn't seen him smile that wonderful smile in years, and it pained her. She noticed. But to others, it had become imperceptible, so skilled had Wasdin become with minimizing any kind of facial movement, because of the way it would trigger the beast that is Trigeminal Neuralgia and the unbearable pain it inflicts. Sufferers say it's like feeling a charley horse coming on and trying to catch the gathering cramp, stretching your leg before it grabs hold. But there is no stopping TN. And when it does grab hold, it grabs hold, not of one's leg, but the side of the face, the searing pain most times surging throughout the entire head.

Dr. Spencer knew Wasdin was dealing with a disorder, but he didn't know the extent of it, or even its name. But now he had a parishioner, a friend, inquiring about suicide, and so he soon learned more about Trigeminal Neuralgia.

TN is a neuropathic disorder that affects the six branches of nerves – three on each side of the face – that pair with the cranial nerve and travel across the face. It causes an equal opportunity pain, reaching into the ears, eyes, lips, nose, scalp, forehead, cheeks, teeth and/or the jaw. Sufferers describe the pain in different ways – like being stabbed about the face and head with a fiery ice pick, like being submerged in boiling water, like a sustained electrical shock running from the face into the brain. Medical professionals say it's one of the most painful conditions known to humans.

As the two men talked in Dr. Spencer's office, a painting of a smiling Jesus beamed down at them. The pastor preferred the painting over ones depicting the Messiah being crucified. He felt the vibrancy it conveyed better matched his own personality, and his outlook on life. Perhaps it's also why the pastor and Wasdin had become friends. He liked Tom for the same reasons he liked that painting, and had enormous respect for him. Rather than ever really noticing the pain Wasdin suffered from, Dr. Spencer instead saw a vibrant man in full vitality, even though he was approaching his mid-60s. "This was a man who embraced life, who took it on," he said. Dr. Spencer saw a strapping, broad-shouldered fellow, handsome, with sandy brown hair and an athlete's gait and presence. And then there was Susie, his beautiful wife and partner in life.

Tom Wasdin had it all, and more. Or so it seemed.

Wasdin, Dr. Spencer also knew, was a community leader, a successful businessman, a developer worth multimillions of dollars, and a generous philanthropist; someone widely admired and respected. In his younger years, he'd been a winning basketball coach. He was the man who once recruited and coached future Naismith Memorial Basketball Hall of Famer Artis Gilmore to Jacksonville University. And then, as an assistant coach, he helped the 1970 Dolphins advance all the way to the NCAA Championship Game against the mighty, John Wooden-coached UCLA Bruins. It was the ultimate David vs. Goliath story, and it captivated the nation. It also epitomized Wasdin's own life, a serial overachiever, someone who routinely slew Goliaths by outworking, out-planning and out-hustling them. This was a man born into the Great Depression, whose mother died when he was an infant, who rose from the hardscrabble farm lands of rural North Central Florida to someone who had pictures hanging in his home of him and Susie standing next to world leaders.

It was quite a journey. Wasdin had accomplished so much, with seemingly so much more to achieve – or overachieve, depending on the point of view. He was, after all, always the underdog, always the guy coaching at the smaller school, working for the smaller business, the guy constantly going against the Goliaths – and winning.

But this Goliath, this Trigeminal Neuralgia, was a giant he couldn't bring down. Sometimes it brought him down. Literally. "There was one time," Susie said, "when he was so delirious from the medication he was on, just trying to control the pain, that he fell and fell hard. He hit his head on the coffee table. It was bad. I lived in constant fear that Tom was going to fall, hit his head again, and die from that."

Nothing seemed to work. As he sat in Dr. Spencer's office, Wasdin told the pastor of the surgeries and procedures he'd had over two decades. Five of the six branches of nerves running across his face had been numbed, effectively killed, in order to kill the pain. The process also left him unable to feel most of his face. When he ate, food would unknowingly dribble out of his mouth. He practically had to learn how to talk again, and this was a man who was a dynamic public speaker. But now Wasdin was down to one good nerve, one nerve that gave him a semblance of feeling in his face. It gave him the faint ability to chew, to talk, to have a sliver of a normal existence.

And now the Trigeminal Neuralgia had hijacked that nerve, too, and the pain was unbearable. Susie used to find comfort when she saw her husband sleeping, because she felt it was a sanctuary, temporarily bringing Tom relief. What she didn't know is how the pain would awaken him, again and again, in the darkest hours of the night. It would jar him upright, that jolt of electrical pain traveling from his face into the recesses of his brain. He didn't complain, but he didn't think he could go on like this. The cure – and nothing was certain – was to deaden the sixth and final nerve. If it worked, it meant the pain would no longer be there. But it also meant Wasdin would be unable to chew food, talk clearly or have any more feeling in his face. It would be like dealing with the aftereffects of a dentist's Novocain, only all over the face, and 24 hours a day, seven days a week, every single day of his life. In short, it wouldn't be a life.

"As we talked, I began to realize that it had to be an incredible amount of pain," Dr. Spencer said. "He shared with me how just moving his jaw, just smiling, could trigger it. I could see it in his eyes; that he was getting to a place where he wasn't going to be able to live the way he wanted to live."

Prior to that meeting, Dr. Spencer, like many people close to Tom, had no idea of the relentless suffering Wasdin was dealing with. He'd only seen a man whom others envied and wanted to trade places with – the exciting history as a basketball coach, the successful business ventures, the millions in wealth, the physical stature and good looks, the smart and attractive wife who was 14 years his junior; a community leader and successful businessperson in her own right.

Yes, this was a man others envied; a man who even in his middle-age years people still called Coach; a man Dr. Spencer thought he knew. But he really didn't. Few did.

Nobody, not even Susie, knew he was there that day to talk suicide. Oh, she'd heard her husband mention once or twice how thankful he was that they didn't keep guns in the house. And she, more than anyone, knew the excruciating pain he lived with. TN hadn't taken away Tom's soul, but for years it had taken away his smile. But she still believed in his overriding optimism and his fighting spirit. She believed in her David. After all, she'd witnessed him so many times overcoming so many Goliaths. Little did she know, though, that Tom was already contemplating a trip to Oregon, where he'd heard something about how they allowed assisted suicide.

Dr. Spencer had seen enough in his years as a pastor to know that what you see and what is really going on can often be two different things.

"I took Tom seriously that day," he said.

They talked more.

"I knew firsthand that the residue suicide leaves is extremely painful," he said. "I made Tom promise that if it ever got close, that he would give me a call. He said he would."

When he left that day, thinking about his life, about the things most important to him – his wife, his family, his health, his standing with God – Tom Wasdin wasn't thinking about the tens of millions of dollars he'd made, the great games he'd coached, the boardroom battles he'd won.

"I couldn't help but think," he said, "that the world looks a lot different when you think you're going to die."

Chapter 2

GROWING UP WALDO

"We were poor, very poor, but we didn't know it. We always had food on the table and clean clothes to wear." – Tom Wasdin

The world Tom Wasdin was born into didn't hold much promise. By the mid-1930s, the Great Depression had ravaged America's terrain, steadily drying up hope. The prospects were even more barren if you were born several miles outside a rural North Central Florida town called Waldo. This is where Thomas Errol Wasdin entered the world on July 30, 1935, barely three months before his mother exited it.

Eddie and Faye Wasdin were farmers; a young couple of little means who were on their way to having a large family. Dorothy arrived first in 1933, delivered on the family farm by a midwife. When Dorothy was barely more than a year old, Faye Wasdin became pregnant with Tom, and he, too, was delivered on the family farm by a midwife. But before the family could grow further, Faye Wasdin fell victim to blood poisoning from an infection that had worked its way into, of all things, a pimple on her face. As her condition worsened and her fever reached dangerously high levels, she was rushed 60 miles northeast to a Jacksonville hospital, where she died, only 20, leaving behind a heartbroken husband and two children too young to have had any memory of her.

It was overwhelming for Eddie Wasdin, just 27. In addition to the everyday work of the farm, he also had to care for two children still in diapers, one a newborn. But what folks of that era lacked in material wealth was often richly made up by family. Just a few hundred yards across a field, walking distance away, were Uncle Wilbert and Auntie

Estelle Gunter, Eddie's sister. The couple badly wanted children, but couldn't conceive. After Faye's death, Eddie's father, who was the original Thomas Wasdin in the family, encouraged his son to take his two small children and move into the Gunter's tiny home, a rectangular structure lifted off the ground by blocks, barely 600-square feet with a fireplace and a wood stove in the kitchen. It had no running water, no electricity, no heat in its two bedrooms and no indoor plumbing. What it did have, though, was love, and lots of it.

The days turned into weeks, the weeks into months and eventually Eddie moved back into his farmhouse while little Dorothy and Tom stayed with Uncle and Auntie. It just seemed better that way – for everyone.

Tom Wasdin's mother, Faye Wasdin, who died of blood poisoning when she was 20. Tom was only three months old at the time. Shortly afterward, he and his sister Dorothy moved in with their Uncle Wilbert and Auntie Estelle Gunter, who raised them.

Once a Coach, Always a Coach

Tom Wasdin's paternal grandparents, Essie and Thomas Wasdin.

Dorothy and Tom loved their life with Uncle and Auntie, especially because they sensed they were deeply loved. "We were poor, very poor," Tom said, "but we didn't know it. We always had food on the table and clean clothes to wear."

Still, it was a hard life. After doing his homework next to the bright glow of a kerosene lamp, Tom slept in the home's closed-in front porch, where in the wintertime frigid winds whistled through cracks in the wood. The only remedy was more blankets, piled on until Tom was mummified; not wanting to emerge when the cocks began crowing before daylight. In the summertime, it was the opposite, with the heat so suffocating Tom could feel streams of sweat rolling across his ribs that poked against his flesh. Inside the house, Uncle and Auntie had a small bedroom, as did Dorothy. In the back was an open porch. Once a week during colder months, on Saturday night so as to be fresh for church the next morning, water was heated and poured into a galvanized tub that was brought into the kitchen, where one by one each family member bathed. Outside, a barrel held about 10 gallons of water with a hose protruding from it – a farmer's version of a shower for when the weather was warmer. Burlap bags provided a measure of privacy. Farther away was the outhouse.

The Gunter farm was primarily a chicken farm, but "we also had fresh vegetables, lots of good food," Tom said. "Because it was a chicken farm, we ate a lot of fried chicken, chicken gizzards, chicken liver, and we always had eggs. If it was a special occasion, we'd have pot roast. It was very Southern. We drank a lot of sweet tea and lemonade. Since we also had cows, we always had fresh milk and homemade butter. A typical breakfast was eggs, bacon, biscuits, honey and grits. Auntie made the very best biscuits."

What the Gunters also provided the young Wasdin children with were values. Uncle Wilbert was a deacon in the First Baptist Church of Waldo – "a Christian's Christian," Tom said. Life revolved around the church, and Uncle was a regular at the deacons' meetings. Tuesday night was choir practice. Wednesday night was a prayer meeting. Thursday night was visitation night, particularly if someone was sick. And Sunday? Sunday was an all-day affair at church, starting with Sunday school, then the church service. Later in the day was the Baptist Training Union and evening service. Tom attended all the weekly activities, never missing one until his senior year in high school, when there was a rare football game on a Wednesday night, which conflicted with the usual Wednesday night prayer meeting. Since Uncle drove the team bus to all the games, he happened to miss that night, too.

Dorothy and a young Thomas Wasdin, right, shortly after their mother died and about the time they moved in with their Auntie Estelle and Uncle Wilbert.

"The values I received growing up," Tom said, "I don't know if I could've gotten better values."

He realizes that now, just like he now realizes how many life lessons he learned during his youth. One lesson he learned early and often was the value of hard work, a trait that later served him well as a successful basketball coach and then as a multimillionaire developer. These weren't always easy lessons, though. Once, as a young boy of about 12, while noticing the free time some of the other children had, especially on weekends, Tom began feeling sorry for himself, and he expressed it. For him, work was constant, beginning early in the morning before school.

"Nobody loves me," he whined to his uncle, starting to cry. "I can't go fishing. I can't go swimming. All I do is work."

Tom was cleaning one of the chicken houses that day, a Saturday, getting it ready for new chickens. His sobs grew stronger. Uncle looked at him for several seconds and then broke off a switch from a nearby bush.

"I'll give you something to cry about," he said with an even tone, before administering about a dozen whacks. When Uncle stopped, he let the boy cry a little more until the whimpers subsided. Then he pulled Tom close to him and said, "Son, I don't want to spank you. I love you. Someday, you'll appreciate what I'm doing for you. When you have your own kids, you'll understand. You'll realize that you were one of the most loved children in the world."

Then he pulled the boy closer, hugging him.

"I love you," he said again.

The boy nodded, wiped his eyes. Then the two went back to work.

Years later, Tom realized that the winds of the Great Depression, and all the hard work he and his family did to overcome it, were always blowing at his back throughout his life. The work ethic he learned as a youngster served him well.

And to be sure, there was a lot of work to do. Between Uncle and Daddy's farms, there were chickens, eggs, cows, hogs, turpentine gathered from pine trees, beans, corn, squash, tomatoes, pecans, watermelons and other assorted produce. Chickens were cleaned and often sold to restaurants. Produce was hauled to Jacksonville in a truck, to be sold either at the Farmers' Market or the A&P grocery store. On those days when the truck came to pick up chickens, Tom would rise at 3 a.m. and groggily feel his way into the coal-black chicken house. Once there, usually with the headlights of the family truck providing some needed light, he'd gather and crate chickens for morning delivery, dodging hanging feeders and stumbling over water trays. Then he'd feed the other chickens. It was a lot of work. After all, Uncle's chicken coops could house 10,000 chickens a year. When Tom was done and the sun started to peek into sight, he'd get ready for school.

Uncle paid Tom about $2 to $4 a week for doing his chores. "I always remembered how hard it was to earn it, so I was reluctant to spend it," he said. "I also remembered little expressions like, 'You don't go broke making a profit.' 'A dollar saved is a dollar earned.' 'You always spend less than you make, and that will take care of your finances.'"

It was all good, but it was those two main things – the value of hard work and the comfort of always having money in his pocket – that proved to be a pair of veins Tom mined throughout his life.

Waldo in the 1940's provided other lessons, as small towns often do. And it was definitely a small town, about 12 miles northeast of Gainesville, where the University of Florida sat. Waldo's population was approximately 800 people, with those who resided in town called "townies", and those who lived in the outlining farm areas, as the Wasdins and Gunters did, known as "country." When Tom was in junior high school the big news one day, both in town and in the country, was about how Mansel Ayers, who played on the high school football team, had been drinking and wrecked his car, missing a curve when he was returning to town from Ocala. Ayers almost killed himself and his girlfriend. The remains of his crumpled car were hauled to a local garage, where the townspeople stopped by to view it as if it were an open casket.

"It was totaled, just wrecked completely," Tom said. "It made a lasting impression on me about drinking and driving."

Yes, sometimes fate was fueled by alcohol. Sometimes it was prodded in other ways. And sometimes it just happened – inexplicably and unforeseen. Tom had an uncle named Gordon, his mother's half-brother, who had a paper route as a boy. Gordon was a cautious youngster, but one foggy morning while delivering the *Gainesville Daily Sun* on his bicycle, riding along Highway 26, a hit-and-run driver struck and killed him. The police later found the man who had done it. It was, after all, hard for the man to hide in nearby Gainesville, especially with a car suddenly damaged, with clumps of hair on it. The tragedy, and the sadness that engulfed his family, made Tom more careful when he got his first bicycle, a Sears Western Flyer, one of only two bikes he owned during his childhood. Uncle bought it for him when he was about 7. His only other bike was a Schwinn that Tom bought with his own money later as a teenager, purchasing it at Beard Hardware on the square in Gainesville.

Though he had cried and complained about all the work he had to do early in his youth, Tom did like the money it put in his pocket. He also didn't want to give Uncle and Auntie much trouble. He learned early that it wasn't worth it, and that he hated to disappoint them. Even at a very young age Tom was a people pleaser, seeking approval, a trait that has stayed with him throughout his life. He also quickly learned that if he got in trouble at school, the news would arrive home before he did, even though there were neither phones nor electricity to carry the message.

As he got older, he appreciated that work was a part of everyone's life. It wasn't uncommon for the family to gather at Tom's grandparents' house, where they would have a family hog killing, or perhaps make cane syrup together. "We called them work parties," Tom said. "We'd get together with relatives, family, friends and we'd work together. Everybody donated their time and then got a part of what we did, whether it was some of the meat or the syrup. We considered those work parties to be social events."

It wasn't always work, though. There was play time. When they were real little, Dorothy and Tom created a world of their own under the back corner of their house, beneath the dining room. In that little corner they built their own town, one where metal toy cars traveled across dusty roads before pulling up to houses made of dirt. For hours, the cute boy with the dishwater blond hair played with his older sister, absorbed in their make-believe world.

There was laughter, too, like the time one Sunday morning when Tom was dressed for church, antsy and full of a boy's boundless energy, barely paying attention to his surroundings. Suddenly, he backed into the galvanized bathtub that was still in the kitchen, toppling into the cold water. "When he got out, he was completely drenched," Dorothy said.

They laughed then, and they still laugh now.

Another time, when Dorothy and Tom were staying at Daddy's house, Tom awoke in the middle of the night needing to use the bathroom. Instead of having to navigate in the evening blackness to an outhouse, most families, like the Wasdins, kept a slop bucket handy. Tom relieved himself in the bucket, only to learn the next morning that it was the milk bucket.

Again, it was another event the family laughed at whenever they recalled it in the coming years.

Some events, however, were more fraught with drama. Clothes were not easy to come by during the Great Depression. Auntie was constantly darning socks and patching holes. She even made shirts for Tom and dresses for Dorothy out of the cotton bags that once contained chicken feed, which came in attractive floral and other print and textured designs. So it was a bit alarming when one winter night, while playing with something on the mantel above the fireplace, Dorothy's coat caught fire. By the time it could be put out, it was ruined. "You just did what you had to do and moved on," she said. "Life happened."

It was a life slowly emerging with new technology. Nobody in Waldo had a TV. They weren't even invented yet. But cameras were around. Tom was about three when he saw his first one. Timid for a family photo, he kept hiding behind Uncle. He was a shy boy in general, and while Uncle and Auntie were the best parents he could've had, he was painfully aware that he didn't have the woman who'd given him life. Maybe that's what drove him during his youth and later as an adult – to work harder, to do more, to make a name for himself, to want acceptance and to be liked. He doesn't know. All he knows is the pain he occasionally felt, knowing he didn't have what other children had.

"I'd be sad sometimes because I didn't have a mother," Tom said. "I had Uncle and Daddy. I had an Aunt, and I knew she loved me. But I didn't have my mother. I'd cry sometimes because I'd hear other kids talk about their mothers. 'Mom this, mom that.' It hurt."

By the time Tom was four, Daddy had gotten remarried to a woman that he and Dorothy called Miss Edna. They also got a stepsister, Greta

Fay, and eventually four half-siblings – Erlene, Shirley, Jerry and Arvita. Tom and Dorothy visited Daddy regularly, and he was always good to them, but his home was never their home. "It was always more like we were guests," Tom said.

When he was set to start school, Tom didn't want to go. Waldo High School housed all the children in the area, grades 1 through 12. All totaled, there were about 120 kids. His first day, Tom was intimidated. Actually, he was frightened. Then he saw a face from church, his friend that he knew as Fred Jr., a skinny kid who stammered. His father, Fred Donaldson Sr., owned the local grocery store. "Once I saw Fred Jr., a familiar face, I was okay," Tom said. "I never minded going to school after that."

The two friends progressed through each grade together, eventually graduating to nearby Gainesville, where they became Kappa Sigma fraternity brothers at the University of Florida. But that was a long ways away. There was still a childhood to live and more hard times to endure. If it wasn't bad enough growing up in the deep shadow of the Great Depression, there was the historical event that visited the United States when Tom was just 6. Tom and Uncle were driving back from Waldo one chilly winter day in the family truck, a Chevrolet Model A with the cabin removed and a flatbed rigged in the back. The truck had a windshield, but no doors. Country roads were dirt and narrow. When another car approached, it was customary to slow down and lean off the road with your two side tires, allowing the other vehicle to pass in the same manner. But nobody passed without first stopping to chat. That wouldn't be neighborly. On this day, the talk from the passing car was excitable.

"The Japs just bombed Pearl Harbor!"

At Daddy's house that night, Dorothy and Tom's father hushed them when the news scratched across the family's battery-powered radio. It was a Sunday night, a time when they usually visited their father and stepmother. Daddy was known to be a prankster, jovial. But he sternly quieted the family as his face tightened, leaning it into the voice emanating from the radio, the news now seeming more official as it crackled across the dining room.

"The expression on Daddy's face was suddenly serious," Dorothy said. "There was just this heavy atmosphere. You could feel it. I'm sure what was running through Daddy's mind is if he would have to go to war."

Eddie Wasdin didn't. But life around Waldo began changing, as it also did around the country during the 1940's. The war brought jobs for scores of local people, particularly at a nearby training station known as Camp Blanding, where there suddenly was work building barracks for thousands of soon-to-be soldiers-in-training. "They hired carpenters at Camp Blanding and paid them $1 an hour," Tom said. "Meanwhile, farm labor was about 20 cents an hour." Camp Blanding gradually expanded, consuming 170,000 acres while serving not only as a training center, but as an induction center, a separation center and a German prisoner of war compound. Some 800,000 soldiers received all or part of their training there.

Tom was just six when war was declared, the conflict in Europe shifting into the overdrive that came to be known as World War II. He was still too young to fully understand. He was just a boy starting school; starting his life. He countered the world's seriousness by quickly developing a love for recess – "my favorite subject," he would often joke later in life. As he grew, recess turned into what would become a lifelong passion for sports. By the time Tom reached his high school years, he liked to say, "If I couldn't shoot it, pass it, dribble it or date it, I wasn't interested in it." Sports, school, church, chores. "That was my life," he said, "but mostly sports and church. Sports because I wanted to and church because I didn't have a choice."

It was a stable life. The Gunters only moved once, when Tom was 12, going from the tiny 600-square-foot house to a home a little more than twice as large that had indoor plumbing and a stand-alone garage. The house sat on 40 acres of land. More importantly, it sat near the two-lane road that was Highway 301, which meant the family could now get electricity. The home also had three bedrooms, which meant Tom didn't have to sleep on the front porch anymore. Around the same time, Tom's father became the first man in Waldo to own a tractor. Prior to that, Eddie Wasdin worked his crops the old-fashioned way – behind a mule. Even with the modern convenience of a tractor, and other societal advancements, it was still an innocent and simple time, with families huddling around crackling radios at night, listening to programs like Amos 'n' Andy, The Shadow, Captain Midnight, The

Once a Coach, Always a Coach

The house Tom Wasdin moved into when he was 12. It was the first time he lived in a house with indoor plumbing and electricity. It sat on 40 acres of land off Highway 301, just outside of Waldo, Florida.

Lone Ranger and The Green Hornet. Then one day, Tom saw the future of communications at an appliance store in Gainesville, something that would change the world – a snowy black-and-white television set, able to broadcast the one station from Jacksonville.

Like millions of other boys around the country, television animated Tom's curiosity, making him more aware of a bigger world, one that he wanted to explore. He loved Waldo, but he knew he'd one day want more than what the small rural town could provide. There were times when he couldn't wait to grow up. In fact, in some ways he was growing up faster than most boys. When Tom reached the 8th grade, he was already showing precocious athletic abilities. At the request of a local fellow named Floyd "Sonny" Tillman, Tom joined a town baseball team, playing second base. Not only was he the youngest player on Sonny's team, he was the youngest player in the league. He liked Sonny, and saw something in him. "Sonny was best friends with my Uncle Ralph, so I knew him fairly well," Tom said. "Sonny was a thinker, a guy who'd organize things, someone who always had ideas on how to do things."

Years later, their lives intersected in Brevard County on the East Coast of Central Florida, where Tom was Cocoa Beach High's basketball coach and Sonny worked as a cook at Fat Boys' Bar-B-Q restaurant in Cocoa. It was during that time in the late '60s when Sonny assessed the operation at Fat Boys' Bar-B-Q and thought to himself, "I can do better than this." So he decided to give it a try, opening his first restaurant at the corner of 520 and US1 in Cocoa. But it was in Gainesville, fittingly located on Waldo Road, where he officially opened the first restaurant that he would call Sonny's Real Pit Bar-B-Q. It later became a franchise, and it made Sonny a multimillionaire. Tom, too, would one day become a multimillionaire, with both men also becoming University of Florida boosters. Sonny never went to college, but UF would be Tom's alma mater.

First, though, there was high school to attend, where sports took greater shape in molding a life that was only beginning.

Chapter 3

A Boy Becomes A Man

"I knew there was more to life than there was in Waldo." – Tom Wasdin

From the time boys are old enough to talk, adults ask them what they want to be when they grow up. Little boys think they know, but of course they don't really. Usually, it isn't until they reach their high school years when clearer ideas form. And that's what happened with Tom Wasdin. But for him, those years weren't so much about framing a picture of his future. Instead, it was the opposite.

"Mostly, I was figuring out what I *didn't* want to do," he said. "And I knew that the one thing I didn't want to do was farm."

Even in rural North Central Florida the world was expanding for him during those post-World War II years. Tom was coming of age and becoming aware of an emerging world of popular culture and of people doing things other than raising crops and chickens.

"I knew there was more out there than what there was in Waldo," he said, even though he loved the small town he grew up in and always cherished the happy upbringing he had.

But he still wanted to see more, to experience it and to live it.

Tom found himself drawn to the voices crackling from the family radio. The news intrigued him, especially political news. On WRUF radio, he followed the Democratic Party race for U.S. Senator between two men who seemed so different – the young George Smathers and the old Senator Claude Pepper. It began a lifelong interest and eventual involvement in politics. Newspapers also were ubiquitous. Everyone in Waldo got a newspaper. Tom usually read the *Jacksonville Journal*, an afternoon newspaper. It is how he kept up with sports, particularly his favorite baseball teams, the Boston Red Sox and Cleveland Indians, and the great players both franchises fielded; players like Ted Williams, Bob Feller, Lou Boudreau, Early Wynn, Bob Lemon and Larry Doby. That new invention called the television, with one station beaming in from Jacksonville, gave Tom glimpses of the world and of other sports, like boxing. The Wednesday night fights sponsored by Pabst Blue Ribbon beer were a favorite for him and his friends, as were the boxers, men like Joe Louis, Rocky Marciano, Kid Gavilan, Sugar Ray Robinson, Jersey Joe Walcott and Rocky Graziano.

Many Saturdays, the family went into Gainesville to shop. It was only about a half-hour drive from the back roads and farm fields of Waldo, but Gainesville was a world bright and vibrant with activity, indicative of a college town. The University of Florida was the hub of everything in Gainesville, the school Tom would eventually matriculate at. But as a boy growing into manhood, he noticed other things beyond a formal education that shaped his thinking. In Waldo, Tom had begun to see the nicer things in life. For instance, at Margaret Ann's Grocery Store, he saw expensive meats like sirloin and ham. But all of that was larger, bigger and better in Gainesville.

In Gainesville, Tom saw other boys in the downtown square, selling food items, and it impressed him. Tom always had money in his pocket, and his trips to Gainesville usually included stops at Sears, Woolworth's, McCrory's and Beard Hardware Store. At the Woolworth's lunch counter, he liked to get a sandwich and a drink. He especially liked that he could eat a filling meal for less than a dollar. But Tom kept noticing the boys his age selling parched and boiled peanuts at a nickel a bag. After he bought a bag of peanuts, eating them as he walked through town, throwing the hulls in the street, he thought: "Here I was spending money, and they were making money. That impressed me. Not only was I impressed that people were making money, but I'd see the new cars, nice stores, people wearing nice clothes. People were eating at nice restaurants, and they had the finer things money could buy." At Gainesville's Florida Theatre, Tom saw his first movie, "Song of the South," and he soaked in the Hollywood glamour, and it reinforced in his mind that "there was something better out there."

How to get from Waldo to where Tom wanted to be seemed to also include Gainesville. Though he never considered himself a good student, or really very interested in education, he could see the importance of it if he wanted to have the kind of future he was getting glimpses of from the radio, newspapers and television; not to mention from family trips to Gainesville and Jacksonville. He saw a little bit of that from Waldo, too, when he regularly observed college students disembarking at the train station, carrying their suitcases and an air about them of something exciting. And even though Tom knew he didn't want to farm for the rest of his life, he saw from farming the importance of having a measure of intelligence. His father, Eddie Wasdin, was an astute businessman, one of Waldo's most successful farmers, a man who had worked his way up to owning hundreds of acres of land.

"He was a smart guy, even though he only had about an 8th grade education," Tom said. "He was good with numbers. I remember how he taught me the difference between compound interest and regular interest, which is something I never forgot."

Tom, too, was discovering that he had an aptitude for numbers. "I liked business courses and really enjoyed a class in general business," he said. "I had two years of algebra, even physics. Having subjects like that in high school was big for a little ol' country town. I took bookkeeping. I also took other courses, things like English, history and social studies. But I really didn't like them. I did enjoy math, though. It seemed to come easier for me. I was much better at non-verbal than verbal."

There were two others things he liked – dating girls and playing sports. Though not always in that order. Even now, Tom likes to tell people that "if I couldn't shoot it, pass it, dribble it or date it, I wasn't interested in it."

It seemed Tom always had a girlfriend, even before puberty, during those earlier years as a boy when having a girlfriend carried a sissy stigma to it. His first girlfriend, back around the 4th grade, was Evelyn Norwood. It was innocent, just two children playing in the schoolyard, building make-believe homes out of Spanish moss. "I liked having a girlfriend, but I didn't want anybody to know it," he said. Later, in high school, having a girlfriend took on a more macho meaning, and Tom's close female friend was one of his classmates, Anita DeSha. "It was about the same time when I was noticing the outside world that I was also noticing girls in a different way,' he said, "and that they were different than boys." It was Anita DeSha who talked Tom into taking a girlfriend of hers from Lake Wales to the senior prom, which was a big affair at a pavilion on the water at Keystone Lake, where the young men and women danced and laughed and sang the lyrics from their favorite Faron Young song: *"You call everybody darling and everybody calls you darling, too."*

Movies went from Walt Disney's "Song of the South" to more adult films that featured sexy sirens like the busty Jayne Russell in "Outlaw," and the cooing Marilyn Monroe.

Tom was about 14 when he learned how to kiss. That first lesson came in the back of Uncle's pickup truck, on a long trip from Highway 301 to US1 and up the coast to Savannah, Ga. Actually, for Tom, it really didn't seem that long, because in the back of the pickup truck was a cabin that Uncle had built, where he sat with his sister Dorothy and Dorothy's friend Betty Jo Koons. At the girls' direction, Tom learned how to pucker his lips and perform grown-up kisses with Betty Jo. "And if you wanted it juicy," he said, "they told me I had to lick my lips."

It was all so innocent. And it wasn't Tom's only interest. Sports had wedged its way into a busy life of school, chores and girls, and Tom was good at it. There had already been an inkling that he might excel as an athlete back in the 8th grade, when he played on a town team assembled by Floyd "Sonny" Tillman, who later went on to establish the chain of restaurants known as Sonny's Real Pit Bar-B-Q. Not only was Tom the team's youngest player, he was the youngest in the league. Just like having a girlfriend or figuring out numbers came natural for Tom, so did sports. Not that he was the best or found it easy to excel at; but Tom found that he had an aptitude for sports and a natural desire to apply himself to improving his conditioning, strength and skills.

When he was 12, and the family moved into the house on the 40 acres of land near Highway 301, it didn't just mean they now had electricity, it also meant that Tom had a basketball goal, built on a dirt patch. It wasn't much, just a post with a wobbly backboard fastened together with 2x8 strips of wood. Sometimes it had a string net, sometimes it didn't. Either way, it didn't matter, because Tom played any chance he had, sometimes spending hours on the dirt court, dribbling, shooting, practicing, honing his skills until the moon started to rise.

"Basketball became my favorite sport because I could play it by myself," he said.

It wasn't the only sport Tom played. There was baseball, of course, and also football and track, where Tom competed at Alachua County track days as a middle distance runner. In a small town like Waldo, it was difficult for any boy to gauge just how good he was, because Waldo High School rarely, if ever, competed against big schools. But for a small-town boy at a small high school, Tom was always one of the better players for his age.

Since Waldo was just a tiny dot on the map, the high school team played 6-man football, which was basically the same as 11-man football, but modified for schools not large enough to field full-fledged teams. It was tackle football, for sure, and players wore helmets without facemasks, which was the norm at the time, along with shoulder and hip pads, and cleats. Though there were several outstanding players on the team, it was Tom who played quarterback, as well as defensive back. Not only did the quarterback position naturally feed into his physical abilities, but it also meshed well with his skills as a leader. Tom was never known for being exceptionally fast, but he was quick and savvy; a heady player with an accurate arm, and it led to impressive individual numbers and an undefeated team record his senior season.

The 1952-53 Waldo High School football team. Standing from left to right: Head Coach Hugh Noe, G.L. Lester, Jimmy Norwood, William Ward, Thomas Wasdin, Fred Donaldson, William Rountree. Kneeling from left to right: Winfield Tillis, Richard Dougherty, Earl Brooker, Milton Miley, Marvin Osteen, Nolan Simmons.

One of Tom's foremost abilities was escaping danger and then throwing on the run, attributes that brought the approval of Coach Hugh

Noe, who named Tom the team captain. It also was no coincidence that Tom was assigned jersey number 77, the same as the great Red Grange, a legendary player during that era who was noted for his ability to both run and throw, and also for the nickname – "The Galloping Ghost."

When it all came together for that exceptional senior season, Tom Wasdin's name grabbed several lines in the record book. He set the national record for most touchdown passes in a season with 26. He set the national record for the highest completion percentage with a minimum of 100 attempts – a staggering 75.9%. He also helped the team finish second in defense, yielding just an average of 6.4 points per game, as well as seventh in the nation in offense, scoring an average of 48.6 points per game.

"I was just a good football player for a very little school," Tom insisted. "Nobody knew I existed except the *Gainesville Daily Sun*."

Even still, the Waldo High Blue Devils finished 9-0, and since they played in the only 6-man conference in Florida, they were the de facto state champions. And while Tom might've thought that nobody outside the nearby Gainesville newspaper noticed him, he did draw interest from Deland's Stetson College as a two-sport player in football and basketball. But then Stetson dropped football, and interest in Tom waned with it. But Tom's interest in sports only increased, especially in his favorite sport – basketball.

As in football, the basketball team had adjustments to make because of Waldo High School's small size. The biggest adjustment was that their basketball court wasn't in a gym. It was outdoors, in a small park in downtown Waldo, right off Highway 301. Fans could watch from two sets of bleachers, or they could drive up and watch from their cars, as if it were a drive-in movie, honking their horns for the home team. The Waldo High Blue Devils played in what was called the Little Ten Conference, and the other schools were Anthony, Summerfield, Bronson, Chiefland, Bell, Hawthorne, Cedar Key, Dunnellon and White Springs.

The basketball team wasn't as dominating as the football team was, but they were plenty good enough, and Tom, who never saw a shot he didn't like (or usually take), was the team's leading scorer. It wasn't uncommon for him to pour in 25 points when the next leading scorers managed only 16 or 18. But just like in football, where they didn't play any bigger schools, the same was usually true in basketball; so it again was difficult to measure one's talent and know exactly just how good you were. Tom did, however, get an inkling of his athletic prowess after a game where he scored 52 points against Newberry High School, which Coach Noe told him was a state record. That was when one of the officials who was also a principal, a fellow known as Tiny Talbot, came to him after the game.

"Are you going to college?" Talbot asked.

"Yes," Tom replied.

"Where?"

"At Florida."

"Are you going to try out for the basketball team?"

"I don't know."

"Well, you're good enough to play for them," Talbot said. "You're better than any freshman they have now. You need to go out for Florida."

Even earlier in his teen years, folks had noticed Tom's basketball abilities. One day, during 8th grade PE, Coach Marvin Hodges observed Tom playing pickup ball on a little clay court and approached him.

"Why don't you come out for the basketball team after school today?" he said.

Tom was thrilled to do so, but he had one problem. He didn't have sneakers with him at school. So after school he quickly went to the nearby Alexander's dry goods store, and bought the only pair of sneakers they had in stock. This is where he encountered another problem. The sneakers were two sizes too small. By the end of practice, his feet were killing him and he could barely run, but he made the team.

"I know your feet are hurting," Coach Hodges told him afterward, noting that he could tell that he was wearing sneakers too small. And then coach told him to be ready for a game the next night against Trenton High School. Tom was ready, or so he thought. When Coach Hodges told him to go into the game with just a few minutes remaining, with instructions to guard a particular player, his nervousness almost overwhelmed him. But natural competitive instincts took over and soon he was regularly coming off the bench for Waldo High, feeling comfortable.

The basketball court in Waldo, Florida, where Tom Wasdin scored 52 points one game his senior year at Waldo High School, setting a state scoring record.

What became uncomfortable was his father's disapproval. Eddie Wasdin thought sports was a waste of time.

"You're ruining that boy," he told Uncle, explaining that the time Tom spent playing sports could be better spent working.

Uncle thought otherwise, so he took young Tom aside and had a talk with him. He explained to the boy that he didn't mind him playing sports, that he thought it was good for him and kept him out of trouble, and that it didn't really cost any money.

"I told your dad that you like it and that you seem to be good at it," Uncle said. "We agreed that you can play sports as long as you do your work. But you've got to do your work first."

And so Tom did. Playing sports never became an issue again, and as Tom continued to grow and improve, more and more people noticed that he stood out from most of his peers, especially during his senior basketball season in 1952-53, when he scored 500 points, averaging 25 per game. Along with Tiny Talbot, other people were telling Tom how well he played, and it was good to hear. But Tom wouldn't allow it to go to his head. Instead, he kept playing hard, trying to improve himself individually while helping his team win.

As in football, Tom was quick on the basketball court, a smart player with an explosive, if not sneaky, move to the basket. He scored a lot of points mainly because of his ball-handling skills and an ability to hoist what some might consider an occasional unconventional shot. These were not unconventional shooting methods to him, though. He had perfected them through years and many hours playing H-O-R-S-E. Tom also had a keen ability to drive to the basket. He knew that the closer you got to the basket, the better the odds were of making a bucket, and he didn't mind mixing it up with bigger players, even though he was average in size at 5-foot-11 and 175 pounds. But whether the opposing team employed the zone or man-on-man defense, it was always difficult for them to prevent the Wasdin kid from knifing through their coverage en route to the basket. Tom combined his quickness with a longer than usual, last-second stride just as a defense was collapsing on him, zipping through several bodies for an easy bucket.

"Sometimes I'd hear Coach Noe holler, 'Don't drive against a zone,' and I'd think, 'Whaddaya mean?'" And then he'd drive against the zone and score, and score and score, and then score some more.

It helped that Tom applied himself to physical fitness. Working on a farm figured into that, but Tom also took extra steps to build his body. The summer before his senior year, he concentrated on getting faster, and he did it the old-fashioned way – by running. Everywhere.

"We'd be working in the chicken house, and Uncle would say, 'Thomas, I need you to get me some 10-penny nails.' The shed was maybe a few hundred yards away, and I would run all-out to it, in a full sprint." And that's the way the summer went – running everywhere. All out. When he showed up to 6-man football practice later that summer, Tom found that he was just as fast as kids who could outrun him a year earlier.

The fastest kid in his class was a boy with a similar background as his. Like Tom, who was known as Thomas to his friends when he was growing up, Marvin Osteen also lost his mother. Unlike Tom, who lost his mother during his infancy, Marvin's mother passed away when he was 14. The Osteen family was large (seven children) and extremely poor. Marvin's father had worked on Eddie Wasdin's farm, but he moved around too. When Marvin's father had the family living in Plant City, Marvin decided to move back to Waldo and support himself during his high school years. For three-and-a-half years he lived in a log cabin behind a truck stop where he also worked. At first, Marvin made $2, and then $3 a week, doing things like mowing the grass with a push mower, pumping gas, painting, waiting on tables, emptying trash ... whatever was needed.

"I was Johnny On The Spot," Marvin said. "The important thing is that I got room and board."

He'd occasionally do work for Tom's father, and he found Eddie Wasdin to be a hard worker and yet a good-natured jokester that most people knew him as. "You'd be riding down the road with him, maybe going to Jacksonville, because I sometimes went there with him to the Farmers Markets, and I'd be about to fall asleep, and Eddie Wasdin would lean over and slap you on the leg and give you a big laugh. But he was a worker, too. He'd buy a brand new truck, but it would be a working vehicle, for sure. He'd drive it through the woods, get it nicked here and there. If there wasn't a clear road, that didn't matter much to Eddie Wasdin. He was always out and about; always doing something and always working."

As much as Marvin liked Eddie Wasdin, he particularly liked Uncle and Auntie, as everyone in Waldo called them; not just Tom and his sister Dorothy.

"I really admired Uncle and Auntie," Marvin said. "They were good, solid people, and great examples for me. They were kind and friendly to everyone, very hospitable. Uncle was a deacon in the church and he drove the school bus, so I was around them a lot."

Of course, Marvin was around them a lot because he was also around Tom a lot. The two became good friends during their high school years together. And just like Uncle and Auntie were good examples to be around, so was their nephew whom they were raising. "Thomas was a really good kid," Marvin said. "He kept his nose clean, he was a good student, and he treated his peers with respect. I don't ever remember him getting into a fight or even arguing with anybody. He was always involved in things, participating, always in church. He was just a nice kid."

The two boys often walked home from school together, and whenever it was time for the Wednesday night fights, Marvin would walk a little over a mile from his house to watch them with Tom. They even double-dated for the senior prom.

But during all those times together, they never talked about the commonality of losing their mothers and then living apart from their fathers.

"I don't know why we never talked about it," Marvin said. "Years later, I think about how we had that in common, although Thomas lost his mother much earlier in life than I did, but for some reason we never discussed it."

Years later, Marvin also sees how there were signs when they were boys that Tom had the type of leadership skills that later propelled him to become a successful basketball coach and then a successful businessman. Marvin, too, became successful in the business world. After serving in the Marines, he put himself through Jones Business College in Jacksonville before a career working for Barnett Bank.

"Now that I look back on it, Thomas was the type of guy who took charge of things," Marvin said. For instance, there were times when Marvin and Tom shoveled chicken manure from one of Uncle's chicken houses, loaded the manure onto the back of a truck, and then hauled it to a farm field for fertilizer. "When we did that, Thomas was the one in charge, even though he wasn't officially in charge. He knew where to go and what to do. He was the leader."

The same held true when the boys played on the football and basketball teams, where Tom's leadership skills were even more evident. "To be a quarterback, you have to be a leader, and that's what Thomas was," Marvin said. "And on the basketball court, Thomas was the guy who brought the ball up-court and ran the plays that coach called. To do that, you also had to be a leader. And he had talent, too. He was a great quarterback, and in basketball he was our best shooter."

But Marvin saw the same things in his friend that young Tom Wasdin saw in himself – that he wasn't the biggest, the fastest or the best athlete among them. But he sure worked hard at it. In addition to doing things like improving his speed by running everywhere he went during the summer before his senior season, Tom also discovered other ways to improve his body – some coming from manual work, and some coming from applying himself to innovative methods. In the summers before each of his high school years, Tom toiled in the watermelon fields, and it was grueling labor. The work was six days a week, starting at 7 a.m. and going hard until sundown. From Mr. Dell, who owned Dell's poultry and had a bad back, Tom learned the proper way to bend from the knees and lift watermelons. If he wasn't lifting them, he was tossing them onto a pair of waiting hands on the truck. Sometimes he was the guy catching and packing the watermelons. As he got older, he was entrusted with driving, and it's how he learned how to drive a tractor trailer and the skill of maneuvering one in reverse. Lifting, throwing and packing watermelons made him stronger. He never lifted a weight until he was in college, but Tom's muscles showed definition through his bronze summer skin. He liked that byproduct of the hard work, but he didn't like the work itself. It was low-skilled labor. In fact, though he was far from racist, Tom couldn't help but notice that he was often the only white guy working in the watermelon fields, which was not a good sign in what was America in the late '40s and early '50s.

"Again, what I was learning was what I *didn't* want to do," Tom said. "And I didn't want to do something the rest of my life that was so physical."

If the muscle definition he was getting from working in the acres and acres of watermelon fields wasn't enough, Tom sent away for Charles Atlas' secrets from an advertisement he saw in the back of a friend's comic book. It was the same ad many boys saw for decades in comic books. It featured young Charles Atlas as a 97-pound weakling who had sand kicked in the face, only to return bulked up with muscles to pummel the offending bully. Nobody was bullying Tom. That wasn't his motivation. His motivation was simply to get bigger, stronger and better for the sports he loved to play. Self-improvement, whether physically or mentally, would be something he'd pursue the rest of his life. What Tom learned from Charles Atlas was the power of dynamic tension; a series of different exercises where a person provides resistance against himself. Tom would go through the exercises every morning when he awoke, and every night before he went to bed. And he would be in bed before 10 p.m., because that was one of the stipulations in the Charles Atlas program.

"I worked harder than most athletes," he said. "I don't think I was a great athlete. I wasn't the best football player on my team. One of my teammates, G.L. Lester, his initials stood for General Lee, was offered a football scholarship to Mississippi State. A couple of guys, Nolan Simmons and Marvin Osteen, were faster. But I think I worked harder than most."

Because of his work in the watermelon fields and the dynamic tension exercises he learned from Charles Atlas, Tom had tight core muscles, a broad, strong back and arms bigger than most boys his age. He was a formidable opponent in arm wrestling, and he could outdo anyone in one-armed pushups. In fact, years later, when he was a young man in the National Guard and stationed in Fort Stewart, Ga., he did 50 one-armed pushups on a challenge from the company commander.

Waldo High School Class of 1953. Standing from left to right: Fred Donaldson, Earl Brooker, Marvin Osteen, Thomas Wasdin, William Ward. Sitting from left to right: Teacher Emily Boring, Evelyn Norwood, Joyce Webb, Anita DeSha.

Nobody else came close to his tally, not even when doing pushups in the traditional two-armed way.

All of it – the hard work around the farm, the discipline of rising

Thomas Wasdin's Waldo High School graduation photo. Class of 1953.

early and working late, the sports, the education – transformed Tom into a well-rounded young man as he graduated from Waldo High School. He had also participated for many years in the Boy Scouts, learning various survival skills as well as solid lessons in citizenship. There were times when he and other Boy Scouts would be dropped off at Cedar Key without adult supervision, where for a couple of days they would fend for themselves with their camping skills. In the Future Farmers of America, Tom learned all aspects of farming and how to judge cattle. He also sang in a quartet, was on the debate team, received instruction in public speaking skills and learned Robert's Rules of Order on how to conduct a meeting.

Mostly, though, he was learning that as much as he loved growing up in Waldo, he wanted more. His father gave him a car when he graduated from high school, a dark green 1946 two-door Ford sedan which he soon painted a fire-engine red. Tom was on his own now, but for the time being he wasn't going to go far. He had decided to go down the road to Gainesville, to pursue a college education at the University of Florida. He briefly toyed with idea of going to work after graduating from Waldo High School in a class of eight students. The summer after his senior year, he worked at W&J's Upholstery Shop and he liked it. It

Tom Wasdin's first car, a 1946 two-door Ford sedan that he painted fire-engine red.

was steady work and the pay seemed good – a dollar an hour. But Uncle had a talk with him.

"If you don't get an education now, you probably never will," he told Tom. "You can always do these other things."

Tom agreed. And now, with his mind made up, he was all set to go to UF. But there was one more conversation he had to have, and this one was with his father, who was pulling Tom in a different direction. Eddie Wasdin took his son and showed him a section of the hundreds acres of land he owned.

"Thomas," he said, pointing, "you see that oak tree over there?"

Tom looked and saw a stretch of farm land where an oak tree stood.

"If you get a good woman and marry her, I'll build you a house on 40 acres of land, and you can help me work the farm. This farm can get a lot bigger with help, and you're a good worker and you don't throw your money away."

Tom thought about it, but he really didn't have to think long.

"Daddy," he said, "I appreciate it, but I'd like to go to college."

Eddie Wasdin must have heard the conviction in his boy's voice, because he didn't say anything more about the farm or the land. Instead, he stuck his hand out and shook the hand of the boy who'd now become a man, saying three words that sent Tom Wasdin off into the future.

"Good luck, son."

Chapter 4

FIFTEEN MILES TO THE FUTURE

"I had this attitude that I can do it. If I relied on self-discipline, drive, motivation, my competitive nature, I can do this. And there was one other thing I knew I had. Those other kids might've been smarter than me, but I knew I could outwork 'em. I guarantee I can outwork 'em."
– Tom Wasdin

From Tom Wasdin's Waldo home to the center of the University of Florida campus in Gainesville was 15 miles. It may as well have been 15 light years. Sure, Tom had gone into Gainesville many times growing up. He even attended several UF football games during his senior year in high school. None of it, however, prepared him for the cultural shock of going from a rural country boy to a student at a major college.

"It changed my life completely," Tom said.

It could've very easily crushed him instead.

From what he observed at the Waldo train station, Tom knew there was something different about college students – the way they dressed, the way they groomed, the way they carried themselves. He knew he was on the outside looking in. He didn't realize, though, until he got to UF that outside was a greater distance than 15 miles.

It wasn't that he was without a plan. Growing up in Waldo, the three most important and influential people were the Baptist minister, the coach and the school principal. He wasn't going to become a minister, and he saw how the coach and principal had nice cars, lived in nice houses, and had good families. He also liked the idea of eventually marrying a teacher and then having summers off to do things together as a family.

So Tom was prepared, and he announced that his major was going to be physical education. What he wasn't prepared for was the reaction he received. "Every time I talked with someone, they were going to be a doctor, or a lawyer or a businessman. When I said that I was majoring in PE, it was, 'Oh, PE. Really?' It certainly didn't bring a sparkle to anybody's eyes. I learned pretty quick that you weren't earning a whole lot of people's respect getting a degree in physical education."

There was another thing he learned – that he had a lot to learn. Not that Tom had gotten a bad education at Waldo High School. It prepared him well for a life in Waldo – farming. It just didn't prepare him for college. Tom hadn't helped himself either. He never really had to apply himself to schoolwork, and so growing up he didn't. When he started attending his first classes, he noticed other students with notebooks, jotting down what the professor was saying. "Not only had I never taken any notes in school," he said, "but I didn't even know how to take notes."

The realization that he was in way over his head came after the first week, when he got his paper back from the writing lab. Students were required to write a two-page story on any non-fiction topic. Tom had never had to write a paper before, and it showed.

"When I got my paper back a week later, it looked like it was bleeding there was so much red ink marked up on it," he said. Out of all the markings, the one that caught his attention was the one at the top of the page – a fat, scarlet U.

"You either got an S for satisfactory or a U for unsatisfactory," he said. "Maybe there were some other students who got a U, but I didn't see any. I didn't show my paper to anybody, but some of the other students showed me theirs. When I read what they wrote I knew it was way beyond my capabilities."

All of it caused Tom to think back to freshmen orientation, just before school started, when UF interim president J. Hillis Miller addressed the incoming students.

"Look to your left," Miller told the freshmen.

Each student looked to the student standing next to him on the left.

"Now look to your right," Miller said.

The students looked to the students standing next to them on the right.

"By this time next year, they probably won't be here," Miller said, concluding the exercise.

The message was clear. Two out of three students would fail out. If that message wasn't clear enough to Tom before school started, it had crystallized for him now. He thought about Uncle, and how he didn't want to disappoint him. He thought about Daddy, and those three insincere words he had sent Tom off to school with – "Good luck, son."

Tom might not have realized it at the time, but whatever he lacked in education and experience, he possessed other traits that he could – and would – tap into. This is where his background in athletics and the discipline of growing up working on a farm came into play.

"I knew I wasn't stupid. I just hadn't applied myself," he said. "Now I'm at a crossroads. Was I going to take the easy way out, or was I going to work at it? I remember thinking to myself, 'I know I can get better at this if I work on it like I did with my athletic skills.'"

This was a boy, after all, who had increased his foot speed the summer before his senior year in high school by disciplining himself to run all-out everywhere he went, and who also had sent away for Charles Atlas' strength training secrets and religiously applied himself to them.

"I had this attitude that I can do it. If I relied on self-discipline, drive, motivation, my competitive nature, I can do this. And there was one other thing I knew I had. Those other kids might've been smarter than me, but I knew I could outwork 'em. I guarantee I can outwork 'em."

He set his mind to do just that. It was competition, and as a lifelong athlete, competition was something he both understood and got natural motivation from. He wasn't without a plan, though. One of the first things Tom did was go to a reading lab and get evaluated. The result was to be expected, given the rural education he'd received in Waldo.

"The reading test that I took evaluated your speed and comprehension," he said. "My reading was slow and my comprehension was average. I knew that if you were slow and average you weren't going to make it." He knew that best, of course, from sports. Tom also came to realize that he read ... one ... word ... at ... a ... time. So he went back to the reading lab, often two and three times a week, for more work and personal help. He bought vocabulary books, did the newspaper crossword puzzles, and purchased other types of puzzle games that challenged his mind and forced him to connect logical thoughts.

"It wasn't long before I doubled my reading speed and improved my comprehension," he said. "Now I was on a more level playing field."

He got organized for his classes, learned how to take notes and fell into studying with students whom he saw were excelling; while avoiding the ones that he could sense were on the road to flunking out.

Still, it was a struggle. In retrospect, it was a mistake to minor in biology. "Sometimes guidance counselors gave me bad advice," he said. "The thinking was, 'You're a farm boy, son. That's botany, biology, trees. You need to minor in biology.' I thought it was a good idea, too, because then I could coach and be a biology teacher. But I soon found out that I was in classes with guys who were pre-med, who knew all about botany, biology, genetics, things like that."

Despite all his efforts and hard work, school was a constant struggle, especially because of the minor in biology. Tom's GPA his freshman year, which was 1953-54, was 1.84. "I don't think people around me knew I was a bad student, because I kept my mouth shut," he said. "I learned that it's better to be thought a fool than to open your mouth and remove all doubts." Maybe his grades weren't as high as other students, but that Wasdin work ethic never wavered. He kept applying himself, kept persevering and kept progressing.

He also integrated himself more and more into the college life, while still keeping one foot firmly planted in the kind of social scene he felt most comfortable with. Instead of dating college girls, which he never did, he dated local girls. Instead of college functions, Tom might instead be found square dancing in Newberry. "In that culture, I was somebody," he said. "In the culture of the University of Florida, I was nobody." Plus, even though he was the type of guy who always had money in his pocket, it wasn't the same money that his fellow students from well-to-do families had.

He felt that the "playing field was a little more level" when he traded in his Ford for a Studebaker, a convertible, baby blue with white leather interior. It was a car that appealed both to the guys and the girls. Mostly, though, the guys liked Tom because he was a good athlete – a physical specimen, really. He was a chiseled 185 pounds, which in the late '50s

America was big enough to play offensive line on UF's football team. What Tom really wanted to do, though, was play basketball for the Gators. It seemed the thing to do to go out for the freshmen team, which Tom did. That didn't mean he didn't play other sports. While trying out for the freshmen basketball team, Tom was also playing 11-man tackle football on the weekends. One weekend, while playing quarterback and trying to run around a defender, Tom took a direct blow on his thigh. It bruised so severely that it even developed a blood clot, forcing him out of action for three weeks. By then, the basketball tryouts were over, leaving Tom with a lifetime of wondering: What if?

Even his old high school coach, Hugh Noe, always wondered what might have been.

Years later, Coach Noe ruminated on his former star player, saying: "Thomas Wasdin was captain and quarterback of the Waldo High six-man football team that was ranked number two in the nation. He set two national records in six-man football. He was an outstanding basketball player and set a state record in basketball that stood for years. If he had not gotten injured, he would have played basketball at the University of Florida. In my opinion, he was better than most of the players at Florida at the time. He was the best all-around athlete to come out of Waldo. I never had a moment of trouble out of Thomas as a player or student. He was a natural leader. I have enjoyed following his career as a coach and businessman."

In his later years at Florida, while playing intramurals, Tom was always one of the leading scorers and one of the best – if not the best – players. He competed against guys who played basketball for UF's varsity team, and knew how his skills matched up. Others knew, too. Once, an AAU referee who also served as an SEC official pulled Tom aside, "There's nobody on Florida's team who can drive to the basket like you," he said. The reason why was because Tom was way ahead of his peers. He had figured out that if you landed on both feet, you immediately had two pivot feet established, creating more options. And because of his years playing H-O-R-S-E, Tom was very creative. Couple that with his quickness, and he was a difficult player to defend, much less stop from driving to the hoop. So even though he never formally played basketball for the Florida Gators, Tom was noticed, and he was definitely known. In fact, years later, when UF basketball coach Jim McCatherin was celebrating his 95th birthday, Tom was at the event, prompting instant recognition from McCatherin.

"There goes the Waldo Flash," the old coach said.

To that, all those years later, Tom flashed a smile.

Still, though Tom was so well-accepted via sports into the college culture, there were times when even playing sports reminded him that he was different from most of his contemporaries. "I didn't dress like them, I didn't talk like them, I didn't act like them," he said. He was reminded of that while playing intramural flag football. As usual, Tom played quarterback. A kid named Julius Byrd was the speedy receiver on the team. Once, when Byrd was streaking downfield on a post route, Tom chucked the football as far as he could, but it came up short. When Byrd returned to the huddle, Tom apologized.

"I throwed it as hard as I could," he said.

Byrd looked at him and laughed.

"*Throwed* it," he said. "What do you mean *throwed* it?"

More than a half-century later, Tom still remembers the exchange.

"He wasn't trying to hurt my feelings," he said. "But I got the message."

As much as sports brought him inside the college culture, he never really was an insider. It was why, when he started school, he felt most comfortable living with Fred Jr., the same boy and familiar face who brought him a sense of ease years earlier on his first day of public school, back in Waldo. The two first lived together in a rooming house and later above the Florida Bookstore on University Avenue across from campus, on the same floor as a barber shop.

Eventually, Tom wanted to join a fraternity, even though doing so reminded him that "I didn't have as much as they had." The flipside of that, however, was that it made Tom even more determined "to one day have what they had."

He had rushed Kappa Alpha as a freshman, though not seriously. They wanted Tom mostly for his athletic skills, and Tom felt comfortable with KA because of its reputation as a Southern fraternity, attracting young men from similar, small-town backgrounds like his. He never pledged Kappa Alpha, but it was where he switched from being called Thomas, as he had been his whole life growing up in Waldo, to simply Tom. It seemed the thing to do, and the shortened name stuck.

The fraternity Tom did join, pledging his freshman year, was Kappa Sigma. Like KA, the Sigs liked Tom's athletic skills, especially since he was all-campus in flag football and basketball, and he was just a good guy to have around.

Tom was branching out in other ways, too, although not by his own volition. ROTC was mandatory, but not the National Guard. If anything, World War II in the prior decade and the Korean War in the earlier part of the '50s convinced Tom that whatever conflict was brewing now in Southeast Asia, he wanted no part of it.

"We all had people who were either killed or injured in World War II," he said. "I had one relative who lost a son in World War II, and she always had a gold star on her front door. That's what you did back then if you lost a family member to the war. It was always there, that gold star, and it always made an impression on me. I knew early on that I didn't want to be in the service."

The National Guard became a happy middle ground, and it also served Tom well. He learned a lot about leadership, which fed into his already natural leadership skills, and he quickly moved up the ranks. He started as a private and finished as a tank commander. Along the way, he learned how a chain of command operates as well as how to give orders, skills that later served him well in coaching and the business world.

But he still had a lot to learn. Some of those lessons came painfully, and stuck with him the rest of his life.

Eventually, Tom's dating of local girls led him to Sharon St. Peter. They met the summer after Sharon's senior year at Gainesville High School. She was pretty, pert, about 5-foot-2, with blonde hair and an outgoing, bubbly personality. She was smart, too. A city girl with a lot of dating experience, whereas Tom was a naive young man fresh off the farm. She'd gotten a scholarship for education and planned to become a teacher one day, which appealed to Tom since he'd always envisioned himself marrying a teacher. Sharon came from a good family. Her dad, Milton St. Peter, owned Gainesville Concrete Block & Supply Company. Soon, Tom was working for Mr. St. Peter. But then again, he was always working. Uncle paid his tuition and gave him $320 a year toward expenses. Tom made up the rest by working at Brownlee Seed & Feed, Dell Poultry and at that backbreaking job of loading watermelons in the summertime.

He once even thought of buying a Tom's Peanut Route – a route that covered Bradford and Alachua counties. What appealed to Tom more than anything was not having to study. Striking out on his own in the business world meant he could leave school and all its stresses behind. So he went to his father and asked for a thousand dollar loan to buy the route, but his father turned him down. "Son," he said, "I don't think it's worth a thousand dollars, and I don't think it's something you'll enjoy doing."

What made working for Milton St. Peter a natural course to take was the fact that three months after he met his daughter Sharon, they were married. It was an abrupt wedding because of the obvious reason that Sharon was pregnant. The wedding came between Tom's junior and senior year. The young couple honeymooned at the Roosevelt Hotel in Jacksonville, and it was the first time Tom ever stayed in a hotel. They were a young couple – too young, really. Tom was only 20 and Sharon 19, and soon trouble arrived. First, though, a baby arrived, one that the young couple named Thomas Wasdin. For a while the marriage was happy. Sharon was good for Tom in that she was an excellent student, and she helped him with his study habits. She also typed his papers and put them smartly into folders that made them look professional. But the young couple was fighting.

"We were too young and too naive to make it work," Tom said.

Yet, he still worked at it, while also working toward a degree and preparing for a future as a coach and educator. He did some student teaching at Buchholz Junior High School, his first formal experience in actual education. And the first time Tom ever coached, it was guiding the University City Kiwanis Little League team, which he did for two baseball seasons. The thought process was that when he graduated and sought a paying job as a coach and teacher, he could point to Buchholz Junior High and the Little League as his hands-on experience.

It was in Little League where Tom learned early coaching lessons that later served him well. "I learned things like how to handle players, how to select a team, how to pick the starters and then tell the other kids they weren't starting without destroying them. I learned to keep players happy, how to play them all while still trying to win. And one of the most important things I learned was how to deal with parents, or they will become your biggest problem."

His natural leadership qualities were coming into play again, even though he didn't realize it at the time. Years later, after a successful career as a high school and Jacksonville University basketball coach, and then as a developer, a letter found its way to his home in Cocoa, Florida. It was from one of his former Little League players who went by the name of Cappy Rappanecker – a kid Tom remembered as someone he instilled confidence into as a pitcher, but didn't think much of it at the time, or even years later, when he got the letter. It didn't start with any formal salutation. Instead, the letter got straight to the point:

> When your name first became prominent in the press as the '70 JU basketball coach, I wondered whether or not you were my Little League coach at University City Kiwanis in the summer of '57.
>
> When I saw that you were a Waldo native, I thought to write. I called a classmate of mine from high school – mainly to find out if you were really you (the coach that I knew). You were. At any rate, I remember quite clearly – after 52 years – your having asked me to throw a few pitches to you. You wanted to evaluate my potential. After three or four pitches, you said, "I just found a pitcher for next year."
>
> Those were very important words to a 10-year-old with a vague reluctance – maybe shyness – to get involved with things. I hit the ground running, as they say, and haven't really looked back.
>
> All of that was important because it gave me the overall confidence in my abilities to the end of being able to successfully compete with anyone. Not that successful competition is the great reward, but that was a model for later-in-life activities.
>
> So I suppose you really were a major contributing factor to my development.
>
> Good luck to you, and thanks.
> Cappy #4

Even though Tom was coaching and molding young lives through sports, he was not done competing himself. He played AAU and city league basketball. He played city league softball. For a time, he played Tobacco League baseball. That was a semipro league similar to what Sonny Tillman, who later founded Sonny's Real Pit Bar-B-Q, had operated with a team from Waldo, when Tom was an 8th grade boy going up against adults.

The first team Tom Wasdin coached was the University City Kiwanis Little League baseball team in Gainesville, Florida. Standing from left to right: Henry Leggett, Ken Ellis, Bill Thompson, Ty McCoy, Robert Stearns, Head Coach Tom Wasdin. Kneeling from left to right: Jeff Williams, Jerry Jones, Bruce Leavitt, Bill Boyd, Ricky Waglow, Cappy Rappernecker.

In a small way, Tom also got involved with something else that would later become a big part of his life – politics. As a boy, he'd been enamored listening to WRUF radio, following the Democratic Party race for U.S. Senator between George Smathers and Sen. Claude Pepper. Now at UF, in his senior year, Tom got involved with student government as a representative for the College of Health, Physical Education and Recreation, and found that he enjoyed it.

At the University of Florida, Tom Wasdin was on the Student Government's Executive Council. He's standing in the back row, second from the right.

His grades also were coming up, to where he eventually graduated with a 3.0 GPA. He was gaining more confidence, learning social skills and integrating more easily with fellow university students. But the marriage to Sharon was falling apart. Within months after Tommy Wasdin was born, Tom and Sharon separated, with Tom spending his last year at UF living in the Kappa Sigma house. Tom and Sharon still saw each other, though, and in 1958, Larry Wasdin was born. After the divorce, Sharon met another man, a successful businessman, whom she married. The St. Peter family approached Tom, asking if he'd allow the boys to be adopted by their new stepdad in an effort to make their upbringing less conflicted and complicated. Tom agreed, and Tommy and Larry were adopted by their new stepdad.

"In my heart, I thought it would be best for the boys," Tom said. "That's why I agreed to let Sharon's new husband adopt them. I thought it would be in their best interest."

So much was happening, and more was yet ahead. It wouldn't be happening in Gainesville, though. Tom graduated from UF – the first Wasdin to ever earn a college degree – the first semester of 1958. That January, he had several directions he could've gone with jobs, but it boiled down to two – teaching physical education and biology while coaching varsity basketball at Mayo High School, or becoming a physical education resource teacher at the elementary school level in Jacksonville's Duval County. Mayo was a small rural town, like Waldo, while Jacksonville was big time, with more opportunities there to move up. Although there wasn't a coaching job immediately available, Mike Houser, Duval County's supervisor of physical education and athletics, promised Tom that he wouldn't have to wait too long for such a job. So Wasdin chose Jacksonville, and it proved to be a life-altering decision.

In barely more than four years, Tom had gone from a country boy to the college life in Gainesville. Now he was going to the big city of Jacksonville, where even bigger moments in his life waited.

Chapter 5

A Merging of Magic

"Yes, we had a special group, but Coach Wasdin was enlarging on what we had." – Steve Pajcic

Would Lewis have accomplished as much without Clark? Would Lennon have become the same legend without McCartney – or vice versa? What if, rather than being brothers, Orville and Wilbur Wright were distant relatives? What if Simon had grown up several thousand miles away from Garfunkel, instead of several thousand feet? We'll never know. History is rife with exclamation points that erased the question marks of what might've been had not the right circumstances converged.

Tom Wasdin wonders what his coaching career would've been like had his first job out of college not taken him to a lower income section of Jacksonville, where a special group of children were growing up, poised to accomplish special things with their lives, seemingly waiting for just the right role model to enter their small stage. Wasdin will tell you that those young people made him. They, however, will tell you the opposite. What history tells us is that it was a merging of magic.

Even though he was the first member of his family to ever graduate from college, there weren't many jobs waiting for Wasdin after he was handed his degree from the University of Florida in January of 1958. So he grabbed the one that took him to the outskirts of Jacksonville, to a blue-collar part of the city where most folks either farmed, worked at the Cecil Field Naval Air Station, or labored on the local railroad. The area, not surprisingly, was known by many as the wrong side of the tracks, both literally and figuratively.

Wasdin was given the title "Resource Teacher" and the responsibility of five elementary schools: Pinedale, Lackawanna, Biltmore, Reynolds Lane and Annie R. Morgan, the latter three of which fed into Paxon High School. Wasdin's charge was to teach teachers. Specifically, his assignment was to instruct classroom teachers on how to teach physical education and get the maximum benefits from what was traditionally a throwaway time during the school day – recess. So he traveled from school to school, teaching teachers even while teaching elementary school children things like team sports, dancing, how to play Dodge Ball and H-O-R-S-E.

Wasdin appreciated the job and the opportunity to impact lives at such a young age, when the clay is still soft and moldable. It was the genesis of his coaching career, one that in a little more than a decade would take him all the way to college basketball's National Championship Game, going against John Wooden's UCLA Bruins. He was already moving forward, but years later, when he looked back, he saw better what he had accomplished during those formative years as a coach, pouring himself into those children.

"I was ready to set the world on fire as a coach – not to move on or up, but for those kids," he said. "That's always been my philosophy, to give whatever I'm doing my full attention and best effort. I didn't realize how involved I was with their lives and what it meant to them, and really to me. I used to think success was coaching against UCLA, but I had more success in more meaningful ways during those early years in Jacksonville, impacting lives when I was coaching in public schools."

It was a special group of kids, too, and as much as he impacted their lives, they did the same with him.

At Annie R. Morgan Elementary School, Tom remembers one precocious youngster, just 11, who greeted him before a PE class.

"Mr. Wasdin," little Steve Pajcic said, "I have everyone lined up and on a team. We're ready to play. You don't have to do anything."

Later, Wasdin pulled a fellow faculty member aside and marveled at the boy's intelligence and leadership skills.

"That Steve Pajcic boy is going to be governor of Florida one day," Tom predicted.

Barely 15 years later, that precocious youngster began the first of six terms in the Florida House of Representatives, where – perhaps not surprisingly – he concentrated heavily on issues dealing with education.

Once a Coach, Always a Coach

In 1986, Pajcic became the Democratic nominee for governor of Florida, tapping into Tom Wasdin to be his Brevard County campaign manager. Pajcic, though, lost to Republican Bob Martinez. Today, he is a successful Jacksonville-based attorney who still fondly remembers Coach Wasdin, as do many of the other children from that era.

"He's one of a few people who makes an impact on a whole lot of people's lives," said Pajcic, who saw in Wasdin someone who was like them, but who was also so much more.

"He was cracker, but he was cool," he said. "The way he carried himself, the way he thought about himself, good-looking, smart, fun. He was like royalty to us. Even though he was from the sticks like us, he had street smarts. He understood the ways of the world. But he never talked down to us. He always communicated at our level. And even though he knew a whole lot more than us about life, he was open to our thoughts and our input. He was always learning."

Yes, they learned together; grew together.

As Wasdin moved up the ranks through Jacksonville's public school system, his ascent mirrored that group of kids he first met in elementary school. And what those young students recognized from their vantage point, looking up to Coach Wasdin, Tom's superiors saw

The coaching staff at Paxon Junior High School. From left to right: Coach Jones, Tom Wasdin, Ed Cunningham, Bob Meeker, Glen Bates, John Ferrari, John Guido.

as well. It didn't take long for Wasdin to receive promotions. After working a semester as a Resource Teacher, he became the 9th grade basketball coach at Paxon Junior High in the fall of 1958, teaching math and physical education. One of his PE classes had over 90 students, but Wasdin loved the challenge, loved the environment and especially loved his first real coaching job.

It was a learning experience, and much of what he was learning wasn't just X's and O's – it was also about himself. He knew he was competitive as a player on the court, but what surprised him – stunned him, really – was just how competitive and animated he was as a coach, especially in game situations. It surprised other people, too.

Wasdin's first game as a coach came against Kirby Smith Junior High School, and it was an eye-opener in many ways. "I had heard they pressed," he said, "but nobody told me about the zone press. We couldn't get the ball up the court. My players were shell-shocked, dribbling the ball off their knees, their toes, and Kirby would intercept passes and go in for an easy layup. If we got the ball past midcourt, it was a victory. We lost by more than 50 points."

Afterward, Wasdin ruminated over the loss.

"All during the game, I kept thinking, 'I know how to beat this thing, but I can't now.' I felt like I'd let my team down by not having them prepared before we played Kirby. That's when I learned the value of scouting and how important it was to be prepared. I knew that we were going to play them one more time, later in the season, and that next time we were going to be ready."

When the two teams met later in the season, Paxon lost again to Kirby, but this time the score was much closer, with Kirby winning not because Paxon wasn't prepared, but simply because they were a better team with better players. You can accept those losses better.

Wasdin kept coaching, kept competing ... and kept getting a reputation. He wasn't just animated courtside, he was over the top. His voice was loud – big and booming – and he used it not just at his players, but at the officials, too. It was at the end of the season, after a game against John Gorrie Junior High, when the school's veteran coach pulled Tom aside.

"Tom," he said with a sage voice, "you need to settle down. You're going to have a heart attack. When you get all excited, your players get all excited. And when you're yelling at the officials, telling them what to do, they don't like that. That's not helping you or your players."

Tom was thankful for the older coach's advice, and he had to admit he was right. "I really appreciated his wisdom," he said.

There was a learning curve, for sure.

"I learned not only how to handle myself, but also how to handle players," he said. "Again, I was learning how to pick five starters and select a team, and how to tell the other kids that they weren't starting without destroying them and how to keep them motivated and involved. I also learned how to deal with parents, because if you don't know how to deal with them, they'll be your biggest problem."

Some of the lessons he learned growing up, and when he coached Little League while a UF student, proved helpful.

"The thing Little League taught me is that every kid is different, but you have to treat them the same and hold them all to the same standards. You have to be fair with all of them. You have to be. If you're not, if you're not sincere or honest, they will see right through it, and you'll lose them. If you have rules, you'd better be ready to enforce them."

He worked his players hard, too. If anything, they were in shape.

There were, however, certain things Tom didn't have to learn, things that were ingrained into the fabric of his being. He never used profanity, not even in his later years when he coached college ball. He never demeaned or berated players in front of their peers.

The more he coached, the more he learned, and the more comfortable he became. It just seemed ... well, natural. He still had aspirations of being a school principal someday, but for the time being he loved coaching, and he loved the impact he had on young lives.

"It was fun having your own team, having them do what you told them to do and then seeing them be successful with that, seeing them win. Making something, doing something, building something. It was very rewarding to watch kids get better right before your eyes. Coaching is teaching, and I like to teach."

He'd better have liked it, because teachers back then didn't make a lot of money. His job as a resource teacher earned him $3,500, the same as what he was paid at Paxon Junior High, where his coaching supplement was $200.

Tom was only 23, with a lot of life still ahead of him. It was in September of 1958, though, where one chapter of his life ended. That was when his divorce from Sharon became final. It was about that same time when he saw a picture in the newspaper of "Miss Flame of Duval County." Each community had a volunteer fire department, and each community had a beauty contest feeding into an entire Duval County competition – hence the name Flame.

Of course, Miss Flame had a double meaning – as in hot, hot, hot.

Being a young red-blooded male, that's certainly what Tom thought when he saw the photo of "Miss Flame of Duval County" – a perky petite brunette named Glenda Adams.

"My first reaction was, 'Boy is she pretty,'" he said.

And he had an even better reaction when a friend told him, "I know her. I'll introduce you."

His friend did, and before long Tom and Glenda were enjoying their first date at the local zoo. She was even prettier in real life. Tom, however, still had the goal of becoming a principal and marrying a schoolteacher. Toward that goal of becoming a principal, he enrolled into a Masters program at the University of Florida. But as for the latter goal of marrying a teacher? Well, looking at Glenda convinced him to ditch that idea. After his first marriage, and the hard lessons he learned from it, Tom changed a lot of his priorities. "I was looking for purity, and Glenda was all that," he said. "She had a great figure, but she had a reputation for being a prude, and I was fine with that. She was also one of the sweetest, nicest persons I'd ever met. She thought I was the greatest thing, too. We never had an argument."

There were religious differences, though. Tom grew up Baptist, and Glenda was Mormon. But they thought they could work around it as they continued to date, and a romance blossomed. Tom didn't know how serious it was until he saw her compete for Miss Jacksonville. While being interviewed on stage, Glenda mentioned her boyfriend, someone whom "I plan to get to know better, whom I love very much. I hope we get married."

In the audience, the words floored Tom.

"I was so happy," he said. "I was thinking, 'Well, I guess she likes me more than I thought she did.'"

They continued to date, and in the fall of '59, they married. They were young, in love and happy, but the religious difference they thought wouldn't divide them eventually did become an issue.

"Initially, I was thinking that I'd go to my church and go to Glenda's and then decide which one to stay with," Tom said. "But every time I went to the Mormon Church, they spent all their time telling me why the Baptists were wrong. They'd be telling me what was wrong with the Baptists and not why I should become a Mormon. I wanted to go to church to learn, not be blasted every time I'd go."

So, as anyone who felt they were constantly under attack would do, Tom stopped going and went back to the Baptist church.

What really helped the marriage, however, was that Glenda was the perfect coach's wife, pouring herself into his career, her life revolving around the next basketball game, following him through his career path that took him from junior high school to high school and eventually to Jacksonville University.

"She attended every game, and was very supportive. She was a great coach's wife. I can remember those times after a big win at Paxon High School, when we'd stay up until the paper was printed, and then about 12:30 or 1 a.m. we'd get a street edition and read what they said. It was exciting times. We were very happy."

Though the climb up the coaching ladder was steady and eventually very heady, there were humble beginnings. Tom and Glenda's first home was a two-bedroom trailer that someone in the Navy had owned and then abandoned. It was a mess, with rotting food still in the refrigerator. The young couple cleaned it, fixed it and by the time they moved in, it looked new. It was Tom's first piece of real estate, and he instinctively developed a mindset that later served him well when he became a multimillionaire developer.

"My philosophy, which is one of my philosophies in life, is to live within your means and don't go into debt. Be happy with what you have. We were very happy in that trailer."

It was an exciting time. Many of those kids Tom first met in elementary school followed him from Paxon Junior High to Paxon High School. Or maybe he was following them. Either way, it was a mutually beneficial relationship.

Steve Pajcic, the precocious boy who had the kids lined up and ready to play years earlier, had an equally impressive younger brother named Gary. Both would grow up to become prominent attorneys. The boys were very competitive. Tom coached Steve three years in junior high school and then all three years in high school. There were other great athletes who were simply special kids – James "Spunk" Bryant, Gary "Foots" Harrington, Jim Hackendale, Dennis Womack, Ben Thompson, Billy Nelson, Mark Wright and Ronnie Sellers, who later played in the NFL.

"Yes, we had a special group," Steve Pajcic said, "but Coach Wasdin was enlarging on what we had. He had an eye for talent, and he knew how to develop it. He enticed, encouraged and expanded on what we had."

Everything was moving up, and in many ways, too. That's why it seemed curious that after Tom's second season at Paxon Junior High, the athletic director, Glenn Bates, called him in. Bates wanted to discuss the up-and-coming 9th grade team.

"Do you want to have a championship team here at Paxon?" he asked Tom.

"Yes," Tom replied.

The answer seemed obvious. What wasn't so obvious was Bates' line of reasoning. But once he spelled it out, Tom was on board.

Bates wanted Tom to leave coaching the 9th grade team and go back and coach the 8th grade team, and let Coach Ed Cunningham, who was currently coaching the 8th grade team, to move up and coach the 9th grade team. Cunningham was a good coach, but Bates saw something special in this young Wasdin guy. Paxon had never had much success in sports, even though they had talent. They needed to develop that talent, nurture it, and do so from the ground up. Sending Wasdin back to coach the incoming 8th graders, and then grow with them, was the plan.

Wasdin jumped at the idea, immersing himself into the game plan as if it were exactly that – a game plan. He handpicked students for his PE class so he could teach them basketball all year long. He honed in on the best athletes who were the best students. He not only singled out the ones who were the tallest, but the ones who also had the tallest mothers and/or fathers. He developed an intramural basketball league that played Monday through Thursday and made sure the games were properly officiated, so the boys could get used to basketball played with a whistle. He organized a basketball league for every Saturday morning during the summer and kept the gym open all day, giving individual instructions.

"If they weren't playing another sport, they were always in the gym," he said. "I kind of took over their lives that way, and they loved it. It also gave me the opportunity to develop a feeder program and the talent I already had to work with."

It was a brilliant idea, brilliantly executed. Four years later, that group of 8th grade boys would win the high school state championship. In fact, while earning his Masters degree at the University of Florida, Wasdin wrote a paper for one of his classes on the success of this project. It is also how he formulated his tenets for basketball success; things that were unexciting and simple, but necessary:

Play without committing turnovers
Play without giving up offensive rebounds
Play without giving up fast-break baskets
Play without committing useless fouls
Do hit your free throws
Do get the other team in foul trouble
Do win the loose ball battle
Do out-hustle the other team
Do draw offensive charges

As special as the relationship was that Wasdin developed with that 8th grade team, there was another relationship that he developed that season, one that would alter his life.

The first game of the season was against Terry Parker Junior High. He'd never met the other coach, a fellow by the name of Joe Williams – a tall, slender, good-looking guy. Williams was young, too, just a couple of years older than Tom. But he was just as energetic and fiery as Tom was when he started coaching.

Several times during the game, absorbed in the action and shouting orders, Williams walked past his bench, past the scorer's table, *past* where Wasdin was coaching, and then all the way down to the end of Paxon's bench, barking orders at his team.

Finally, Tom had had enough. Politely, but firmly, he told Williams, "Coach, you oughta stay down by your own bench."

The words caught Williams by surprise, as did his position on the court. He looked around, stunned that he had wandered so far away from his prescribed area. It was almost as if awakening someone who'd been sleepwalking.

"You're right," Williams apologetically told Wasdin. "I'm sorry."

Williams was definitely different. But he sure could coach basketball.

"I thought we had a really good team, and we had worked so hard," Wasdin said. "But here this guy I'd never heard of came in and beat us. There was something about him that I liked."

The next day, Wasdin noticed that Williams had forgotten his jacket on a chair – a tan London Fog overcoat. Sure enough, Williams called to see if he'd left the coat at Paxon. When he came to get it, he and Tom struck up a conversation, this time away from the frenzy of a basketball game, and a friendship developed. Later that year, when they played each other again, Wasdin won.

Tom Wasdin's 8th grade basketball team at Paxon Junior High School that won the Duval County Championship. Notable players were No. 11 Ronnie Sellers and No. 4 Gary Pajcic. Both later became All-American football players at Florida State.

They both proved to be on their way up in the coaching ranks. For Wasdin, that meant heading from Paxon Junior High to Paxon High School at the start of the 1961-62 school year. His primary job was coaching varsity basketball. But he also coached golf and junior varsity football. Once again, the kids from the supposed wrong side of

Once a Coach, Always a Coach

the tracks that he first got to know as an elementary school Resource Teacher were mostly the same students he had now in high school. As always, he was impacting lives.

Tom Wasdin also coached the golf team at Paxon High School. Standing from left to right: Billy Harrell, Head Coach Tom Wasdin, Ken Barnett, Ronald Linenger. Kneeling from left to right: Ray Castleberry, Kirby Phillips, James Barnett.

One of those high school kids was an outstanding athlete whom he had known for years now – a boy by the name of Ronnie Sellers. Wasdin wanted him to play on the JV football team, but Sellers didn't think he'd like to play football. He didn't like the idea of all that hitting.

"He thought it was kind of stupid to go out there and beat each other up," Wasdin said. "I convinced him to come out for the JV team. I saw in him a wide receiver. With Gary Pajcic playing quarterback, I knew we could split Ronnie out and have him catch all the passes. I told him I'd keep him away from all the contact."

Sellers bought into it, and became a star player for Paxon High.

Several years later, Ron Sellers became an All-American wide receiver for Florida State and later enjoyed an all-star career in the

NFL. In 1988, he was inducted into the National College Football Hall of Fame, becoming the first FSU player to be so honored. All totaled Sellers is in 10 Halls of Fame.

"When Coach Wasdin came to me to play football, I was 6-foot-1 and about 150, at the most," Sellers said. "I didn't think I was a football player, but Coach Wasdin saw something in me. Once I got into it, I loved it. I owe a lot to Coach Wasdin. In my career, I've played for a lot of great coaches, guys like Joe Gibbs, Tom Landry and Don Shula, and Coach Wasdin in so many ways was equal to them. He was one of the best coaches I ever had. He was my mentor and teacher and somebody I've always turned to for advice throughout my life. I love the man."

Once, during Sellers' pro career, a sports reporter asked him about his most embarrassing moment in football. Sellers' mind went straight to that JV team Wasdin had coached. He told the story of a game against Jackson High School's JV team; a game that was knotted at 0-0 with one play left in the contest. Jackson tried a desperation pass. Wasdin had the sure-handed Sellers in the game playing safety. By now, he had integrated him into other facets of football that involved hitting.

"Of all the kids I coached, Ronnie Sellers was probably the best all-around athlete," he said.

On that last play, Sellers recounted to the reporter how he'd intercepted the pass and returned it about 70 yards. The reporter had no way of knowing it, but it was a sensational run that saw Sellers juking, changing field a couple of times and skillfully eluding would-be tacklers. The game was on Jackson High's field, which didn't have goal posts on the end that he was running toward. Wasdin had always instructed the boys to run *through* the goal posts, just to make certain you scored. But without any goal posts in sight, Sellers estimated where the goal line was, and estimated wrong, stopping just short of the goal line and dropping the ball to the ground as he did.

"It wasn't a spike or anything like that," Wasdin recalled. "He wasn't showboating. But it was ruled a fumble instead of a touchdown, and the game ended in a tie."

Sellers never forgot the incident, telling the reporter: "I was embarrassed, but I was more worried about what Coach Wasdin was going to do."

When Wasdin got to Sellers, the boy was crying uncontrollably.

"I was a sensitive kid," he said, "and I hated that I'd let my teammates down."

Wasdin never yelled at Sellers. First of all, that wasn't his style, and he could obviously see that the boy felt bad enough. But it was that kind of respect and admiration he instilled in those kids. They wanted to do well, but even more so they wanted to do well for *him*.

"Son," the coach said with a consoling voice, "that was one of the greatest runs I've ever seen in my life."

"He had just the right things to say," Sellers recalled.

Years later, Sellers went on to become the successful business owner of Ron Sellers and Associates, a company that deals in corporate insurance, estate planning and wealth management.

Most all the kids whom Wasdin followed from elementary school – or were they following him? – seemed to have significant successes in life. Lawyers, politicians, college athletic directors, college bowl directors, educators, business professionals, bankers ... and on and on.

One of those kids was Butch Cronon, who not only mirrored Wasdin's ascent from elementary school to junior high and then high school, but later went to Jacksonville University when Wasdin was coaching basketball there. Like a lot of the children who came from their side of the railroad tracks, Cronon grew up poor, and from a broken home. His mom was divorced and he never met his father until he was 23. He and his mother and sister lived with his grandparents in a tiny two-bedroom home, with Butch sleeping on the back porch. Poor? They didn't get a hot water heater until Butch's senior year in high school. Making matters worse was the fact that his grandfather was an alcoholic.

"Coach Wasdin was very much that male authority figure in my life that I needed," he said. "He took an interest in me, even though I wasn't a very good athlete. I didn't play for him beyond the 7th grade. But he always had time for me. His interest in me was genuine. There was genuine concern. And he listened. At every stage of my life, Coach was there."

Cronon recalled a time at Paxon High School when he and two classmates drove to Pensacola to root for their basketball team at a holiday tournament. "I don't know how, but Coach Wasdin found out we were sleeping in our car at an abandoned drive-in theater," Cronon says. "He got word to us to come to the hotel and stay with the players. That was so typical of him."

Later in life, as he became a successful professional, Cronon found himself tapping into so many of the life lessons he learned from Coach Wasdin. He rose to the ranks of director for AT&T, then president of the North American Telephone Co., before he and his wife Pat founded the Hand n' Hand Child Enrichment Center, which they still own and operate in Orlando, Florida.

"Outside of my mom, I don't think anybody took more pleasure in my professional accomplishments than Coach. He's meant a lot to me, and I know I'm not the only one who feels that way."

He's right.

Ask any of the men and women who grew up in that section of Jacksonville during that era, and they all carry the same common sentiments about their coach and mentor and that magical period of time they shared together.

As Spunk Bryant, who became a St. Johns County Commissioner, says, "It was a unique situation. Coach Wasdin had a lot to do with where I think all of us got to in life. He instilled in us that competitive spirit. He believed in us, and we believed in him. He taught us about winning and how to win, the kind of life lessons that carried over into the rest of our lives."

As Gary Harrington, who became a successful insurance agent and businessman, says, "He was full of energy with tremendous enthusiasm, excited about everything, and he got everyone else excited. He convinced us that we could be something, and we bought into it. He was a hard worker and he got us to work hard. He was good at dealing with people, sizing people up and figuring out what each individual could do to contribute to the success of the team. He was a great leader."

Harrington's father wanted him to do what so many others from his side of the tracks were doing, and that was to work for the railroad. But Wasdin convinced the boy that college should be his future.

"Without Coach Wasdin's influence, I never would have gone to college. And I'm just one example of one life he touched. He gave all of us a vision. He was able to paint a picture of what we could do."

As Dennis Womack, who became the baseball coach and then the assistant athletic director at the University of Virginia, says, "My first encounter with Coach Wasdin was in elementary school, at Annie R. Morgan. One of things I remember is that he taught us how to walk. I know that sounds strange. But he taught us to walk not with our feet out, but with our feet straight in. He told us that there are very few athletes who walk with a splayed foot. I took that to heart. The other thing I remember that was unique was that in elementary school most of the teachers were female. But now here was a guy right out of college, a man, coaching us. He had our attention."

Womack was with Wasdin all through his years growing up, through elementary school, junior high and then high school.

"As I look back and think through my career choices, there are two, maybe three, coaches who influenced me, and Tom Wasdin was one of them. He was the first coach I ever had and the first male influence. He taught me perseverance, hard work, leadership and just a never-give-up attitude. He had a personality you responded to. If not for him, I really didn't have any guidance. He's just a special, special person. I also think we were a special group that followed him. But we were very fortunate to have Tom Wasdin coach us. I don't think anyone taught me any more than Coach Wasdin. Yeah, it was primarily on the athletic fields and courts, but those lessons stick with you throughout your life. I think we were a good fit for him, and I know he was good for us. He was the perfect fit for us."

As Angela Briggs, who became a paralegal and business owner, says, "Tom was a great role model for us. Being a girl, just in elementary school, I noticed he was handsome, very friendly and he had a great way with kids. He was respectful. He taught us sportsmanship, respect for fellow players, how to play fair. He wanted us to win, but he wanted us to win fairly. I was with him all the way through school growing up, and we've been friends all these years. He never coached me, but I still learned so much from him; things that spill over into everyday life. It was a special time. I'd like to think we were a special group of kids and Tom is a special man. We were close-knit and we've remained that way throughout our lives."

It was indeed a special time – magical.

Some of the impact wasn't realized until years later. Jim Hackendale was a shy kid, lacking in confidence. His parents had divorced and his father lived in Michigan and the distance between the two wasn't just measured in miles. "I only saw my dad three times from the time I was 12 years old until I was 40," Hackendale said. "Coach Wasdin became a great role model for me."

The memories for Hackendale are vivid, going back to when he first laid eyes on Coach Wasdin at Paxon Jr. High. "He was wearing red gym shorts and a white T-shirt and had a flat-top haircut. The first order of the day was to make sure we all had our jockstraps on. Coach was a strong guy, the most competitive guy I ever met, with an aggressive personality and a big, wide smile, with curly blond hair on those big forearms. He was an impressive guy to a 13 year old."

Hackendale learned that Wasdin got his strong hands and forearms from doing isometric exercises, "and to this day," he says, "I still squeeze and twist my steering wheel when I'm driving."

What Hackendale remembers most, though, is that even though Coach Wasdin was tough, demanding and worked them hard, "he loved us all. We were his guys."

The 1961-62 Paxon High School basketball team. Standing left to right in front of Head Coach Tom Wasdin: Steve Pajcic, Gary Hartley, Jim Hackendale, Tommy Smith, Mark Wright, Ben Thompson, Wayne Hague, Gary Harrington, Spunk Bryant, Johnny Wainwright.

Once a Coach, Always a Coach

A lot of those guys arrived at Paxon High School at the same time as Wasdin, where the young coach wasted no time building a basketball program – indeed, a basketball power. Paxon only went 10-15 his first year, but the foundation for greatness was laid. Still, he wasn't there just coaching hoops. There was golf and JV football, where he also had success. In fact, in only his second year, the JV football team played for the conference championship.

Head Coach Tom Wasdin and Assistant Coach Jim Foster celebrate with their team after a tournament victory.

But it was in basketball where he was really making a name – for himself and for Paxon. After that 10-15 first season, the Eagles went 26-3 in Tom's second year, becoming state-ranked for the first time in school history. Adding to that, Wasdin was awarded the Duval County's Coach of the Year honors and the Sportsmanship Award, the latter quite a testament for a coach whose initial sideline demeanor bordered on out of control. The Paxon Eagles went far that season; farther than any other

PHS team had ever gone – becoming the first team in school history to win the county, conference and district tournament. In the first game of the state tournament, though, Pompano Beach High school trounced the Eagles, 70-53. Pompano Beach was no slouch, however, evidenced by how the Golden Tornadoes went on to win the state championship.

Paxon High would eventually win the state championship, too. In fact, it came just two years later. Wasdin, however, coached the Eagles just one more season, during the 1963-64 school year. Paxon High was ranked as high as second in the state that season. The Eagles won the Gateway Championship and were undefeated in conference play for the second straight year. Tom was also awarded the Duval County's Coach of the Year and Sportsmanship Award for the second straight year.

The 1962-63 Paxon High School basketball team. Standing from left to right: Mike Novak, Gary Pajcic, Gary Harrington, Mark Wright, Billy Nelson, Ben Thompson, Manager Preston Matthews. Kneeling from left to right: Rick Webb, Ronnie Colbert, Dennis Womack, Edward Smith, Steve Pajcic, Spunk Bryant. Not pictured: Ronnie Sellers and Rester Bryan.

But this time, Paxon fell short in the regional finals, losing to Pensacola High School, 46-45, in Pensacola under a cloud of dubious officiating, especially in the closing ticks of the game clock, which saw the Fighting Tigers shoot four foul shots in the last 10 seconds to win.

"To this day, that loss bothers me, as I think it does all of us," said Womack, who was a senior that season. "Billy Nelson, our big man, got into foul trouble and that hurt us. And then those fouls they got in the closing seconds did us in. To lose by one point, that was tough."

Like Pompano Beach High the season before, Pensacola High went on to win the state championship, winning the semifinal and final game each by more than 20 points.

It was the core of that Paxon High team that came back the next year to finally capture the school's first state championship. But Womack was gone, off to college. Tom Wasdin was gone, too, off to a new high school along Florida's Space Coast. It was where new adventures awaited and also what would eventually be business opportunities that would one day lure him from coaching and into becoming a multimillionaire developer. In between, though, he would return to Jacksonville a few years later, but not to coach public school children.

What he left behind was never to be repeated.

But then again, how do you repeat the merging of magic?

Chapter 6

A NEW OPPORTUNITY LAUNCHES ALONG THE SPACE COAST

"I remember sitting on the floor with the principal, looking at the blueprints for the school. It was exciting to see the plans for the coaches' office, the gym, the weight room, and it was all going to be brand new. It definitely was the place to be in Florida." – Tom Wasdin

Tom Wasdin didn't recognize the voice, but he sure recognized the name. Eddie Feely had been a football legend in Gainesville, first as a quarterback at Gainesville High and later at Florida State. Everybody from North Central Florida knew of Eddie Feely, especially Wasdin, since Feely had also married a local girl from Waldo.

"He was one of those guys who was a big man on campus," Tom said.

Now Feely wanted Wasdin on *his* campus. It was a new campus at a new school, and it would be known as Cocoa Beach High, located in the heart of Florida's Space Coast during a time when the area was the most exciting stretch of real estate in the Sunshine State. The year was 1964, and NASA was pressing the gas pedal on its space program, racing against the Soviet Union to fulfill President John F. Kennedy's edict to put a man on the moon by the end of the decade. Brevard County was booming. New schools were opening and the area was abuzz with excitement and energy.

"I want to talk with you about coming to Cocoa Beach High School," Feely told Wasdin.

Wasdin was open to the idea, especially if it meant better pay – and it did.

"My wife Glenda was pregnant and she was working at Prudential Insurance Company as a clerk," he said. "I always believed that when a woman has a baby, she should stay at home until the child goes to school. We were two people living on two salaries in Jacksonville. But with what they were offering at Cocoa Beach, we could go to three people living on one salary. Duval County was one of the lowest paying counties in the state for teachers and Brevard County was one of the highest. They offered me a salary of $5,800 a year at Cocoa Beach High, which was more than Glenda and I were making together in Jacksonville."

Some friction had also developed at Paxon High School. The athletic director, Jack Jones, didn't mind the success that Wasdin's basketball program was having, he just didn't like that some athletes were playing hoops instead of football.

"He thought I wanted guys to play basketball at the exclusion of football, but that wasn't the case," Wasdin said. "Ronnie Sellers and Gary Pajcic both played football in addition to basketball. In fact, I was the one who got Sellers to play football. But not every boy wanted to play football. Steve Pajcic wouldn't play football. The athletic director thought I had something to do with that. He thought I was too influential. The next thing I knew, I wasn't teaching PE anymore. I was in the classroom."

The time seemed right to make a move. Wasdin was closing in on getting his Masters degree from the University of Florida, and he still wanted to get into public school administration, eventually becoming a principal. He saw Cocoa Beach High as a place that afforded him a better opportunity, and the upside of Brevard County seemed limitless.

Little did Tom know at the time, but the biggest part of his future awaited him along the Space Coast – both professionally and personally. And it had nothing to do with public school education. He couldn't have possibly seen that coming, though. All Tom saw in 1964 was the excitement of a new high school and a good paying job coaching basketball in an area that was exploding in growth. He went down for an interview, impressing Feely and the principal so much that they offered him the job before he could leave.

It certainly was a heady time.

"What turned me on was that it was a new school with an unlimited budget for athletics and physical education," he said. "I remember sitting on the floor with the principal, looking at the blueprints for the school. It was exciting to see the plans for the coaches' office, the gym, the weight room, and it was all going to be brand new. It definitely was the place to be in Florida."

Wasdin had also gotten interest from Carol City High School in Miami. Had he gone there, he would've coached a young man named Ted Hendricks, who not only later became a star linebacker in the NFL, but Hendricks was also named to the Florida High School Athletic Association All-Century Team. Wasdin, however, decided to not even interview at Carol City. Cocoa Beach seemed the place to be, and he was eager to go there. There was, however, one thing tugging at his emotions, and that was leaving behind those special kids in Jacksonville whom he had essentially grown up with.

The coaching staff at Cocoa Beach High School. Standing from left to right: Coach Kelley, Coach Fernandez, David Burgess, Jimmy Morgan, Ben Bindschadler, Bill Hancock. Sitting from left to right: Eddie Feely, George Cummings, John Levings, Tom Wasdin.

"I really didn't want to leave those kids, especially guys like Gary Pajcic and Ronnie Sellers," he said. "We really had it going at Paxon, and I knew we were going to have a powerhouse coming back."

They did. In fact, that team Wasdin built at Paxon won the state championship the season after he left.

By then, though, he was building something special at Cocoa Beach High, employing all the things he had learned in Jacksonville, confident it would work again.

"I knew how to build a basketball program," he said. "I could build it from the ground up."

Which is what he did.

Alan Zimmerman recalled during the summer of 1964, playing basketball at a local gym, when "in walks this fellow who we had never seen before. He looked like a Marine home on leave. He asked if he could join us. After several rousing games, where he basically had his way with us, we took a break. He asked two of us if we were going to the new high school, and if we were going to try out for the basketball team. We said we hoped to. He said good, and proceeded to tell us that he was the new head coach. Our chests were sticking out about a foot. We thought we were in. As he walked away, he stopped, turned around asked us, 'By the way, what year are you going to be in school?' Seniors, we replied. His face lost its smile and he abruptly turned and walked away without another word. This man was rebuilding before he even had a team!"

He certainly was – rebuilding and building. Wasdin started a Bitty Basketball League at the Cocoa Beach Recreation Department, getting things going at the grassroots level, developing a feeder system. He modeled the program after what he'd learned from Deland High School head coach Murray Arnold, who later became a college coach. They used 8-foot baskets and a smaller ball for the 5th and 6th grade boys. Six teams played on Saturday mornings, with Tom involving his high school assistant coaches and varsity players as youth coaches. The Bitty League teams played the same offenses and man-to-man defenses that the Cocoa Beach High Minutemen played. Everything had a design, and everything pointed to the future.

"It was only when I got older that I realized what the hell he was doing," said John Casbon, who was a 10th grader when Wasdin arrived.

Casbon went on to become a multimillionaire, primarily through owning title insurance companies, and he traces a lot of what he learned that made him successful back to Coach Wasdin. "All the things I've accomplished in my life, I go back and say, 'Thanks, Tom.'"

It was years later when Casbon could see what he called the "brilliance" of what Coach Wasdin was doing at Cocoa Beach. By having his players teach Bitty League basketball, Wasdin benefitted on many different levels. First of all, one of the best ways to learn something is to turn around and teach it to someone else.

"Here I thought we were just out there teaching these little brats how to play basketball," Casbon said. "But we were really reinforcing to ourselves what Tom was teaching us. And he could also see, by the way we were coaching those kids, if we were really getting it. If not, he knew what he needed to work on with us."

Then there was the importance of developing a farm, or feeder, system, and mentoring that young talent that was coming up. It was yet another valuable tool Casbon took away from Wasdin, something he employed throughout his successful business career.

Finally, there was the importance of having a plan, and then having the discipline to stick with it.

"He had a plan for us right from the beginning," Casbon said. "I later learned that it is, indeed, all about the plan. If you want to be successful, you have to have a plan. Tom put together for us a roadmap where we could see that if we connected the dots we could be successful. And we were. Once we figured it out, we were hell on wheels. We could take on anyone and win. And it wasn't just that we were winning, it was that we knew *how* to win. There's a difference in winning and showing us how to get there. Tom showed us how to get there. We were always prepared. Always. All of those things were lessons I took with me throughout my life."

In addition to a basketball program, Wasdin was building other things, too – namely a home and a family. Little Lori Wasdin was born in November of that year. Tom also built his first home, a two-bedroom, one-bathroom house on Merritt Island. Like Cocoa Beach, Merritt Island was booming with growth. In fact, in 1965, the year after Cocoa Beach High opened, Merritt Island High became a new school. Having two new high schools was good for the area, but it also divided the talent pool. Whereas everyone in Central Brevard used to go to Cocoa High School, which had developed a great basketball program, winning a state championship in 1960, now there were two new high schools in the area vying for the top athletes.

Tom had met one of those stellar athletes on Merritt Island, a boy by the name of Vern Thortsen, who had a cute younger sister named Susie. Susie Thortsen was active in school clubs, as well as a cheerleader who later became Cocoa Beach High's Homecoming Queen. Later still – many years later, in fact – she would even become Mrs. Tom Wasdin. But such a thought was the furthest thing from either of their minds in 1964. Tom was trying to build a basketball program and the Thortsen teenagers were trying to decide which school they wanted to go to – established Cocoa High or the new Cocoa Beach High.

Just a year earlier, in 1963, the Thortsens had moved to Merritt Island from Spirit Lake, Iowa, where their father, a postman, had grown weary of delivering mail in sub-freezing temperatures. One day, while watching the Huntley-Brinkley evening news report on TV, the family saw footage of a rocket launch with people viewing it from the beach, the women wearing bikinis. The month was January. That's all it took. Soon afterward, Gordon Thortsen moved his family to Merritt Island, where the kids enrolled at Edgewood Junior High and Vern quickly excelled at sports. His coach there, Bob Corley, told Eddie Feely that this was a boy he'd want at Cocoa Beach High. But would they be able to get him? Susie, active in the band and with various clubs, wanted to go to Cocoa High, which had a reputation for a great band program. And there was the new high school opening soon on Merritt Island. It was Tom Wasdin, already exhibiting recruiting talents, who, along with Feely, convinced the family that Cocoa Beach was the place to be. It was quite a selling job, because it meant the Thortsens also had to move to the beach.

It turned out to be a good move. Not only did Vern excel at sports there, he got a football scholarship to Georgia Tech, where he played for the legendary Bobby Dodd. Meanwhile, Susie immersed herself in all types of activities – choir, the Beta Club, student government, cheerleading, Homecoming Queen and the band, where she was the majorette.

"I was pretty busy," she said.

She also felt intimidated by Coach Wasdin, the man who would one day, years later, become her husband. As a coach, Wasdin knew that girls could be a distraction to his boys, so he liked them to keep a distance from his players.

"The girls, the cheerleaders, were all a little bit afraid of him because he wouldn't talk to us," Susie said, laughing now at the memory. "He would just give us that Wasdin look. He was all business, and we knew it."

Glenda, the former beauty contest winner, was also intimidating to the girls.

"We were in awe of Mrs. Wasdin," Susie said. "She'd walk into the gym and it was a show-stopper. It was like, 'Wow!' She was so attractive."

The age difference seemed a lot back then, but it really wasn't.

"Tom was only 29, but to us that seemed so old," Susie said, laughing again.

Tom was too busy assembling athletes and building a basketball program to really notice what was going on with the girls, other than he wished they weren't always around his players. But they were good kids, so there weren't any complaints.

"I remember Susie being very active in school activities," Tom said. "She was always involved, always around. She was Vern's little sister, so she was friends with my players, too."

The Thortsens weren't the only folks Wasdin recruited to Cocoa Beach. Another family, the Newsomes, had also moved into the area, arriving from Fort Lauderdale. Brett Newsome was a junior baseball player, and a good one. But he told the Cocoa Beach High coaches that his older brother Toby, who had stayed behind in Fort Lauderdale to finish his senior year at Northeast High School, was an even better athlete. Toby had been All-Broward County his junior year, and was now living with his uncle and aunt, visiting his family in Cocoa Beach every other weekend.

After hearing how good of an athlete Toby Newsome was, Wasdin called the house and spoke to Mrs. Newsome, asking her to bring her son to Cocoa Beach High the next time he was in town, just to talk. She did, and the next thing Toby knew, he was transferring to a new high school.

"Coach Wasdin could recruit," he said. "He was really some recruiter, very personable. He could talk paint off a wall. He thoroughly convinced me that I shouldn't play for anyone else."

Newsome not only liked Wasdin, but also the other Cocoa Beach High coaches, particularly in baseball, since that was really his best sport. He also liked that it was a new school, shiny and sparkling with brand new facilities. Besides, he did miss living with his family. So two months into the school year, he transferred to Cocoa Beach High and started practicing with the Minutemen basketball team.

Immediately, Newsome had second thoughts, regretting his decision. He'd gone from a high school in Fort Lauderdale where he had played with the same guys since 7th grade, and played very well, to a ragtag team of mostly inexperienced players, some of whom really didn't know how to play basketball.

"That first practice, my jaw dropped," Newsome said. "The team was really raw. I think I was the only guy who'd played varsity basketball. I really thought I'd made a mistake going there."

Soon enough, though, Coach Wasdin dispelled those concerns. Sure the team was young and inexperienced, and Wasdin knew it. Admittedly, there were probably times when he might've also entertained second thoughts.

"I could not believe how little talent we had on this team compared to what I left at Paxon, a team that went on to win the state championship that season," he said. "Many of those players at Cocoa Beach had never played organized basketball before, much less played high school basketball, with the exception of Toby."

So what Tom did is what he'd done throughout his life, from his youth growing up in Waldo, to the way he applied himself at the University of Florida, to what he'd done as a young up-and-coming coach in Jacksonville. He simply worked harder than anyone else. He also worked his players hard.

"The conditioning was like boot camp," Newsome recalled. "A lot of guys quit. Coach then took the remaining kids and taught fundamentals. He could coach basketball, you could see that. He knew how to win and he had a game plan. It's hard to explain just how raw that team was, but he molded it into a team."

Newsome didn't realize it at the time, but he was fortunate enough to have missed the team tryouts. Mike Henry, a red-headed rabbit-quick guard will never forget the first day of tryouts.

"There were about 60 or 70 guys there that first day, waiting for the tryouts to begin, and it was just a circus act," Henry said. "I was astounded by the amount of people. Surfers, goofballs and maybe a few guys who could play. Coach Wasdin came in, rolled out the basketball rack, collected all the balls and said, 'Boys, you're not going to even see a basketball for two weeks. I want to see what kind of shape you're in.' I like to call what happened next suicides – the exercises, the calisthenics and the running, the endless running. Every day the number of guys dwindled until there were about 30, and then Coach whittled it down from there. Even still, we weren't much. I remember a newspaper reporter coming out to a practice and hearing Coach Wasdin tell him, 'We're short, but we're also slow.'"

But they worked and worked and worked, with Wasdin often telling his players, "My teams will never get tired in the fourth quarter."

Wasdin also called the team together several days before the season opener, again setting the tone for what lay ahead. He had a bunch of knee pads he'd bought with his own money. "Boys," he said, "you're going to need these kneepads, because we're going to be doing a lot of scrambling and scraping."

Said Alan Zimmerman, the boy who had met Wasdin earlier that summer, playing pickup basketball, and who now made the squad: "We looked more like a wrestling team than a basketball team. We were the only team in Brevard County who wore knee pads as part of our uniforms. We full-court pressed entire games."

"He knew," Henry recalled. "He absolutely knew that if we were going to have a chance of winning any games, we were going to have to be rug burners, fighting and scratching and clawing every second of the game."

And that's exactly what that inaugural team of Cocoa Beach High Minutemen were – a team with heart and hustle, determination and desire.

But could they play basketball?

Newsome remembers the trepidation they all felt going into the season's first game, on the road against Titusville High School in a packed gym, and the pregame speech Coach Wasdin gave them.

Once a Coach, Always a Coach

"Guys," he said, serious, "I've never been shut out before. And let me tell you, it's embarrassing to get shut out in basketball."

"It fired us up," Henry said.

Fighting and pressing on every play, Cocoa Beach led Titusville at halftime, but the much more talented Terriers pulled away in the second half for the victory. Still, the tone was set for the season.

The Cocoa Beach High School basketball team from 1964-65. Standing from left to right: Mike Henry, Steve Fletcher, Wes Morris, Vern Thortsen, John Casbon, Dave Amman, Ralph Featherman, John Gibney, Alan Zimmerman, Dave Rhodes, Joe Echarte. Kneeling left to right: Head Coach Tom Wasdin, Toby Newsome.

"I think from that point on," Henry said, "Coach knew he had a team that wasn't going to go down without a struggle. We were scrappy and we were going to hustle. What we lacked in talent, we didn't lack in desire. And we weren't going to back down from anyone."

Henry's play was indicative of how Wasdin's team approached every game. The Minutemen pressed constantly, stressing defense. Wasdin employed what he called a 3-2 scheme whenever the opposing team inbounded the ball. Two players would be in the inbounds passer's face, jumping up and down, disrupting him, while a third player hovered about 10 feet away, ready to steal a short pass. Henry and usually Vern Thortsen were the two defenders downcourt, lurking like football safeties, hoping the inbounds passer would throw the ball deep in a spasm of panic. Often he did, and often Henry would be waiting.

"Oh my god, I intercepted a lot of passes that way," he said.

Still, Cocoa Beach had growing pains. It didn't help that the Minutemen had to play their first six games on the road until their new gym was finished. They went 1-5 in those games before beginning a winning streak. Things were starting to click, with roles coming into focus. Newsome clearly was the star player, and Wasdin built the team around him. He even had a play called the "Toby Special" that required the rest of the team to screen for Newsome until he got an open shot. But it wasn't all just Toby Newsome. Other players contributed to Cocoa Beach's success.

"He had an ability to get the most out of every kid," Newsome said. "He just kept teaching and instilling the fundamentals. He was very focused that way."

After that 1-5 start, the Minutemen went 9-9 the rest of the way to finish 10-14. For a new school, undersized and undermanned, and one that started two sophomore players, it was an impressive and auspicious beginning.

"We had the smallest student body of any public school in the county," Wasdin recalled. "We also had the shortest team. This was one of the least talented teams I ever coached. But it was also one of the hardest working, scrappiest, committed groups I'd ever been around. We won a lot more games than anyone thought we would. What they lacked in talent they made up in other ways. They were a joy to coach."

Years later, Newsome talks about how special that season was, and the special bond it created. "Those guys are still my friends today," he said. "The camaraderie we developed is still there. We have reunions all the time."

The character of the Cocoa Beach kids and their quick progress only served to fuel Wasdin's passion to build the Minutemen program into the basketball power it would eventually become. After the season was over, he opened the gym for players to work on their skills. During the summer, he opened the gym for pickup games. He tutored some players individually all summer long. He even took players to basketball camps, like the prestigious one at Stetson University,

Once a Coach, Always a Coach

The 1965-66 Cocoa Beach High School basketball team. Standing from left to right: Jim Kennedy, Wes Morris, Bill Kabboord, John Casbon, Jim Fisher, Steve Masek, Jude Acuff, John Longacre, Fred Jones, Joe Echarte. Kneeling from left to right: Head Coach Tom Wasdin, Vern Thortsen, Manager John Pilcher.

where legendary coach Glenn Wilkes presided. When school started back, he'd often meet players before classes began for conditioning and skill drills.

After going 10-14 that first season, the Minutemen completely turned things around in year two, going 14-10, finishing as district runners-up to Bishop Moore Catholic High School in Orlando.

"I thought we were on our way to building a good basketball program," Tom said. "It seemed a little like Paxon."

John Casbon recalled how even as Cocoa Beach developed into a winning program under Wasdin, the coach never took his foot off the gas pedal. There is one game against Satellite High, in Casbon's junior year, which he still remembers vividly. Casbon's mind was somewhere else during that first half, as the Minutemen steadily fell behind their arch-rival Scorpions. Who knows where his mind was at? It could have been anywhere. Casbon was still a teenager after all.

Wasdin called timeout. On the sidelines, he grabbed Casbon by the stomach and held it in his clenched fist; with the coach's jaw clenched even tighter.

"He wouldn't let go until I looked him in the eyes, which didn't take long for me to do," Casbon said. "I had absolutely disappointed him. Coach was no wimp. He had big arms and a very intense look. He got my attention real quick. I went back out there and pounded the boards, which was my job. We got the lead and ended up beating Satellite."

That was the other thing Casbon came to appreciate about Wasdin, something Casbon also carried with him years later into the business world – the ability to motivate people. No, not by grabbing them by the stomach. But rather by instilling in them a desire to *want* to excel; a desire to please their leader.

"Tom definitely knew how to motivate," Casbon said. "He knew how to get that something extra out of you. Listen, we were just a bunch of surfers, some of us pot smokers, who played basketball but didn't really know how to play. We would've been just a bunch of bumbling guys if someone hadn't come in and showed us the way. He turned us into a machine that believed we could beat anyone."

More often than not, they did.

Once again, it was exciting times, and not just because of what Wasdin was doing at Cocoa Beach High, but also because of what the burgeoning space program was doing to the area. Celebrity sightings weren't unusual along A1A, and there were many places where young couples and singles could go – places like the Mousetrap, Ramon's (famous for its Caesar Salads), Bernard's Surf, Johnny's Hideaway, Wolfie's Restaurant and Sandwich Shop at the Ramada Inn, Heidelberg for jazz music and German food, the Alibi Lounge, Lee Caron's Carnival Club with its famous pink elephant out front ... and on and on. It wasn't unusual to see an astronaut or two, usually one of the original seven, driving a Corvette convertible straight off the car lot of former Indianapolis 500 winner Jim Rathmann.

Susie Thortsen remembers hearing the news one day that President Lyndon B. Johnson and Lady Bird Johnson were at the Cocoa Beach Country Club, and subsequently getting to see them there.

Once a Coach, Always a Coach

Tom Wasdin also coached the Cocoa Beach High School golf team. Standing from left to right: Jim Painter, Jim House, Becky Montgomery, Bryan Clark, Head Coach Tom Wasdin. Kneeling from left to right: Jimmy Leist, Bob Roth.

As a young family man, Tom wasn't much for the night life. He wasn't only busy coaching basketball. He was also the assistant football coach and the head golf coach. But his name was sure getting known in the community. One day at school, he noticed a man walking around the hallway, looking lost. He wasn't very tall, and was wearing thick glasses.

"Can I help you?" Tom asked.

"Yeah," the man replied, "I'm looking for Tom Wasdin, the basketball coach."

"That's me. What can I do for you?"

"I'd like for you to coach my basketball team in the Cocoa Beach City League," the man said.

Still a young man in his late 20s, Tom had a better idea.

"I don't want to coach your team," he said, "but I'd certainly like to play on it."

The man's name was Rick Stottler, and he immediately took a liking to Wasdin, not only as an athlete, but as a person. Tom played on Stottler's Brevard Engineering basketball team and then later on his traveling slow-pitch softball team. Stottler also had an architectural firm, Stottler Stagg & Associates, which sponsored other teams. Eventually, his Stottler Stagg softball team became a perennial state power, even competing nationally. But these were just the formative years for that, and also for the friendship that would develop for the two men. They played other sports together, and often spent endless hours just talking – about sports, business, school, goals and just life in general. Little did they know at the time, but coming together in sports and recreation would later lead to a successful and lucrative business partnership.

"Rick liked sports, and he was a very bright guy with a lot of ideas," Tom said. "We hit it off great. We became very close personal friends, so close that his kids – Michelle, Dickie and Lori – called me Uncle."

Wasdin was establishing roots along the Space Coast, roots that would not really take hold until years later. That's because something would soon happen that would take him back to Jacksonville; something he never saw coming. He was too busy, after all, building a basketball program. The Bitty Basketball League was gaining momentum, establishing a feeder system that would propel Cocoa Beach High into a basketball power well into the 1970s.

Tom wouldn't be there to see it, though. One day, just like he'd come to Cocoa Beach via an unexpected job inquiry, he got another unexpected job inquiry. It came while he was teaching a swimming class during the summer of 1966. Things were progressing professionally. Eddie Feely had left Cocoa Beach High to coach football at Merritt Island High, where he would eventually win a state championship in 1972. Tom thus became Cocoa Beach High's athletic director, as well as the dean of students and dean of faculty. He was now in administration, which had been his goal all along, working toward becoming a principal.

But at the pool that bright summer day everything changed when he looked up and saw the angular figure of his old friend Joe Williams walking toward him with that same easy grin he always remembered. Williams had just completed his second year as head coach at Jacksonville University.

"I want you to come to JU and be my assistant coach and head recruiter," he told Tom.

It might've sounded like an easy sell, but it wasn't. Stottler caught wind of the offer and put the full-court press on his friend to convince him to stay.

"Tom," Stottler said, "you're the kind of guy we need in our community. You're a great role model and a great coach."

Stottler said he'd come up with the funds to match Jacksonville University's salary figure, as well as provide a place for Tom and his family to live in Cocoa Beach. It was a tempting offer, especially given Tom's long daily commute from Merritt Island in one of the high school's Drivers Education cars. For the next several days, he and Glenda agonized over the decision.

"In the end, Joe's dream for JU was too compelling to turn down," he said. "He made JU sound like the greatest place in the world and he was going to pay me more than what he was making as the head coach. The more I thought about it, the more attractive it was. Competing at the college level, playing in the Jacksonville Coliseum, flying to away games ... it was big time. And Joe made me feel really wanted and needed. Glenda also missed Jacksonville, where we had made a lot of friends. We decided to go. As it turned out, it was one of the most important decisions I ever made. The next phase of my life would change me forever."

Even while the Wasdins moved back to Jacksonville, there were still some strings attached to Cocoa Beach.

"I did promise Rick that I would come down the next summer and play softball for his team," Tom said.

Stottler also had other ideas in mind for his friend, things that would eventually change Wasdin's life again. For now, though, an exciting new adventure awaited at Jacksonville University, where two young coaches named Joe Williams and Tom Wasdin were about to rock the college basketball world.

Chapter 7

A BIG ROLE ON THE BIG STAGE

"You know how you can meet certain people and immediately have a bond? That was Joe Williams and Tom Wasdin. There was a sincerity about them that they were going to get it done at Jacksonville University." – Rex Morgan

Sitting in the front seat of Joe Williams' car in a dark driveway as the clock pushed past midnight was not what Tom Wasdin envisioned when he went to Jacksonville University to be his old friend's assistant coach. Williams' easy smile that creaked from the corners of his mouth was nowhere to be found that night. His head, which Williams naturally carried hunched, like a tortoise emerging from its shell, hung a little lower.

The two men didn't need to say much, but then again they did. Things weren't working. That was a given, and no amount of words could amplify that more than the game they had played – and lost – earlier that evening. It was now year two of their four-year plan to make the Jacksonville University Dolphins a major player in Division I college basketball. Williams and Wasdin knew there would be growing pains. But the pain from earlier that evening was almost too much.

The Dolphins were coming off an 8-17 record the year before, when their recruiting budget was a paltry $750 and their overall budget just $43,332.76. Two of those eight victories came against The Citadel, whose scrappy senior guard, Pat Conroy, later became a bestselling author. In one of Conroy's books, a memoir titled *My Losing Season*, he chronicled those two losses to JU. It would be a nice footnote years later for Joe Williams, who had always aspired to be a writer. But at the time, Williams and Wasdin could ill-afford their own losing season at JU. Sure, they could rationalize that their 8-17 record came in the Dolphins' first season in the NCAA's major college division, and that they'd also lost All-American center Dick Pruet for a chunk of the season due to a severely sprained right ankle.

The 1966-67 Jacksonville University team was Tom Wasdin's first year as an assistant coach. Standing left to right: Manager Steve Carnine, Assistant Coach Bill Curtis, Ernie Gilbert, Wayne Kruer, Kent Stewart, Dick Pruet, Gene Martineau, Danny Lee, Head Coach Joe Williams, Assistant Coach Tom Wasdin. Kneeling from left to right: Alan Treece, Tom Erney, Mike Kellam, Al Kramer, Skip Bumbico, David Blaisdell.

Still, it was obvious that it was going to take more than calling themselves Division I to make JU big time. The Dolphins realized that when they played Georgia Tech late in the season, and a writer from the *Atlanta Journal* wrote in his preview that the Yellow Jackets were playing the "small college" Dolphins. Williams confronted the sports writer, whom he knew because the writer had formerly worked in Jacksonville.

"We're not small college," Williams told him. "We're NCAA major college. Now you can say that we're the sorriest major college team in the country, but we *are* major college."

Sure enough, in the next day's *Atlanta Journal*, after a double-digit loss to Georgia Tech, the sports writer referred to JU as "the sorriest major college team in the country."

Then came the 1967-68 season. This was the season that was supposed to show enough improvement to demonstrate that their four-year plan wasn't a pipe dream. If not, if Williams and Wasdin posted another season with more than twice as many losses as victories, then they might not even get to that fourth year. The two men knew they needed to show improvement, and soon.

They didn't.

Their second season together started with the Dolphins losing their season opener to a Florida Gators team led by dominant 6-foot-10 junior center Neal Walk, who scored 37 points and grabbed 25 rebounds against them. A year later, Walk would be the No. 2 NBA draft pick behind UCLA's Lew Alcindor, later to be known as Kareem Abdul-Jabbar. Though the loss to UF was expected, the lopsided 109-73 score still stung, even if the road game in Gainesville was perceived as a payday for the Dolphins and a tune-up for the more powerful Gators.

It was the Dolphins' second game, a home-opener against the University of North Carolina-Wilmington, an anemic Division II school, which was supposed to get things going and signal improvement.

"They were the weakest team on our schedule," Williams recalled.

The night was a disaster. The Dolphins lost 75-73 to a UNC-Wilmington team that was so talent-thin, even as a Division II school, that it would go on to finish the season 9-16. To make matters worse, the game was officiated by Kermith "KC" Hall and James "Shorty" Long, two locals from the Jacksonville area, and it seemed apparent to a lot of folks that the Dolphins were getting some generous calls, especially down the stretch, when one JU player after another went to the foul line. Problem was, they kept missing free throws.

"People thought we'd gotten every break in the book, especially from the officiating, and we still couldn't win," Wasdin recalled.

That night, a bleak overcast evening that felt as dark as Wasdin's mood, Tom started second guessing his decision to leave Cocoa Beach High, where he was Dean of Students and moving up the faculty ladder, to go be an assistant coach at JU. The Dolphins had good players, sure. But they were good on a Division II level, not Division I; and certainly not against a major university. And now JU had lost to a weak Division II team in UNC-Wilmington even while they'd gotten home cooking from the officials.

Something needed to change, and as Wasdin sat with Williams in the head coach's driveway, he heard his friend cut the solemn silence between them with a suggestion so radical it stunned him.

"Tom, this is going so bad," Williams said. "I want you to be the head coach and I'll be your assistant."

It took several seconds for Wasdin to process Williams' words and gather his thoughts. His friend was already paying him more as the assistant coach than Williams was making as the head coach. But this was something entirely different.

"No, Joe," Wasdin replied. "You upgraded the schedule and you recruited these players. They're not my responsibility. They're yours, and you're going to have to coach them."

Tom didn't want to tell his friend the rest of what he was thinking, that he was questioning whether he'd made the right decision in coming to JU. He was questioning whether the two of them could get it done. But he wasn't a quitter. If they were going to climb that mountain to the summit of Division I college basketball, then they were going to have to work smarter and harder, the latter of which Wasdin never feared.

"I always knew that Tom was a hard worker," Williams said. "Going back to when we were junior high coaches, I saw how hard he worked with his players. That's why I wanted to get Tom to work with me. I figured with both of us working together, we could get twice as much done."

The two men talked some more, late into the overcast evening, sitting in the front seat of Williams' car. Mostly, they talked about how they simply needed the talent level and the caliber of their players to be much better in order to compete at the level they aspired to be at.

"It's hard to coach foul shooting," Wasdin told Williams. "Either you can shoot foul shots, or you can't. We have to go out and recruit those types of players. We have to get better players."

In just a few years, JU had gone from NAIA to Division II to Division I. In fact, just a decade earlier the Dolphins were a junior college program. It was a speedy and heady rise, for sure, but at the same time the program was sinking.

"We simply needed to improve our level of talent," Wasdin said, "and that was going to require me turning most of my attention to recruiting. So after that night, recruiting became almost a full-time job when I wasn't teaching my three or four classes. I'd teach my classes, go to practice, and then hit the road. Sometimes I'd miss practices or even games altogether, just so I could be on the road recruiting. We felt that recruiting was either going to make or break us. Every place Joe had been, he'd won, and every place I'd been, I'd won. If we could just get the players, we felt we could coach them well enough to win."

So Wasdin hit the recruiting trail while Williams hit up the community. In addition to players, they needed fans and funding. The recruiting budget from the university was a woeful $2,000 a year. The coaches didn't even have a credit card. Williams started the Century Club for boosters, which cost $100 to join, producing a kitty that the coaches could tap into for recruiting trips. Williams visited a local businessman named Prime Osborn, who was president of Jacksonville-based Seaboard Coastline Railroad and prominent in the city. He told Osborn of his goal to build a big-time basketball program in Jacksonville and how Jacksonville University represented the city.

"You need to help us represent Jacksonville the best way possible," Williams told Osborn.

Williams didn't know how Osborn would reply. He also didn't know that Osborn also happened to be chairman of the board for Jacksonville University.

"I probably could've gotten fired for going to him like that," Williams recalled.

But Osborn didn't get him fired. Instead, he measured the young coach in his gaze.

"Son," he finally told Williams, "I like you. You've got a lot of balls. I'm going to help you. What do you want me to do?"

Williams wanted Osborn to help with a ticket drive, and Osborn did just that, assembling the presidents of other major companies in Jacksonville to do so. The primary responsibility for ticket sales still fell on Williams and Wasdin, which meant that when they weren't coaching basketball and doing all the other ancillary duties that came with their jobs, they were selling tickets and raising funds.

It was nonstop, but it was what they believed they had to do.

Wasdin was determined not only to recruit the best players, but to also become the best recruiter he could possibly be. He recalled what it felt like when he was a successful high school coach, and what did and didn't work when college recruiters like Stetson University's Glenn Wilkes visited him and his players. He figured out early on that "somebody in every player's life is the most influential person to him. That meant it was my job to find out who that is. If you find out who is going to make the decision, then you're not wasting your time with other people. It could be a parent, an uncle, a coach ... but whoever it is, you have to find that person and deal with them."

He remembered how, at Paxon High, the smart recruiters like Wilkes not only came to visit the top players like the Pajcic boys, Ron Sellers and others, but how they also made a point of getting to know their coach. "I noticed how they complimented me, figured out what I was interested in and would talk about that," Wasdin said. "They showed a personal interest, and that meant a lot. When I started recruiting, I reflected back to those times when people tried to recruit my players and implemented what I liked and what I could see that worked."

At a coaching clinic outside of Philadelphia, Wasdin met a young black assistant coach at Villanova University named George Raveling, who would later become a very successful major college head coach. The smart coaches in the late '60s could not only see that integration was coming, but that it was necessary in society. The South, of course, was slow to change. Wasdin and Williams didn't want to drag their feet. They wanted to be ahead of the curve, and ahead of slow societal changes. When Wasdin was coaching at Cocoa Beach High, he played AAU basketball in a league that had black players like Dick Blake, a former Florida A&M standout who later became the first black principal of an integrated high school in Brevard County. From firsthand experience playing with and against guys like Blake, Wasdin knew how good and how untapped the talent level was with black athletes. So he asked Raveling for guidance about recruiting black players. Raveling was generous with his knowledge, some of which might've seemed obvious and common sense years later. But in the '60s, it wasn't.

"Don't ever call a black player a boy," Raveling instructed.

Tom thought about that. When he coached, especially in high school, it was common for him to address his players as boys. Not in a demeaning way. But in the sense where he'd say something like, "Boys, we've got to tighten up on defense."

He could see now, listening to Raveling, that even a general reference using that term could spell danger, so he adjusted.

"And another thing," Raveling intoned. "Don't ever tell a black athlete that you know what they're going through, or that you know what it's like being black, because you aren't black and you don't know what it's like being black or what black people have gone through."

That especially made sense to Tom. He could see how someone might say that to try and empathize, and how wrong that would be.

"Make sure you treat those black players you're recruiting with respect," Raveling added. "You're from the South, and you have a Southern accent. That's not a big advantage for you. You can make up for that by being sincere."

Tom absorbed everything Raveling told him. He also absorbed other things about Raveling that he tried to implement into his own personality. He liked how friendly Raveling was, how he made him instantly feel at ease. "He was one of the most congenial, sincere persons I've ever met," Wasdin said. "When he talked to you, he looked you in the eye and made you feel like you were the most important person in the world. He wasn't looking around the room to see who else he needed to talk to. He was looking at *you*. You were the most important person to him. He made you feel special. That was a great lesson for me. That was the way I wanted to make other people feel."

Armed with his own experiences, along Raveling's good counsel and even better example, Wasdin hit the recruiting trail. Often, he was on the road trying to operate on a travel budget that was miniscule and without even a credit card. The Century Club, where boosters donated $100 each to join, helped offset some of the costs of recruiting, but even still Wasdin often paid for things out of his own pocket.

When he wasn't on the road, Wasdin still maximized his time and resources. He and Williams connected with a man named John "Moose" Montgomery, who worked as a district manager for Southern Bell. A supporter of JU basketball, Montgomery told Wasdin that he could come into the Southern Bell offices after hours and use their WATS line to make toll-free, long-distance calls. It became an almost nightly ritual for Wasdin to spend several hours after practice at the Southern

Bell offices, calling dozens of recruits. For a program operating on a shoestring budget, it was a huge benefit.

"I was working daylight to dark," Wasdin recalled. "But that's the way I always worked, going back to working on the farm growing up."

After developing relationships with recruits, Wasdin would bring Williams into the Southern Bell offices and have a list of calls lined up for the head coach to make. Before it even got to that point, though, Wasdin had already told the recruits about what a great university Jacksonville was, how it was a great city with friendly people, how the campus was beautiful, right on the St. John's River and just a few miles from the Atlantic Ocean. He'd note that there was no football, so basketball was king, and that the Dolphins played in the 10,000-seat Jacksonville Coliseum. Even though the student body was less than 3,000 students, he'd tell the prospective players that JU was big time. In fact, Wasdin was so confident that he'd tell recruits that JU was "the number one place to play basketball south of Tobacco Road," adding that he and Williams were in the process of building a major college program. Mostly, though, he'd tell prospective players what a great guy and head coach Joe Williams was.

"He had already built me up before I even got on the phone with those recruits," Williams said. "And then, when I got on the phone, I'd build Tom up. We were a team. But we had a lot of work to do, and it really helped a lot that Tom was very good at spotting talent."

Some of the talent Wasdin was pursuing during that 1967-68 recruiting period would help lay the foundation for JU's future – players like Vaughn Wedeking, Chip Dublin, Greg Nelson and Rex Morgan.

Getting these players meant leaving Florida and recruiting against some of the top programs in the country. It also meant doggedly going where other coaches didn't go, or perhaps didn't even know about. One example of that was when Wasdin was on a recruiting trip in New York. He was there to recruit a player, but the player's coach told him that there was a kid who was even better whom Wasdin should go see. The player's name was Chip Dublin. Wasdin had heard of Dublin, and knew that he had gone to Loyola University in Chicago. What he didn't know was that Dublin had left school there and returned to New York, where he had been an All-New York City prep standout. Not only wasn't Dublin playing college ball anymore, he was working as a clerk at a Chase Manhattan Bank on Wall Street, which is precisely where Wasdin found him. He convinced Dublin to resume his basketball career, and to do so at JU.

"Chipper was a very likable guy, and he was just perfect for us," Wasdin said. "He was a good kid, very smart, especially street smart, outgoing, the type of young man who communicated very well."

Dublin would also become one of the first handful of black players to play college sports in the Deep South.

The pieces were coming together.

Wasdin especially knew there was talent to be found in basketball-rich Indiana, and he wasn't afraid to go there and spend significant chunks of time trying to recruit players to tiny Jacksonville University. It was in Evansville, Indiana where he found 5-foot-10 Vaughn Wedeking, and saw in him great athletic ability that could help JU's program. Wedeking wasn't highly recruited, partially because there was some uncertainty as to which sport he would pursue. He was the Indiana state champion in the 440, and the University of Tennessee was recruiting him to run track and play basketball.

"We didn't have a track team, but I saw that Vaughn could run Coach Williams' 1-3-1 offense," Wasdin said. "We wanted that kind of speed, and he was also smart, a good ball-handler and an outstanding foul shooter (who made 91.9 percent of his free throws in high school). I spent a lot of time calling him on that Southern Bell WATS line, talking to him and recruiting him. He and Greg Nelson were good friends and they wanted to go somewhere together, which wasn't a problem for us, since Greg was an outstanding player, too."

Nelson was bigger, growing into a solid 6-foot-6 frame. The two of them were leaders, and they helped guide their high school team to 51-consecutive regular-season victories.

"After Vaughn and I played in some tournament, Tom showed up talking with this Southern drawl," Nelson recalled. "He had this bulldog demeanor about him that I liked."

Not recruited by their hometown University of Evansville, Wedeking and Nelson scheduled recruiting trips to Tennessee, Georgia Tech and finally Jacksonville. They enjoyed their trip to Tennessee. Nelson remembers playing dodgeball in a dormitory hallway with some of the Volunteer players, most notably Tom Boerwinkle, a bullish

7-footer who was at the time called the most physically developed player ever for UT. "It was a wonder I didn't get my head tore off playing dodgeball with that guy," Nelson recalled.

The Georgia Tech trip was okay, but uneventful. And then there was Jacksonville. "Tom just exuded optimism," Nelson recalled. "You just believed in him. You believed that you could be a part of something small that could become something big."

They ate a steak dinner in a rotating restaurant atop a high-rise, enjoying a stunning panorama of the city. They visited the beach. The academics impressed them both.

"It wasn't a necessity that Vaughn and I go someplace together, but independent of each other we both decided we wanted to play at Jacksonville, so it worked out well," Nelson said.

There was another player in the Midwest whom Wasdin came in contact with, one who would have a huge impact on Jacksonville's program. However, this player wasn't a kid, at least not any longer. Rex Morgan was a sought-after player coming out of high school in Charleston, Illinois, although at the time he didn't realize that college coaches coveted him. His high school coach wanted him to go to the University of Illinois, so the coach kept letters from other schools in a box, never showing them to Morgan. Going to Illinois, which was only 50 miles away, was an okay idea to Morgan, though he had dreamed of getting out of the cold weather and playing somewhere either in California, Arizona or Florida.

Everything seemed set for Morgan to go to Illinois when the school switched coaches. After 20 years at the helm, Harry Combes stepped down as the Fighting Illini head coach and was replaced by Harv Schmidt. "The new coach didn't know me," Morgan recalled. "I wasn't really recruited by Illinois after they changed head coaches. So I ended up going to the University of Evansville."

Part of the reason why Morgan chose Evansville was because of a player who'd been there just before him, a guard by the name of Jerry Sloan who went on to become a Hall of Fame NBA coach.

"Like me, Jerry Sloan had gone from a small town to Evansville," Morgan said. "He was a 6-foot-5 white guy who played guard, and when I talked to him he was an NBA player. He was the one who convinced me that Evansville was the place to go."

But almost immediately, Morgan didn't like the college experience at Evansville, even though he led the freshmen team to an undefeated season; the first in school history. He told a reporter he didn't like eating meals on road trips out of brown paper bags, and it was a comment that gained legs. "I was real immature at the time," Morgan said. "I was quoted about the brown paper bags, and that got a lot of attention. I also didn't like that we were driving two and three hours to games in cars and vans when other teams were flying."

Two of Morgan's teammates – Mike Owens and Layne Holmes – had been recruited by JU. But their parents wouldn't let them go that far away to a program that wasn't established.

"Mike and Layne kept talking about how they wished they could've gone to Jacksonville," Morgan said. "They'd talk about how great Florida was and how they would have gone to JU had their parents let them. After that first season, we went down to Florida for spring break, and we stopped at a service station somewhere in the South, before we got to Florida. And guess who we run into at the service station? Joe Williams and Tom Wasdin."

Williams and Wasdin were heading to the Final Four in Louisville, Kentucky.

"We just talked," Morgan recalled. "And you know how you can meet certain people and immediately have a bond? That was Joe Williams and Tom Wasdin. There was a sincerity about them that they were going to get it done at Jacksonville University. With both of them, you could tell they were good people. They were like me, trying to find a niche, and I thought, 'Maybe we can find that niche together.' I walked away feeling that, yeah, I can trust these guys. I can play for them."

Knowing now that Morgan wanted to leave Evansville, and that he had an interest in coming to Jacksonville, Wasdin kept tabs on the big, playmaking guard.

"Coach was the ultimate salesperson," Morgan said. "He could sell ice to an Eskimo. But it was more than that. Joe and Tom made it real personal. Tom took the time to get to know me. And they didn't just sell me on the school. They sold me on who they were. They got me to believe that they believed in me. They were telling me that if I didn't come then they didn't have anybody else. They kept telling me that there wasn't anybody as good as me. Jacksonville hadn't had a lot of success, and I had a lot of confidence in myself that I could go somewhere and make a difference."

His childhood friend, Frank Casey, kept encouraging Morgan to stay in touch with Wasdin. Morgan and Casey had grown up playing ball together and although Casey's skills didn't translate to the college level, they still wanted to go to school together somewhere, preferably where it was warm. "Florida sounded magical to a couple of Midwestern cornfield guys like us," Casey recalled. "I was the only guy in Rex's ear telling him he had to go to Florida."

Casey soon found someone in his ear – Joe Williams. The JU head coach asked Casey if he wanted to come to Florida, too, and be a jack-of-all-trades guy for the Dolphins' program, mostly serving as a sort of sports information director. He'd be on scholarship, too. Williams didn't have to ask Casey twice.

On one recruiting trip, Wasdin came into the stands to watch Morgan play, sitting next to Casey and conversing with him and the other young men sitting there, his thick Southern drawl standing out like a breakfast bowl of grits at a steak-and-potatoes dinner. "One of the guys with us was wisecracking, and after Coach Wasdin left, he said, 'Who in the hell was that hayseed?' When I told him he was a coach who was recruiting Rex to go play in Jacksonville, Florida, the guy said, 'Rex can't go to a school with a hayseed like that.'"

But not only did Rex Morgan want to go to Jacksonville, he had actually wanted to leave Evansville after his freshman season and transfer right then to JU. But his coach wouldn't release him. So he returned home and went to nearby Lake Land Junior College in Mattoon, Illinois, where Wasdin kept in contact with him, assuring Morgan that not only was he needed at Jacksonville, but that he'd never have to worry about eating his road trip meals out of a brown paper sack.

During his season at Lake Land Junior College, Williams and Wasdin brought Morgan down to New Orleans on a recruiting trip, where the Dolphins were playing Loyola University. The game didn't go well, at least from a first-impression standpoint. "We played one of our worst games, if not *the* worst game, of that season," Wasdin recalled. "We had the lead and then we blew it, and Rex was there and saw it all."

Afterward, Wasdin found Morgan, hoping he hadn't lost interest in JU.

"Rex," he said, "I'm sure you're not very pleased with what you saw tonight. I don't know why we played so badly. We do have a young team, but I promise you that we're better than this."

"Coach," Morgan replied, "you need me more than anybody else in the country does. I'm coming to JU. And when I get there, I can tell you that this won't happen."

It wasn't what Wasdin was expecting to hear, but it sure was what he liked to hear.

"Rex, you're right," he said. "You're a lot smarter than I thought you were. We do need you, and I know you're going to make a difference."

In the summers, Wasdin was still going back to Cocoa Beach. But instead of it just being for fun and games, playing on Rick Stottler's powerhouse softball team, he was now managing the Canaveral Pier for Stottler. That summer, he got Morgan a job there, solidifying their relationship.

Little did Wasdin realize at the time, but his ongoing relationship and friendship with Stottler was laying the groundwork for the future, and it would be a future away from coaching basketball. Returning to Cocoa Beach during the summers wasn't what he particularly wanted to do, but on his coaching salary Tom needed the extra income. Stottler, though, instinctively knew Wasdin's potential and didn't want to lose him. The first summer Tom managed the Canaveral Pier (later renamed the Cocoa Beach Pier) it was the most financially successful stint in its history, turning a profit. Wasdin ran the Liar's Lounge and Snack Bar along with a bait and tackle shop. He met a surfer entrepreneur named Dick Catri and allowed him to build a surf shop into the pier named Shagg's Surf Shop, which became very successful. Later, when Shagg's moved to a bigger location, Wasdin brought another surf shop into the pier. This one was called Ron Jon Surf Shop, and it eventually would grow into an internationally known tourist attraction. It was also with Dick Catri that Wasdin helped start the Easter Surfing Festival, which became a hugely popular annual event in Cocoa Beach and one where the sport's future iconic superstar, Kelly Slater, first learned to compete.

From these and other experiences with Wasdin, Stottler saw something special, and he knew that offering the coach a summer job managing the pier would only go so far for so long. So he decided to sweeten the pot. Stottler and his partner Charlie Moehle asked Wasdin to meet them at the Melbourne Beach Steak House, an upscale restaurant known for its signature Gomez salad dressing.

"Tom, we'll make you a proposition," Stottler said over dinner. "If you keep coming down to manage the pier and the surf contest, then when we pay off the pier and get out of debt, we'll make you a one-third owner of it."

A deal was struck. Wasdin realized that it not only was an investment for his future, but he also was beginning to realize that he enjoyed the business aspect of managing the pier and liked that he was still involved with young people. His second summer there, he oversaw the opening of a teenage night club called Asylum, which had an electric dance floor with strobe lights and black lights ... but no alcohol. "We had soft drinks," Wasdin recalled, "and you couldn't get in if you were over 21. It was fun. Part of the appeal for me was that I enjoyed the kids." Tom often found himself even tapping into his own inner kid, playing pinball on one of the machines late into the evening after closing up. It was an idyllic, innocent time. But it was also a second job, and Wasdin recognized that. His primary responsibility wasn't building a business; it was building a basketball program at Jacksonville University with his friend Joe Williams.

The influx of basketball talent Wasdin helped recruit to JU had immediate results, which was evident at the start of the 1968-69 season. The team was returning Rod McIntyre, Danny Hawkins, Ken Selke, Kent Smith and Tom Erney, and the players could sense that even though they were incumbents, nobody's starting position was guaranteed. Practices were spirited and intense. One day, a flare-up between Rex Morgan and Tom Erney evolved into a fistfight, which required Williams and Wasdin to reign in the players and channel their competitive drive toward the common good.

The competition on the outside was fierce, as well. One preseason poll had the Florida Gators in the Top 10. Florida State had an outstanding center named Dave Cowens, who would later become an All-Star NBA player with the Boston Celtics and a future inductee into the Naismith Memorial Basketball Hall of Fame.

Finally, as the season started, Williams settled on juniors Rex

Morgan and Rod McIntyre and sophomores Vaughn Wedeking, Greg Nelson and Chip Dublin for JU's starting five.

After a tune-up win against Biscayne College, Jacksonville moved on to the Sunshine Classic, where the Dolphins stunned favored Florida, 67-64, beating the Gators for the first time in JU's school history. In the title game, Jacksonville fell to Cowens and FSU, 93-88. Even still, the tournament seemed like a clarion call that the Dolphins were becoming a program to be reckoned with, as well as respected. Indeed, five games later, the Dolphins avenged their loss to FSU, beating the Seminoles, 76-68, following that big win with another against Georgia Tech. Things were rolling.

The 1968-69 Jacksonville University team that beat the Florida Gators for the first time in JU history. Standing from left to right: Assistant Coach Tom Wasdin, Rex Morgan, Greg Nelson, Rod McIntyre, Ken Selke, Mike Drasites, Assistant Coach Bill Curtis. Kneeling left to right: Ken Smith, Chipper Dublin, Danny Hawkins, Head Coach Joe Williams, Tom Erney, Vaughn Wedeking, Mike Kellam.

All of it produced the best season in JU basketball history – a 17-7 record in big-time college basketball that had the program gaining national attention. Morgan, who averaged 26.7 points per game that season, earned All-American honors. Led by Wedeking and his 90 per cent accuracy from the free throw line, the Dolphins became known as a team that could make its foul shots. In fact, JU finished the season as the nation's best free throw shooting squad. But could they reach the national stage that is the Mecca for college basketball – the Final Four? That was the goal, but in order to do so, more talent was needed.

Thus, Wasdin kept his foot on the gas pedal, both literally and figuratively. He knew that what JU especially needed was a dominant big man. He just didn't know if he could get one, much less that he could get two.

Chapter 8

TWIN TOWERS

"PS, my friend is 7-foot-2 Artis Gilmore." – Ernie Fleming

The letter arrived addressed to Tom Wasdin at Jacksonville University, and the assistant coach immediately recognized the name on the plain white envelope. Ernie Fleming was a 6-foot-5 sharpshooter with mutton chop sideburns out of Durfee High School in Fall River, Massachusetts. Wasdin had recruited Fleming, but because his grades were lacking, he encouraged him to go to a junior college and then transfer to JU. And that's what Fleming did, signing with Gardner-Webb Junior College in North Carolina. There was one problem with that, though. Gardner-Webb was becoming a four-year program after Fleming's sophomore season, so Wasdin figured Fleming would stay put and finish his college career there. But his letter said otherwise. Fleming told Wasdin that he was still interested in JU, and that he had a friend on the team who was interested in coming, too.

"PS," the letter said, "my friend is 7-foot-2 Artis Gilmore."

It got Wasdin's attention. How could it not?

Wasdin vaguely remembered Gilmore as a player from Chipley, in the Florida panhandle, who played at an all-black high school and then spent his senior season at another all-black high school – George Washington Carver High – north across the border from Florida in Dothan, Alabama. In both places, but especially in small-town Chipley, segregation was at its worst, with designated areas all over town marked for coloreds. "It was very difficult growing up in my hometown," Gilmore recalled. "It was a very racially motivated area. In a small town like that, things would happen that were off the radar, bad things that didn't receive much recognition. There was a tremendous amount of fright you lived with."

It made Gilmore withdrawn and distrusting of whites. His ticket to a better life would be basketball, but where would it be punched? During his senior season at Carver High, the team played in a prestigious all-black basketball tournament in Montgomery, Alabama. "Coaches came in from everywhere, from all over the country, for that tournament," Gilmore said. One of those coaches was from Gardner-Webb, which at the time in the mid-60s was one of the few schools in the South that was taking black athletes. Since his academics were not solid enough for a four-year university, Gilmore went to Gardner-Webb, where he mostly played under the radar of major college recruiters.

But now, thanks to Fleming's letter, Gilmore was on Wasdin's radar, and since JU was ahead of the curve for integration he was eager to see Artis in action. Wasdin didn't remember him being quite that tall in high school, but if Fleming said he was 7-foot-2 and interested in coming to JU, then he was definitely worth a close look. Wasdin knew, too, that because of segregation and other factors, players often slipped through the cracks. He read Fleming's letter again and again, making sure he was reading it correctly. Wasdin resolved to be at Gardner-Webb's next home game, which was just a couple of days away.

It was early in December of 1967 that Wasdin drove to Boiling Springs, the North Carolina town where Gardner-Webb sits, and bought a ticket to the Runnin' Bulldogs' game that night. He doesn't remember who the opponent was. What Wasdin does remember, though, is that he couldn't take his eyes off of the freshman center.

"I couldn't believe how good Artis was, how high he could jump, and how agile he was," he recalled. "He could've started for us right then. Same with Ernie Fleming."

Wasdin could also see why they might be interested in leaving Gardner-Webb. Boiling Springs was a small, country town west of Gastonia and northeast of Spartanburg – basically in the middle of nowhere. And the college had few black students, which meant that there was not much of a social life for Artis Gilmore and Ernie Fleming.

Soon, Wasdin was burning up the Southern Bell's WATS line that their friend and booster, John "Moose" Montgomery, was letting him use in the evenings to make toll-free phone calls. This way, he could stay in close contact with Fleming and Gilmore and develop their relationship – especially with Gilmore, a quiet, almost reticent young man who required extra effort to get to know.

"I kept calling their dorm room, talking mostly to Ernie, and whenever I could, I kept going to their games," Wasdin said.

Wasdin explained to the young men the virtues of Jacksonville University.

"I told them the JU story, about how it was a great place to play and how we were going to be a basketball power. I told them what a great coach Joe Williams was, how he didn't raise his voice or use profanity, and that players liked playing for him and worked hard for him. I told them we had the nation's most beautiful campus, right on a river, that we had a small student body and that they could expect a lot of individual help. They said they were interested."

Gilmore liked what he was hearing, and eventually when he made a recruiting visit to JU's campus, he liked what he saw.

"Right away, I thought he was pretty special," Gilmore recalled. "Just listening to him, I liked that he was treating me as an individual, as a man. The way I grew up in Chipley, you weren't treated like a person. But here this white man was treating me with respect."

Showing up regularly at Gardner-Webb games posed a problem, though. The college was shifting to a four-year program the next year, and it seemed a foregone conclusion that Fleming and Gilmore were going to stay. Wasdin sure didn't want to tip anyone off that he was there trying to recruit their best player to JU. At the same time, he also knew he had something better to offer the players.

"Gardner-Webb wasn't big time," he said. "They weren't on TV, they didn't play in a coliseum, like we did. Their gym seated about three thousand people, about the size of a high school gym in Indiana. They were playing in the bus circuit, too, going to games in either a bus or a van. I could see why they'd want to come to JU, but I still didn't want anyone to know that."

He noticed that Gardner-Webb had a booster club and that members wore red blazers to games and socialized before and after games, and at halftime, in a little hospitality room. Since Tom owned a red blazer he began wearing it to games, socializing with the boosters in the hospitality room. Everyone assumed he was another booster, and not an assistant coach/recruiter from Jacksonville, and that was fine with him.

"As long as I wore that red blazer, nobody stopped me from going into that little hospitality room," he said. "I told people I was an insurance guy from Charlotte who loved basketball. I just blended right in, talking about how good of a team we had. I always kept that red blazer on. As long as they saw me as a fan of the school, nobody suspected anything."

Still, there was concern that other college recruiters might hear about the growing legend of Artis Gilmore, who would come to be known by the moniker "The A-Train", and try to swoop in. So Tom and Artis developed a plan. They put the word out that Artis was staying at Gardner-Webb, and if he wasn't, then he was going to go to nearby Wake Forest.

"That was our best chance," Wasdin said. "We either had to keep it quiet, or if someone mentioned it, just say that he was either staying or going to Wake Forest. If people knew Artis was interested in leaving, there's no way we could've competed for him head-to-head against all those big schools."

Wake Forest had an aggressive, up-and-coming assistant basketball coach named Billy Packer, who had played at the school and who would later become one of college basketball's iconic broadcasters. What Wasdin knew, and others apparently missed, is that for Gilmore to be able to go to Wake Forest, which had stringent academic standards because of playing in the Atlantic Coast Conference, he would've had to qualify academically out of high school and been what was called a predictor. And he hadn't. It was, after all, why he was going to a junior college in the first place.

Wasdin went to about a half-dozen Gardner-Webb games that season, and then about a dozen more the following year, as Gilmore and Fleming blossomed into even better players. All the while, he couldn't believe he had the inside track on Gilmore, but he did.

"You didn't even want to dream that high," he said. "I sure didn't want to take anything for granted. I continued to sell JU, and after our 17-7 season, I told Artis, 'The one thing we don't have that other schools have is a national reputation as a basketball power. We were 17-7 this year with everyone coming back. If you come, Artis, we can win another 10 games.'"

"Coach, don't worry," Gilmore said. "I'll take care of that."

Wasdin liked that Gilmore exuded a quiet confidence without being cocky. In fact, the more he got to know the big man, the more he liked him.

"What Artis wanted was an education, to play with good teammates that he got along with, and coaches who would treat him like a man," he said. "He was soft-spoken and shy, but when you got to know him you could tell he was thinking deeply about things. I kept treating him like the gentleman that he was. I told him what he needed to hear and not what he wanted to hear. I told him that we cared about him and Ernie, and about their education. I was careful not to say that I know what it's like being black. I was also very careful not to use the word boy or even let it slip out in an innocuous way."

Next on the agenda was getting Joe Williams to see Gilmore play. Williams was reluctant. Florida had slim pickings for big centers, but Wasdin would still drag Williams to see them because it was all the state had to offer. Now, Williams thought, Tom wants to drag me all the way to North Carolina to see another big man who wasn't very good.

"Don't take me to see another slow guy," Williams told Wasdin.

Wasdin kept assuring Williams that Gilmore was not just good, but great. Even still, he had to add some incentive for Williams to make the trip.

"Listen, Joe. I'll drive. And there's a great little barbecue place along the way that I'll take you to," Tom said. "I promise you it'll be worth it."

"Okay," Williams finally said. "I'll go."

Williams knew, as he would recall years later, that "Tom worked tirelessly. He poured himself into recruiting. If this was someone he really wanted me to see, then I owed him that."

It was about a six-hour drive and the two coaches left about noon, driving up in the blue, four-door 1967 Chevrolet Caprice that Wasdin got from Rick Stottler as part of the deal for managing the Canaveral Pier during the summers. Along the way, they stopped at the barbecue joint, where the food was great, just as Tom promised. But would Artis

Gilmore be great, or at least good enough to contribute to JU's mission to become a college basketball power?

Just minutes into the game, Williams got his answer.

As he watched the 7-foot-2 center work both ends of the court, nimble and agile and fast, and able to leap like no player he'd ever seen before, Williams lost sight that he was a coach and morphed into a fan. Soon, he was on his feet, shouting.

"Go, Artis! Go! Tom, look at Artis! Isn't he great?! Go, Artis! Go!"

By the end of the game, Williams was hoarse.

"I had never seen a player like Artis before," he said. "Right from the beginning, I treated him with a lot of respect. I treated him as if he were equal to me as a man, which wasn't how very many black people were treated back then."

From Gilmore's perspective, he saw in Williams someone just like Wasdin; someone whom he could trust and respect.

"When I eventually got to meet Joe, I liked Joe right away," Gilmore said. "He was a mild individual with a great big, huge smile, and very personable. In getting to know those two guys, I never thought that there was a split personality; that suddenly something was going to come up and be negative or different than what they'd been telling me. They were both very genuine. They were the first white people I ever trusted."

Meanwhile, down in South Florida, an 18-year-old young man who had steadily grown to 7-feet tall was working as a car jockey at a Cadillac dealership in West Palm Beach, shuffling vehicles around the lot to different service areas. Pembrook Burrows III had no aspirations about going to college, although his high school coach said he could've worked on getting him a scholarship to Bethune-Cookman College, a black school in Daytona Beach. But Burrows was a late bloomer who didn't start playing basketball until his junior year in high school, and thus spent most of his time on the bench.

"I didn't want to go somewhere and sit on the bench again," he said. "And I wasn't really thinking about what would've been most important, which was getting an education. So after I graduated from high school, I went to work."

Burrows settled into his job at the Cadillac dealership in what would've been his freshman year in college. That following summer, when a lot of his buddies returned home from college, he found himself playing basketball most every day, eventually joining them on an AAU team. It was while playing at a regional tournament in Macon, Georgia, that he came in contact with a former Cocoa High standout named Danny Tharpe, who was now coaching the Cocoa High basketball team. Tharpe had noticed that when the players were introduced pregame, the public address announcer included which college they were attending. However, no such amendment was made for Pembrook Burrows III.

"Are you not playing college ball?" Tharpe asked Burrows.

"No."

"Well, you're at least good enough to go to a junior college and play right away," Tharpe said. "Let me have your name and address and I'll see what I can do."

Burrows gave Tharpe his contact information and then promptly forgot about the conversation. A month or so later, back home in West Palm Beach, he came home from work one day to find "this white guy sitting on my front porch looking like a police officer. I knew I hadn't done anything wrong, but I couldn't figure out what this guy was doing there."

The man introduced himself as Jim Oler, head basketball coach at Brevard Junior College in Cocoa, and based on what Danny Tharpe had told him, he was there to offer Burrows a full, two-year scholarship to play basketball for him.

Oler had already talked to Burrows' mother, who liked the idea of her son going to college. So Burrows signed and headed to Cocoa, where Oler found him housing with an elderly woman. Every day, assistant basketball coach Floyd Horgen, who later became a Hall of Fame golf coach, would pick Burrows up for school and basketball practice. Burrows was largely unskilled as a player, but anybody who knew the game could see his tremendous upside.

Wasdin, of course, was ever-busy on the recruiting trail. With his and Williams' recruiting efforts now in concert, he felt encouraged, though still hard to believe, that Artis Gilmore and his solid 7-foot-2 frame were going to come to Jacksonville University. Still, it didn't stop Wasdin from recruiting other centers, as well as other top players. After all, he and Williams were trying to build a national power at JU and it was going to take more than just one guy to accomplish that.

Down at his old stomping grounds along the Space Coast, Jim Oler was telling him about a raw 7-foot freshman center named Pembrook Burrows III. Wasdin respected and valued Oler's opinion and considered him a friend. Oler, who was originally from Indiana, knew his hoops and consistently fielded winning teams at BJC. When Wasdin coached at Cocoa Beach High, his team and Oler's team would occasionally scrimmage against each other.

"You need to keep an eye on this Pembrook Burrows kid," Oler told him, "because he's going to get better and better."

It helped that Wasdin also maintained contact with the Brevard County area through Rick Stottler and their business relationship with the Canaveral Pier. He was still heading back there in the summers to play softball and manage the pier, and part of the deal for managing the pier – in addition to $100 a week and a place to live – was that Stottler gave him that blue, four-door 1967 Chevrolet Caprice to use. It was, not coincidentally, the car Tom travelled all through the Southeast in, recruiting players.

Being back in Brevard County during the summers helped Tom get to know Pembrook Burrows III better, and offer him help if the young player needed it. "One summer, I saw that Pembrook needed a biology class," he recalled. "Since I was there, it was easy for me to assist him, to make sure he had tutors and went to class."

Even when he wasn't there in the summers, it still seemed to Burrows as if Wasdin was *always* there.

"He came to all the games, or at least it seemed like he was at all our games," Burrows said. "Every time he was at a game, he'd make contact with me and encourage me, and let me know he was there. He really wanted me to go to Jacksonville. He was very insistent. After awhile, as I got to know Coach Wasdin on a personal level, he became someone I trusted. Every recruiter sells their school. That's their job. But he went above and beyond. He was not just selling Jacksonville University, he was selling himself."

Burrows' sophomore season at BJC was also Artis Gilmore's sophomore season at Gardner-Webb. As Coach Oler had predicted, Burrows did indeed blossom into a force in the low post, leading the Titans all the way to the National Junior College Tournament in Hutchinson, Kansas. By now, other recruiters were descending on BJC to recruit Burrows. Wasdin, though, already had a relationship and an inside track. He was sure Burrows was coming to JU, but at the same time he didn't want to be too overconfident. It was the same mindset he had with Gilmore, who had become a force for Gardner-Webb. He, too, had led the Runnin' Bulldogs all the way to the national tournament.

As fate would have it, in a first-round game, Gardner-Webb and Brevard Junior College were pitted against each, with Artis Gilmore and Pembrook Burrows III jumping center in the opening tipoff.

"I couldn't believe what I was seeing," Wasdin recalled. "Here I am at the national junior college tournament, watching a 7-foot-2 center jumping center against a 7-foot guy, and both of them were going to come to JU.

"At least, I hoped."

It helped that Gilmore's recruiting trip to JU had gone well. Real well. There was a hotel restaurant known for its great food and service where Williams and Wasdin used to like to eat. Years later, the same location became a Ruth's Chris Steakhouse. The maitre d' there was a young black man named Lorenzo Reddick. "He was very smooth, very polished," Tom recalled. Since recruiting black players was a fairly new experience, Williams and Wasdin quizzed Reddick about what to do when Gilmore came in for his official recruiting visit.

"You're a young black man, you live here, you know what to do," Wasdin told Reddick. "Where should we take Artis when he gets here?"

Reddick's input was invaluable, and the recruiting visit was a success, with Gilmore impressed both with the city and the school. He liked the campus, and he especially liked the basketball program that Williams and Wasdin were building. Everything seemed set for "The A-Train" to motor south to Jacksonville after Gilmore's sophomore season at Gardner-Webb was completed.

Wasdin was smart enough to know, though, that until you had a signature on a letter-of-intent, anything could happen. He saw scores of other recruiters all around him, and he could see their interest in the two big men. One of those recruiters was Billy Packer, who was there representing Wake Forest, the school Wasdin and Gilmore had thrown out as a possible destination – albeit a decoy – should he leave Gardner-Webb. Wasdin knew Gilmore wasn't academically eligible for Wake Forest. Evidently, though, Packer wasn't aware of that.

Suddenly, Wasdin heard Packer's name paged to a telephone. It was his athletic director from Wake Forest.

"Billy, where are you?" the athletic director asked the young coach.

"I'm out here in Hutchinson, Kansas, recruiting Artis Gilmore," Packer replied.

"Billy, he's not eligible for the ACC," the athletic director told him. "We can't take juco players who were not predictors in high school. You need to come back."

But there were other recruiters to worry about, not just with Artis Gilmore, but also Pembrook Burrows III.

In that opening-round game, Gilmore dominated Burrows and Gardner-Webb beat BJC. Afterward, Wasdin adjourned to the Titans' locker room, where he had access because of his friendship with Coach Oler. When Wasdin emerged from the locker room there were a gaggle of recruiters waiting at the door, wanting to talk to Pembrook Burrows III.

"There must've been about 10 to 15 of them," Wasdin recalled. Burrows had improved so much from his freshman to sophomore season that he was now on the national radar.

Not knowing who Wasdin was, one of the recruiters asked to speak to Burrows. Since Oler had not allowed his players to talk to the media as long as they were still playing in the tournament, the recruiters were eager to finally get to speak to the 7-foot phenom.

"Pembrook is really upset over the loss," Wasdin told the recruiters. "Why don't you guys leave me your cards, and I'll make sure he gets back to you. Right now, he really doesn't want to talk to anybody until he gets back to Florida. He's very upset."

One by one, each recruiter handed Wasdin their business card. When the crowd dispersed, Wasdin found the nearest trash can and threw them all away.

Not too long after that, Burrows signed with JU. And then, shortly after that, Gilmore signed.

It gave Jacksonville University not one, but two 7-footers – with sportswriters calling them the "Twin Towers".

Pembrook Burrows III signing his letter-of-intent to play basketball for Jacksonville University. Sitting and looking up is Brevard Junior College Head Coach Jim Oler. Standing is Tom Wasdin.

It also gave Pembrook Burrows III cause to pause. He'd just been dominated at the National Junior College tournament by Gilmore, and now Gilmore had just signed to play at the same four-year school as him. His original fears about college basketball, that he would just be a bench player, returned to him. He called Wasdin.

"Coach," he asked, "did you guys sign Artis Gilmore?"

"Yes, we did," Wasdin said.

"Coach, you told me I could start. I'm not sure I can beat out Artis."

"Pembrook," Wasdin replied, "I can't talk right now. I'll call you right back. Just sit tight."

Wasdin, knowing that he was on the spot, called Williams and told him about the brief conversation he'd just had with Burrows. Williams knew that they'd given Burrows their word that they would start him, and he didn't want to go back on it.

"What do you think of playing Pembrook at the high post, and Artis at the low post?" Williams asked Wasdin.

"I think that'll work," Wasdin said.

"Well, let's go with that."

Wasdin called Burrows back and told him of their plan to start both he and Gilmore.

"Pembrook, you have a nice little shot from the foul line," Wasdin said. "I think it'll work great for Artis to play the low post, and for you to play the high post."

"Coach, I like that," Burrows said. "I'll see you in Jacksonville. I'll be there."

And just like that, a Jacksonville University basketball team that had gone 17-7 with an emerging 6-foot-5 playmaker at guard in Rex Morgan had added two giants – 7-foot-2 Artis Gilmore and 7-foot Pembrook Burrows III. It was the game's Twin Towers. It not only added height to the team, it also heightened expectations. Any team that went against JU that following 1969-70 season would have to scale those two mountainous players. But could Jacksonville finally scale that mountain that was big-time, Division I college basketball?

Joe Williams and Tom Wasdin and the rest of the world were about to find out.

Chapter 9

WRITING A FEW PARAGRAPHS ON THE PAGES OF HISTORY

"It's like we got up one day and we were playing UCLA in the NCAA Finals." – Tom Wasdin

Whenever anyone flips through the pages of history that is the 20th century, they'll certainly pause and linger for a few moments on the year 1969.

Man landed on the moon that year – not once, but twice. NASA's awe-inspiring Apollo program wasn't the year's only advancement in science and technology, though. The Boeing 747 made its maiden flight and the Concorde jet took its first test flight. The first artificial heart was implanted into a human at the same time that "Marcus Welby MD" debuted on TV. At the Mayo Clinic, the first hip replacement in America was performed. Seiko marketed what it called a quartz watch. And computer scientists succeeded in sending the first message over ARPANET, which later becomes known as the Internet.

Richard Nixon was sworn in as the 37th president in 1969, the same year that the 34th president, Dwight Eisenhower, died. After taking office, Nixon resumed bombing North Vietnam while calling on America's "silent majority" to support him. It was a hard sell, especially after details of the My Lai Massacre detonated on the American public, with Cleveland's *The Plain Dealer* newspaper publishing graphic photographs of dead Vietnamese villagers. In the midst of this, Vietnamese president Ho Chi Minh died.

In the Middle East, Golda Meir became Israel's first female prime minister and Yasser Arafat was elected leader of the Palestine Liberation Organization.

Turbulence, disaster and racial strife marked 1969. Hurricane Camille ravaged Mississippi, killing 248 people. In Washington, DC, upwards of a half-million protesters staged a demonstration against the Vietnam War, which included the symbolic "March Against Death." At Harvard, 340 students protesting the war took over the university's administration building. Black Panther Party members Fred Hampton and Mark Clark were shot dead during a raid by 14 Chicago police officers. In Memphis, James Earl Ray pleaded guilty to assassinating Martin Luther King, Jr. The Chicago Eight trial began, with the three most prominent principals being political and social activists Abbie Hoffman, Jerry Rubin and Tom Hayden, the latter of which four years later married an actress named Jane Fonda. In California, Charles Manson's followers went on a grisly killing spree, the gruesome details of which shocked the world.

The Kennedys were in the news, and more than once. In a Los Angeles court that February, Sirhan Sirhan admitted to killing presidential candidate Robert F. Kennedy. On July 18, Edward M. Kennedy drove off a bridge on his way home from a party on Chappaquiddick Island, Massachusetts, where Mary Jo Kopechne, a former campaign aide to his brother Robert, died in his submerged car. Later that year, on November 18, family patriarch Joseph P. Kennedy, Sr. died.

In the media world, a 38-year-old Australian named Rupert Murdoch purchased Britain's largest-selling Sunday newspaper, The News of the World. After 147 years, the last issue of The Saturday Evening Post was published while the first issue of Penthouse magazine hit newsstands.

Popular movies ranged from "Hello, Dolly!" to "True Grit" to "Butch Cassidy and the Sundance Kid" to "Easy Rider" to "Bob & Carol & Ted & Alice" to the first mainstream X-rated movie, "Midnight Cowboy," which starred Jon Voight, who six years later fathered a daughter named Angelina Jolie. In literature, author Mario Puzo published a novel called The Godfather. Beat writer Jack Kerouac died. On TV, "Sesame Street" and "The Brady Bunch" premiered in America and "Monty Python's Flying Circus" in Britain. Vice President Spiro Agnew labeled "The Smothers Brothers Comedy Hour" as "subversive." In music, "The Ed Sullivan Show" presented a band of brothers from Gary, Indiana who called themselves the Jackson 5, the youngest member of whom was an 11-year-old boy named Michael. The Who released their rock opera "Tommy." Led Zeppelin released its first album. Judy Garland, only 47, died in her rented house in Chelsea, London. Not too far from there, Rolling Stones founder Brian Jones, only 27, was found dead at the bottom of his swimming pool, drowned. The band went on to release Honky Tonk Woman. The Beatles gave their last public performance, doing so on the roof of their Apple records building, and then released their last album together, "Abbey Road," the cover of which sparked rumors that Paul McCartney was dead. In Gibraltar, John Lennon married Yoko Ono.

A music and art festival called Woodstock was held on a dairy farm in upstate New York, drawing an estimated 450,000 people. Several months later, a similar concert was held at the Altamont Speedway in California, where the Hell's Angels were hired to perform security. They ended up stabbing to death a black man brandishing a gun just feet away from the stage, where the Rolling Stones' Mick Jagger was performing.

The first strain of the AIDS virus (HIV) migrated to the United States in 1969, via Haiti, eventually becoming a scourge that took, among other people, Robert Reed, who starred as the father in the "The Brady Bunch."

The first Gap clothing store opened in San Francisco, the first Long John Silver's fast-food restaurant opened in Lexington, Kentucky, and in Arkansas, a young entrepreneur named Sam Walton incorporated his retail store, calling it Wal-Mart Stores, Inc.

In Florida, construction began on Walt Disney World.

Bell-bottom pants and tie-dyed cloths became the rage. Pontiac released a muscle car it called the Firebird Trans-Am. Gas was 25 cents a gallon.

In sports, the New York Jets' flamboyant quarterback, Joe Namath, guaranteed and then delivered a 16-7 victory against the Baltimore Colts in Super Bowl III at the Orange Bowl in Miami. Later that year, in Gulfport, Mississippi, a boy with a dyslexic-looking surname was born. Brett Favre would later go on to become the statistically greatest quarterback in NFL history. Oakland Raiders owner Al Davis promoted his 32-year-old linebackers coach to head coach, making him the NFL's youngest head coach ever. Prior to that, few people had ever heard of John Madden.

In San Francisco, Giants outfielder Willie Mays became the first player since Babe Ruth to hit 600 career home runs. In New York, Yankees outfielder Mickey Mantle announced his retirement. The Amazin' New York Mets won the World Series, beating the overwhelmingly favored Baltimore Orioles, losing the first game before winning four straight. Specialized relief pitching was still an afterthought in baseball, which meant that nobody could've possibly known that a boy born in Panama on Nov. 29th of that year would one day become the greatest closer in the history of the game. His name was Mariano Rivera.

Boxing great Muhammad Ali was convicted on appeal for refusing induction in the U.S. Army. Another boxing great, Rocky Marciano, died in a plane crash on the eve of his 46th birthday.

Out in Los Angeles, the UCLA Bruins basketball team, under iconic head coach John Wooden, prepared to go after their sixth national championship in seven years, and fourth in a row. The Bruins were a preseason favorite, even though they had just graduated their fabulous center, Lew Alcindor, who became the NBA's first overall draft pick in 1969 and later changed his name to Kareem Abdul-Jabbar. What people didn't expect was that on the opposite coast, a tiny school from Jacksonville was about to write a few paragraphs of its own on the pages of history.

Though the Dolphins were coming off a 17-7 season, the national press dismissed their success to their schedule, which was still populated with too many teams from the little-regarded Florida Intercollegiate Athletic Conference. JU head coach Joe Williams and assistant coach Tom Wasdin felt differently. With a frontline of 7-foot-2 Artis Gilmore, 7-foot Pembrook Burrows III and 6-foot-10 Rod McIntyre, Williams was quick to note JU's average size – an even 7-foot – to anyone who would listen. "We are now the biggest college team around," he declared, "and don't bet against us becoming the best."

If the rest of the country was not yet impressed, JU's players certainly were. Rusty Baldwin remembers during the offseason in 1969, before his sophomore season, Coach Wasdin coming into the gym when the guys were scrimmaging on their own.

"Guys," Wasdin said. "We just signed a 7-footer."

Following closely behind was Artis Gilmore.

"He was solid, all muscle, just huge," Baldwin said. "We'd never seen anybody like him. I'll never forget Rex Morgan saying under his breath, 'We can win a national championship with that guy.'"

There was one early practice when the team was scrimmaging and, rather than coaching them, Williams and Wasdin found themselves sitting several rows up in the stands, just watching. For a moment there, they turned into a couple of fans instead of the two coaches.

"Can you believe this?" Williams asked Wasdin. "Can you believe what we have here and how good Artis is?"

They knew.

So did Dr. Duane Bork, JU's team physician.

"Before the season started, I went to a scrimmage and they were very impressive," Dr. Bork said. "That night, I was at one of my favorite watering holes, and I told the boys there that JU has one of the top 10 teams in the country, maybe even the best team in the country. They all suggested that I cut back on the Scotch and take a couple of weeks off to rest."

For sure, it took time for doubts in Jacksonville, much less around the country, to peel away. Some in the local Jacksonville media, however, soon saw that this team had the makings of something special. Gene Pullen of the *Jacksonville Journal*, the city's afternoon newspaper, labeled the Dolphins as "fearsome." Pullen even went so far as to suggest that JU could go 22-3 and average 100 points per game, the latter of which had never been done before in major college basketball, especially at a time when there were no 3-point shots, a shot clock nor dunking.

What had particularly impressed Pullen was a closed-door preseason scrimmage at Jacksonville's Swisher Gym against Davidson College, with the Dolphins dominating the school from North Carolina that had gone to the NCAA Tournament the previous year under coach Lefty Driesell and were entering the 1969-70 season ranked fifth by the AP. "Jacksonville led by 12 points at the half and ate 'em alive," Pullen said, adding that he began telling people afterward that JU had "the look of a national championship team." But Pullen found that whenever he suggested that to colleagues in the

Early in the 1969-70 basketball season at Jacksonville University. Tom Wasdin and Joe Williams are in a discussion with official Poochie Hartsfield.

national media, the response was beyond incredulous. "Everybody was laughing at us," he said.

Wasdin recalled that in that scrimmage, Davidson's three-time All-American forward, a 6-foot-7 black kid named Mike Maloy, who would later play in the ABA and in Europe, attempted to fake one way against Gilmore before attempting a spinning hook shot. "Artis just swatted it in the stands," Wasdin said. "As impressive as it was, it didn't surprise me a bit."

It wasn't just one shot that Gilmore blocked, either. "Artis was blocking shots all over the place," recalled Rex Morgan, the team's senior guard. "He was such a presence defensively in the middle. I remember one play when Maloy went over Pembrook and Artis went up and leaned over Pembrook to go after the ball. He wasn't vertical, he was leaning in, and yet he was still up high enough to pin the ball way up on the backboard. You had to see it to believe it."

So impressed was Morgan early on with Gilmore that he felt certain that the center was the "missing piece" to a team that had gone 17-7 the season before. In fact, Morgan remembers telling guys at a frat party during the first week of school "that we were going to win the national championship." The reaction, he recalled, was similar to what the sportswriter Pullen had received. "Everybody laughed at me," he said.

The 1969-70 team that made it to the NCAA Championship Game. Top Row left to right: Assistant Coach Tom Wasdin, Vaughn Wedeking, Chipper Dublin, Curtis Kruer, Head Coach Joe Williams, Mike Blevins, Danny Hawkins, Rusty Baldwin, SID Frank Casey. Kneeling left to right: Ken Selke, Greg Nelson, Rod McIntyre, Artis Gilmore, Pembrook Burrows III, Rex Morgan.

Greg Nelson remembers the Davidson scrimmage for another reason, although it also involved Gilmore. Someone from the Davidson bench had shouted some racially charged comments at the JU center. "Artis was normally an easygoing guy, but this got him real agitated," Nelson recalled. "I remember going up for a rebound and Artis' big arm coming over me. There was a little bit of anger in him, to the point that nobody was going to get that rebound but him. He accidentally caught me on my head with his elbow, and it knocked me out for a moment, leaving me pretty groggy. I had a goose egg on my head for several weeks after that. Whenever Artis got that way, whenever he got into that kind of zone, it could be scary."

To be sure, the racial overtones of the era, and especially how Gilmore had grown up in Chipley, Florida, left an indelible impression on the quiet big man. "When I was a kid and you'd go downtown, there'd be colored-only bathrooms," he said. "You weren't allowed to express your thoughts, either. It's just the way it was. So whatever I thought, I kept to myself. When I went to Jacksonville, I didn't have a whole lot of confidence; not as a player nor as a person. What Joe Williams and Tom Wasdin did for me was respect me as a person, and that gradually built confidence in me. Because of that, I found a real comfort zone at JU that helped me to flourish. I was a good player before then, and that helped me become a great player. For me, Joe and Tom were more than just father figures. They helped me make a 180-degree turnaround in my life."

There was another preseason scrimmage, this one against Duke in Durham, NC, when Gilmore simply manhandled the Blue Devils' 6-foot-10 All-American center Randy Denton, who later went on to enjoy a career in the ABA and NBA.

It was clear during the scrimmage that the Blue Devils were frustrated at their inability to slow down JU, and especially Gilmore.

"We just dominated them with our size," Wasdin said. "Their coach, Bucky Waters, would blow his whistle and all his players had to come right over and stand at attention. Meanwhile, our guys were as loose as a goose. In those days, college basketball in the South was the ACC and Kentucky, and that was it. So to be able to handle Duke the way we did ... well, we felt pretty good about ourselves."

When the team got back to Jacksonville, Joe Williams got a phone call from an agent who was a Duke graduate. He inquired about Artis Gilmore. "I figured this guy wouldn't be calling me if not for Bucky Waters. Bucky must've gotten on the phone after we'd left and told him how good Artis was."

All the talk about a 7-foot frontline quieted momentarily when McIntyre broke a bone in his foot during practice, an injury that would sideline him for the regular season's first five games. On the plus side (if a broken bone can be viewed that way) it allowed Williams to finesse a situation that worried him and Wasdin all offseason. McIntyre had been a starter the previous two years, and a solid one, too, averaging 12.6 points and a team-leading 11.5 rebounds during the 1968-69 season. But with the addition of Gilmore and Burrows, McIntyre, now a senior, was going to be a player coming off the bench. Same with Greg Nelson, a strong 6-foot-6 junior forward who was second in scoring and rebounding on the team the season before.

Wasdin marveled at how Williams was able to keep everyone happy and involved, noting how eight different players started at different times. "Joe did a masterful job of taking two first-string players who were stars the previous year and blending them in," Wasdin said. "He had recruited Rod McIntyre, and now he was going to have to move him out of the spotlight. Guys had to sacrifice their own scoring and rebounding for the good of the team, and Joe was able to get them to do that. Joe was a smart guy. An intellectual. He was an English major who wanted to be a writer. He liked the arts, literature, music. What he really loved, though, was basketball. And he wanted to win. He was very competitive."

Of course, Greg Nelson and Rod McIntyre could quickly see just how good and dominating Artis Gilmore was, which made it easier to acquiesce to their new roles. "You bring in a guy like Artis and you no longer question who the lead guy is," McIntyre said. Junior wingman Mike Blevins recalled thinking about Artis, whom he later roomed with on the road, "I'm glad he's on my side. He was the biggest man I'd ever met at that point in my life. He was just absolutely huge."

Gilmore's presence on the team came as a surprise to most of JU's players. That's because, in 1969, fresh recruits coming into a program didn't make big news and college recruiting wasn't quite the cottage industry in the media that it would become years later.

"I didn't know who we'd signed until I came back to school that August and showed up on campus for my junior year," Nelson recalled. "All of a sudden, I became aware of these two new guys – Artis Gilmore and Pembrook Burrows. I figured it was just another challenge to keep my starting position."

Nelson tried to meet that challenge during an informal pickup game that some of the players held before preseason practices began. During that pickup scrum, someone set a pick for Gilmore, who used it to make a quick move to the basket. "I broke free from the guy I was defending and jumped up to meet him," Nelson recalled. As high as Nelson jumped with his outstretched arm between Gilmore and the basket, Gilmore's leap still took him considerably higher. That's when Gilmore froze in midair before allowing himself to land back down on the court, the basketball still firmly wedged in the palm of his massive right hand. Everybody stopped.

"Hey man, don't do that," he told Nelson. "I don't want to hurt you."

What had just transpired staggered Nelson.

"Had Artis continued with the play, he would've easily scored and probably broken my hand in the process," he said. "But he had the presence of mind, and the body control, to stop himself in midair. In that instant, as an athlete, you get that immediate recognition of just how good this other guy is. I realized that even on my best day with a jetpack on my back, I wasn't going to stop him. That's when I knew Artis was going to be the entrée for us to something magical that season."

Joe Williams knew, too, that from a marketing and publicity standpoint, starting a frontline that averaged 7-feet was going to create a buzz. And it did. But Williams also knew how important it was to rotate in guys like Chip Dublin and Greg Nelson off the bench. He'd usually do so about 8 to 10 minutes into a game, and often that was when the Dolphins pulled away from their opponent. For a guy who was muscular and physical, the 6-foot-6 Nelson was deceptively quick. And Dublin brought a speed and energy to the floor that was tough for opposing teams to slow down. Suddenly, opponents who had prepared for a towering front line found themselves too slow to keep up with JU's new rotation of players, and it soon showed on the scoreboard.

Williams also had a rule that if it wasn't a fast-break situation, then the rotation of passes had to go through Gilmore. "When he's getting all those rebounds, he's getting *your* rebounds," he'd tell his squad. "So when you're down on offense, he wants to touch the ball." Williams knew that in addition to all his other physical gifts, Gilmore also had good hands and was an adept passer while also being incredibly unselfish. So whenever players weren't sharing the ball, and particularly getting it in to Gilmore, it provided Williams with a built-in reason to rotate personnel in and out, which in turn spread the minutes around.

The two coaches soon discovered that they not only had a talented team, but a gritty, competitive one. Senior guard Rex Morgan had unquestionably emerged as the team leader. Artis Gilmore was the best player, but he was a quiet introvert who was often misperceived and mischaracterized as broody and sullen. Not that the misconceptions bothered him. "I didn't care what other people thought of me," he said. "The most important thing to me was what Joe Williams and Tom Wasdin thought of me. There were so many deep-rooted things with racism that I'd experienced up until that point in my life that it was hard for me to overcome and open up. But the way they treated me with so much respect, it slowly helped me to overcome that. And we had a great team, too, with guys coming together from so many different directions and diverse backgrounds. We all united as one and everybody played their role. I don't remember any kind of negative experience."

As the team leader, Rex Morgan did exactly that; he took the lead and set the tone. The previous season, Morgan finished 10th in the nation in scoring with a 26.7 points per game average. But he put that aside his senior season, and instead led the nation in assists, most of which came when he unselfishly fed Gilmore the ball beneath the basket.

It was a good mix of team chemistry. Vaughn Wedeking, who would later become a dentist and artist, was the team's smartest player. Pembrook Burrows III, a good-natured, jovial young man with an easy smile and laugh, could provide the comic relief. Burrows taught his teammates a carefree jingle that became the squad's, and the school's, anthem. It was called *The Rooster* and it went like this:

Jacksonville had a rooster
And they put him on a fence
And he crowed for the Dolphins
'Cause he had good sense
Hidey, hidey, hidey ho
Oh, oh, oh, oh, oh
Oh what a team
Jacksonville's got a team

The jingle came from Burrows' days at Roosevelt High, a black school in West Palm Beach. He rearranged some of the words and thought it would come in handy when the team had to endure the monotony of conditioning drills, when they had to run around and around the basketball court.

"The guys liked it, and it broke up the drudgery of what we were doing," he said. "Soon we were singing it in the locker room before and after games. Later on, I was amazed that it caught on in the community. Somebody must've heard us singing it when we had an open practice, because it was everywhere, and people always wanted us to sing it."

Then there was Chip Dublin, who was the ideal young man to buffer all the racial tension infecting the country, and especially the South, where it wasn't uncommon for cities like Jacksonville to have race riots. "There was tremendous racial tension in many sections of Jacksonville," Wasdin said. By most accounts, Dublin became the first black player to actively play on a college team in the Deep South, which was quite a burden to take on. Williams and Wasdin helped the situation along by refusing to allow outsiders to impose segregation on their squad.

The year prior, when Dublin was the team's only black player, Williams recalled road games when they'd try to find a restaurant where the team could eat a meal together.

"We'd go someplace and they'd say, 'Ya'all can eat here, but he (meaning Dublin) has to eat in the kitchen.'" To which Williams would reply, "Well then, we'll just all eat in the kitchen."

Wasdin, being the great scout that he was, often did advance work to "make sure that when we went to a restaurant we already knew that they'd serve black people."

To his credit, Dublin rolled with it, refusing to make issues over racial slights or slurs.

"Chipper was the perfect guy for us," Wasdin recalled. "He was an upbeat guy who didn't let things bother him. He was outgoing, articulate, a guy who would make sure he'd shake your hand and engage you in conversation. He was just what we needed."

In that respect, Dublin was the opposite of Gilmore, who initially intimidated Jacksonville's Southern whites not only by his physical stature, but especially when he started to let his hair grow into an afro while sporting facial hair and occasionally wearing a dashiki.

But all of that, all the brewing racial strife of the era, seemed to evaporate once JU's season started and the Dolphins began winning game after game after game, galvanizing the city and shocking the college basketball world.

Gilmore remembers watching in horror one night and seeing a race riot in the city unfold on TV. A Halloween night shooting at Florida Avenue, near the Jacksonville Coliseum and Gator Bowl, had brought the city's black community and the police onto the streets, and the ensuing scene was an ugly one. A local grocery store was torched, the footage of which made national news. It was a restless racial time, not just in Jacksonville, and not just in the South, but throughout the country. But the one thing that rallied Jacksonville, and eventually separated the city from what was going on around the country, was the Dolphins' basketball team. With win after win, the city and community came closer and closer together.

"That team brought the community together as I'd never seen this community come together before," said Dr. Frances B. Kinne, a former JU President and Chancellor Emeritus who at the time was the university's Dean of the College of Fine Arts.

The Dolphins opened their historic season at home with the Sunshine Classic in the Jacksonville Coliseum. It was the official unveiling of Artis Gilmore and the big man didn't disappoint his advanced billing, scoring 35 points, grabbing 13 rebounds and blocking 8 shots to lead JU to a 92-74 victory against East Tennessee State. In the title game, the Dolphins dismissed Morehead State even easier, 117-63, with Gilmore setting a single-game rebounding record for the school with 26. After the game, Morehead State head coach Bill Harrell marveled at JU's size and depth. "If there's a better team in America, I don't want to play them," he said. "Why, I don't think our neighbor (Kentucky) could come down here and beat this outfit." In the visitors' locker room, Harrell pointed toward the floor and told *Sports Illustrated* writer Joe Jares, "See that wastebasket there? You know how easy it is to flip paper in it? It's just as easy for Gilmore to score. I've never seen a player – and I've seen Lew Alcindor several times – dominate a game like Gilmore."

It didn't take Gilmore long to break his own rebounding record. JU's next game was in its Swisher Gym, against Mercer, and again the big center dominated, scoring 34 points, grabbing an astonishing 32 rebounds and blocking 9 shots. In each of JU's first three games, Gilmore scored better than 30 points.

Critics contended that JU was beating up on lower-tier talent. Still, after the Dolphins went 4-0 with a 130-65 victory against Biscayne, they finally cracked the polls – weighing in at No.18 in the AP poll and No.19 in UPI. It was December 16. Plenty of basketball was still ahead.

The next opponent was Georgetown and again it was at Swisher Gym, which was now packed. Momentum and enthusiasm was building in Jacksonville and among its fans, many of them new to the party. The Dolphins once again were dominating, lighting up the scoreboard. With barely more than two minutes remaining before the half, and JU leading 41-26, a fight erupted. Georgetown's best player was Art White, and JU's Mike Blevins was all over him, shutting him down offensively. White was a talented 6-foot-5 forward, but he was also headstrong and temper-prone. Finally, after having enough of Blevins, White decked him beneath Georgetown's basket, breaking Blevins' jaw. White was immediately ejected, and as he walked off the court, Blevins got up and followed him.

"I knew what Mike was about to do, and I tried to rush over there to stop him," Rex Morgan said.

He didn't get there in time. Blevins extended a hand to White as if to shake, and then sucker-punched him. A melee ensued. Joe Williams immediately and instinctively grabbed Artis Gilmore and dragged him off to the bench while other players fought. "I wished I could've dragged Rex Morgan off, too, because Rex was over there trying to break up the fight, and they jumped him," Williams said.

Greg Nelson tackled White and had him pinned on a mat behind the basket, his arm cocked. "I was ready to pop him," he said, "but everybody was grabbing my arm and I couldn't get a punch off."

The sight of Morgan bleeding profusely from a cut above his eye prompted Hoyas head coach Jack Magee to usher his team off the court and into the locker room, where he informed officials that he was forfeiting the game while apologizing for Art White's actions.

Several years later, White, who never finished his college career at Georgetown, was playing professionally in Europe. Greg Nelson was over there, too, also playing professionally. One day in Belgium, Nelson came across a guy who looked familiar. Sure enough, it was Art White. The two men chatted, laughed about the incident from several years earlier and eventually became roommates in Europe.

Wasdin happened to miss the Georgetown game and all the excitement that went with it. "I was in New York City, recruiting," he recalled. "Here I was that night, sitting in my hotel room, when I hear about it on TV while listening to the sports report. I was shocked. I got on the phone right away to find out what happened."

A *Sports Illustrated* writer had been at the game, which Joe Williams was thankful for, because "he could see what happened and that it wasn't as if an opposing team came into our gym and we were running some type of lawless place."

Other than Blevins getting sidelined with a broken jaw, the melee didn't slow down JU's momentum. The Dolphins kept motoring through wins and moving up the rankings. They beat Harvard, 103-64, and saw the AP rank them No.13. Caught in the swelling excitement, a Jacksonville TV station produced a 60-second montage of players in slow-motion action, from Artis Gilmore loping down the court to Rex Morgan spinning toward the hole, synchronizing the film footage to the soaring music of "The Impossible Dream."

To dream the impossible dream
To fight the unbeatable foe
To bear with unbearable sorrow
To run where the brave dare not go

To right the unrightable wrong
To love pure and chaste from afar
To try when your arms are too weary
To reach the unreachable star

This is my quest
To follow that star
No matter how hopeless
No matter how far

The 7-foot-2 Gilmore and 6-foot-5 Morgan had received nicknames, too – Batman and Robin. It only added to the aura of this little school from Jacksonville that few people around the country knew much about. The idea to promote Gilmore and Morgan as Batman and Robin came from the school's sports information director, Laney Yelverton, who had a drawing of the two players wearing superhero capes put on the cover of a game program early in the season. It was meant to garner publicity, and it did, with *The New York Times* picking up on it and writing about it. While he understood the reason behind promoting him and Morgan that way, Artis Gilmore still felt uneasy with it.

"It was okay that they did that," he said. "But my thoughts were that I wanted to keep what we were doing as a team concept, because it was. With Rex and me getting played up like that, as Batman and

The cover of the 1969-70 Jacksonville University Media Guide captured in a creative way the size of the Dolphins' team. From left to right are 6-foot-5 Rex Morgan, 7-foot Pembrook Burrows III and 7-foot-2 Artis Gilmore.

Robin, I felt it was focusing too much on two players and not the team, and I didn't like to exclude anybody. If there was going to be publicity, I wanted it to be as a team."

It *was* a team, and as the season progressed the squad drew closer and closer together. Chip Dublin had started to bring a tape player onto the court for JU's pregame warm-ups, filling the floor with soul music and eventually the strains of *Sweet Georgia Brown*, which the Harlem Globetrotters had made popular. Though dunking wasn't allowed in the college game, it wasn't uncommon for Jacksonville to put on a dunking clinic during their pregame drills, causing even opposing teams to stop and watch.

"Early in my career, I figured out that the pregame warm-ups had little to do with how well a team played during a game," Williams said. "Sometimes when you warmed up the most, the team played the worst. So I let them warm up any way they wanted. I let them devise their own warm-up routine. I figured that allowing them to play their music and having something they liked to do got them loose before the game."

The Dolphins weren't just fun, they were becoming a phenomenon. Nobody had seen a team quite like this, breaking from convention and thumbing their collective noses at tradition. The more they won, the more the old guard claimed the Dolphins were setting the sport back decades.

Little by little, though, JU was garnering grudging national respect. But even though the line of naysayers was getting shorter, they were still there. Next on the schedule was the Evansville Holiday Invitational tournament in Indiana, which featured better opponents. Finally, some thought, this funky upstart squad would get its comeuppance; this goofy, come-from-nowhere team with the green-and-gold uniforms and the letters J-A-C-K-S-O-N-V-I-L-L-E spelled in a semicircle on the front of their tank tops, just beneath each players' number, making their uniform fronts look like a smiley face.

"Now we'll find out how good we are," Wasdin told Williams as they headed to the Evansville Holiday Invitational, which became a phrase Wasdin would routinely say before games all season, as the Dolphins encountered each new challenge.

In the opening game of the Evansville Holiday Invitational,

Jacksonville faced the University of Arizona and promptly dismissed the Wildcats, 104-72, as if they were just another Mercer or Biscayne on their schedule. In the title game, JU handled the University of Evansville in similar fashion, winning by 30 points, 100-70. The tournament marked the first two road games for the Dolphins, and Williams and Wasdin liked what they saw.

"I think we've got a good ballclub," Williams told reporters. "I was looking to see how we'd react to pressure on the road. I'd say we met a real tough situation and passed the test."

The tournament also had a subplot. Two of JU's players – Vaughn Wedeking and Greg Nelson – were from Evansville. Plus, Rex Morgan had played a season for the University of Evansville three years earlier, leading the freshmen team to an undefeated season before transferring while complaining about having to eat road-trip lunches out of brown paper bags. Worse, when Morgan wanted to transfer, Evansville head coach Arad McCutchan refused to give him a release, meaning Morgan had to play a season of junior college ball before heading to JU. Part of the backstory, too, was that Morgan and some of his friends had once toilet-papered McCutchan's house. Not surprisingly, while Evansville fans rode the three JU players with hometown connections, they especially targeted Morgan.

It fueled them.

"I can't deny that Vaughn and I probably had a little extra motivation going against Evansville," Nelson said. "The perception was, when we left there, that Vaughn was too short and I wasn't any good. Neither of us had been recruited by Evansville. So, yeah, we felt some extra satisfaction when we beat them by 30 points."

For Morgan, the tournament proved doubly satisfying. Not only did he answer the catcalls from Evansville fans with his, and his team's, performance, he also got to address some comments that Arizona head coach Bruce Larson had made to him a couple of years earlier. After Morgan had left Evansville and gone to a junior college, Larson had recruited him.

"I actually had a scheduled visit to Arizona," Morgan recalled. "But when I was 1,000-percent sure that I was going to JU, I called Coach Larson and told him not to waste any money, because I wasn't coming. He wasn't too happy about that. He told me that I was making the biggest mistake in my life, and I guess from his perspective it must've seemed that way. Even still, when we beat them, I did feel some sweet revenge."

For a variety of reasons, then, it was a big tournament win. Certainly it was validating. The team knew that it was another answer, and a loud one at that, to their chorus of critics. In the locker room, Pembrook Burrows III gathered his teammates in a celebratory circle for a rousing, sweaty rendition of *The Rooster*.

In the Evansville locker room, Coach McCutchan admitted that part of his motive behind scheduling Jacksonville for his holiday tournament was wrapped in the hopes of beating the Dolphins and showing the local prep talent that there was no reason to head south to play quality college basketball. But now he had to admit that JU wasn't just for real, they bordered on unreal. McCutchan did so, too, with tongue firmly planted in cheek.

"They're very vulnerable," McCutchan deadpanned. "An 8-footer would murder 'em."

Yet another challenge awaited the Dolphins, now No.10 in both the AP and UPI polls, and this one was in Hawaii, where they won again, pushing their record to 10-0. The Hawaii trip actually covered eight days, and it included an exhibition game against the Armed Forces along with two games against the University of Hawaii.

"We were like rock stars out there," Morgan recalled. "*Sports Illustrated* had just done a piece on us. The title was, *Up, Up and Away Go Artis and New JU*. The issue hit the stands just when we hit the ground in Hawaii. Then, when we played that exhibition game against the Armed Forces, we walked into the arena wearing Hawaiian shirts. The crowd went crazy. They loved us."

Artis Gilmore recalled thinking to himself how just a few years earlier he was living in abject poverty in Chipley, Fla., and now he was on this beautiful tropical island in the South Pacific. "I realized that, if not for basketball and my abilities, there was no way I'd be here," he said. "I was not too far removed from the cotton fields and the watermelon patches that I'd grown up around."

Gilmore also roomed with Mike Blevins on that trip, which helped solidify the belief that for them white or black didn't matter. Just like the coaching staff didn't see color, neither did the players.

"We really bonded as a team on that trip," Morgan said. "We spent eight days together, rooming together, eating together, partying together."

In fact, the team probably partied a bit too much. The second game against Hawaii was probably the worst the team played all year. Certainly, it was their lowest scoring output of the season. The team that averaged better than 100 points for the season, becoming the first squad in major college history to do so, finished with only 63 points against Hawaii, winning by just five points. So lackluster was their effort that Williams admonished the team at halftime, telling them, "I didn't bring you all this way to lose."

Not only did they win, they won over a new fan. A talented young writer for *Sports Illustrated* named Curry Kirkpatrick happened to be in Hawaii at the same time, on vacation. Kirkpatrick graduated from North Carolina, so he knew his hoops. But he didn't know too much about tiny JU until he saw several of the players in Hawaii.

"We weren't too hard to spot," recalled Frank Casey, Morgan's childhood friend who served as a jack-of-all-trades, behind-the-scenes guy for the team, whether it was working in media relations, as a traveling secretary, shooting film, or even taping ankles pregame. "Curry became enamored with us. Once you see a couple of 7-foot guys like Artis Gilmore and Pembrook Burrows walking around, it's hard not to take notice, and take an interest. But the fact that Curry was a writer at *Sports Illustrated* who was taking an interest in us got our attention. He loved us. He started touting us after that. He was instrumental in getting us some attention and, in turn, that attention helped us to understand how good we were. When you're in the middle of it, you don't really understand how good you are. But when someone from the outside, someone with the credibility of *Sports Illustrated*, takes an interest in you, it helps everyone feel good about what we were doing. Rex never doubted for a second how good we were, but that's Rex's makeup. For the rest of us, it gave us perspective."

Once back in Jacksonville for a three-game home stint, things were getting frenzied and frenetic. The Dolphins easily handled Richmond, 113-77, before hosting the in-state Miami Hurricanes at

Peter Kerasotis

Dolphins games at the Jacksonville Coliseum consistently set college basketball attendance records in the state of Florida.

the Coliseum. Some 8,500 fans arrived, the largest home crowd in JU history. Considering the school's enrollment was only 2,700, fans were pouring in from all sectors of the community, both black and white, wanting to witness what all the hullabaloo was about regarding Gilmore and Morgan – a.k.a. Batman and Robin. Miami concentrated on Gilmore and seemingly only on Gilmore that game, holding the center to 2 first-half points. What the Hurricanes didn't plan for was just how good Gilmore's supporting cast was. Morgan erupted for 29 points while Burrows recorded a double-double to increase his nation-leading field goal percentage to 68%. Another win, this one against the Virgin Islands, put JU at 13-0 with a road game in Tallahassee against Florida State, coached by Hugh Durham, next on the schedule.

The FSU-JU matchup at Tully Gym was billed as the biggest college basketball game in the state's history and the first game between two Florida schools to be broadcast live on television. JU was now the country's sixth-ranked team, and FSU was No.18. As if the game needed any more hype, the Seminoles enacted an over-the-top pregame ritual where an Indian chief came to midcourt shaking fake snakes and then slaughtering a dolphin fish, chopping its head off, with blood splattering everywhere.

"We'd never seen anything like that," said Burrows, who suffered a back injury that game which caused him to miss most of the contest, hampering JU's efforts.

Governor Claude Kirk attended the game and even called Burrows' mother afterward to let her know that her son was okay. Believing the call to be a prank, Burrows' mother hung up on the governor.

Artis Gilmore's mother, Mattie, was also at the game, arriving from Chipley, which was 90 minutes away. It was the first time Mattie Gilmore, a simple woman from humble means, had ever seen her son play basketball – at any level.

"Afterward, she was so upset," Gilmore recalled. "She felt like it was her fault that we'd lost. She felt responsible. For years to come, she always apologized for that. She didn't understand that she had nothing to do with how we'd played."

For whatever reason, and perhaps it was the hot spotlight of scrutiny that hovered over the game, the Dolphins came out cold, their shots finding more rim than net. FSU's tenacious center Dave Cowens, who like Gilmore would become a Naismith Basketball Hall of Fame member, held the Dolphins' center to a mere mortal 21 points. Nothing seemed to go right. The Seminoles raced to a 16-6 lead and kept the pressure on, taking advantage of JU's uncharacteristically poor 42% shooting to hold on for an 89-83 victory. It ended the Dolphins' 13-game winning streak with a thud.

"I thought some of our guys didn't come to play that game," Morgan said. "Maybe they were intimidated by the big stage. I don't know. Whatever it was, we had some talks and meetings amongst ourselves after that. I remember telling guys that this was a man's game and some of us needed to step up. Not to say that Florida State wasn't good. They were. They were very good. They started four guys who went on to become NBA draft picks. And they only lost three games that season (going 23-3). Had they not been on probation, they likely would've gone to the NCAA Tournament. But I still thought we could've played much better, and I wanted to make sure that kind of game didn't happen again."

The following morning in Jacksonville, the morning *Florida Times-Union* newspaper trumpeted: "The prince has turned into a frog."

Not quite.

"That loss might've been the best thing that happened to us," Burrows recalled. "Up until then, we were rolling over everybody. That game let us know that we could be beat. It was a wakeup call."

Up until then, Nelson said, "Our toughest opponent was each other in practice. We just wailed on each other. Whenever we played a real game it was almost comical because we were winning so big. Everything seemed so easy, especially when you had a guy like Artis Gilmore under the bucket. That Florida State game got our attention."

As soon as the Dolphins' 13-game winning streak ended, they started another, this one stretching to 14 games and taking them all the way to the NCAA Championship Game.

But first things first, and next on the schedule were bounce-back home victories against St. Peter's and Iona before a four-game road trip took the Dolphins to East Carolina, Richmond, Oklahoma City and Loyola of New Orleans. By now, whenever JU came to town, opposing teams saw their home attendance swell. At Richmond, the Spiders drew 5,000 for their game against the Dolphins, an 88-49 loss, just a week after they drew fewer than 1,000 fans.

Jacksonville Journal sportswriter Gene Pullen especially remembers the Richmond game. "Artis was just a freak to those people," he said. "They'd never seen anybody who could jump as high as this guy, as trim and as big as he was. They were yelling before the game, 'Dunk it!' So finally, Joe Williams said to Artis, 'Just throw one down.' Artis jumps up and throws one down backwards and rattles the boards. The people went crazy and JU had to start the game with two technical fouls against them for doing that."

Even while enjoying such moments, and once again breaking free from basketball's establishment, it was still a grueling road stretch, with attention on them increasing and pressure mounting. Wasdin noticed Williams, already a slim and angular man, looking thinner, with his sharp, high cheekbones showing more of an edge and his clothes hanging a little looser on his frame. Williams would often pace the hallways before games, his stomach in knots. "Joe was very cool and calm on the outside," Wasdin said, "but inside he was a mess." By the time the season ended, Williams had dropped more than 40 pounds off his 6-foot-4 body, his weight hovering around 155 pounds. The season fairly consumed not just him, but both coaches, taking its toll on their families, too. When they weren't playing games they were preparing for games. Wasdin wore out his shoes on the recruiting trail, capitalizing on JU's newfound spot on the national stage. Dinner conversation focused on matchups, with Williams often outlining plays and defensive strategies on restaurant napkins.

Though there was success, the coaches didn't let up on practices. If anything, they mashed the gas pedal a little heavier. Early in the season, Wasdin noticed that the team wasn't drawing many charges during games, so one afternoon he held a special drill in practice to demonstrate how to effectively draw a charge. Recognizing that players didn't want to get hurt, and possibly injured, he also wanted to demonstrate the proper way to fall without hurting yourself.

"Who wants to take the first shot?" he intoned as he stood on the court near the basket.

Greg Nelson's hand shot up.

"I will," he said.

Nelson knew Wasdin was strong, a hard-nosed man who could still play the game well and mix it up on the court.

"I was going to give him my best shot and not hold back at all," Nelson recalled. "I just blasted him."

The hit leveled Wasdin, but the coach didn't stay down long. Jumping right back to his feet, he barked, "Who's next? Who wants to do this right?"

Nelson walked away, marveling at his coach, whose eyes beamed with a kind of crazed intensity that only a fellow competitive athlete can fully appreciate.

"I knew I'd hit him as hard as I could, and I knew he was hurting," he said. "But he wasn't going to let on. I thought to myself, 'He's teaching us something here. He's onto something that's going to help us down the road. We can score and probably outscore anyone, but it's going to take more than that to keep winning.' It was a good lesson for us."

As the Dolphins kept winning, another important date waited for them on the calendar, this one circled in red in their minds. It was their rematch against Florida State, this time on their home court. Not only was it JU's homecoming game, the AP also had the Dolphins ranked sixth and the Seminoles now eighth, with the game again slated for a live TV audience. Some 10,500 fans shoehorned into the Jacksonville Coliseum, which was the largest crowd ever to watch a basketball game in the state's history. Like the earlier game in Tallahassee, there were scalpers outside the arena selling tickets to the sold-out game above face value. Once again, Gilmore and Cowens battled with fierce intensity, and once again the score was close. Late in the game, FSU knotted the contest at 59 points before JU went on a 12-2 run, holding on for a slim 85-81 victory.

The game showcased the Dolphins' depth, with Dublin scoring 14 points off the bench. Although Gilmore scored another mortal-by-his-standards 19 points, he pulled in 21 rebounds, maintaining his nation-leading rebounding lead over another player who had somehow eluded traditional big-time college basketball programs – a Massachusetts forward by the name of Julius Erving, who would later go by the moniker Dr. J. Meanwhile, LSU's Pete Maravich and Notre Dame's Austin Carr were battling for the scoring title, which would eventually go to the player they called Pistol Pete.

The revenge victory against Florida State pushed Jacksonville's record to 20-1, with three regular-season games remaining – against Oklahoma City, Georgia Tech and Miami. JU won all three, though not easily. The Dolphins needed a clutch 15-foot jumper from Vaughn Wedeking with just four seconds remaining to dispatch Oklahoma City, 77-75. The other two victories came against Georgia Tech (86-81) and Miami (108-97).

The two wins against Oklahoma City were a bit bittersweet for Williams, for it was his alma mater and OCU's legendary coach, Abe Lemons, was his mentor and a dear friend.

"He had been my freshman coach at Oklahoma City, and he had

Tom Wasdin and Joe Williams celebrating at Fort Lauderdale's Wreck Bar after defeating the University of Miami to end the Dolphins' regular season with a 24-1 record.

helped me a lot as I moved up the coaching ladder," Williams said. "He taught me so much about the game and how to build a program and put a schedule together, and then he helped me by scheduling us. I certainly didn't enjoy beating him."

But there was little time for sentimentality. The NCAA was poised to announce its tournament invites and the Dolphins wanted in on the party. It had been a good season, one they didn't want to see end without an invite to the big dance.

"It was a fun time, a fun group," Wasdin recalled. "Everything fell into place beyond our imagination. A lot of people saw the big number of points we were scoring and focused on that, but we were playing good defense and we weren't turning the ball over. We were also one of the best foul-shooting teams in the nation. Even when we played a bad game, we still found a way to win. We became the darlings of the state. It got so that we couldn't wait for the next day and the next game."

Added Nelson, "There was a three-month stretch there when I don't think my feet ever touched the ground. It was very exciting. After a while, I never thought we were going to lose. It seemed like every game, someone, somehow, lifted us up. Everybody contributed."

There was a perception, though, that JU was anti-establishment, that they didn't really work hard or practice much. Since it was getting them publicity, Williams and Wasdin went with it.

"That was Joe's master plan, to play along with what people were saying," Wasdin said. "He knew people wouldn't believe anything that we said otherwise. It got us an unbelievable amount of publicity. And, of course, recruits love to hear that we're having fun. But to say we didn't work hard or practice hard wasn't true. Nothing could be further from the truth."

Years later, Morgan still scoffs at the notion that JU was a renegade program. "They liked to write that we didn't have a curfew, and that got overblown," he said. "The reason why we didn't have a curfew is because we didn't need one. Did we party? Yes, we did. But did we still get things done the next day? Yes, we did."

It didn't help their image that Williams had taken to wearing a white sports coat at a time when old-guard coaches like UCLA's John Wooden still seemed trapped in the '50s. Some people began calling the Dolphins the "Mod Squad," which didn't endear them to the establishment. What people didn't know is that the garish outfit Williams started wearing late in the season wasn't really his style. He had a TV show in Jacksonville, and on his birthday, which fell on February 27th, a couple of his players surprised him on his show with a new outfit that a local clothier provided.

"It was where I bought my clothes already, so they knew my size," Williams said. "I was making less than $10,000 a year, so I didn't have much to spend on a wardrobe. Since guys like Kentucky head coach Adolph Rupp wore a brown suit, that's what I had – one brown suit that I wore for every game."

What he was now presented with was a white sports coat with powder blue stripes and matching powder blue pants, a watermelon-colored dress shirt and a red, white and blue necktie. Williams wore the ensemble for Jacksonville's next game, which the Dolphins won. So he kept wearing it as sort of a superstitious talisman.

"After a while, people began expecting me to wear that outfit," he said. "If I had a speaking engagement and I didn't dress in that outfit, they thought I was slighting them. So I just kept wearing it."

Even though Jacksonville would go on to finish the regular season 23-1 and become the first major college to ever average more than 100 points a game, in the Dolphins' case 101.3, there was concern that a small independent school from the South would not get an invite to the prestigious National Tournament.

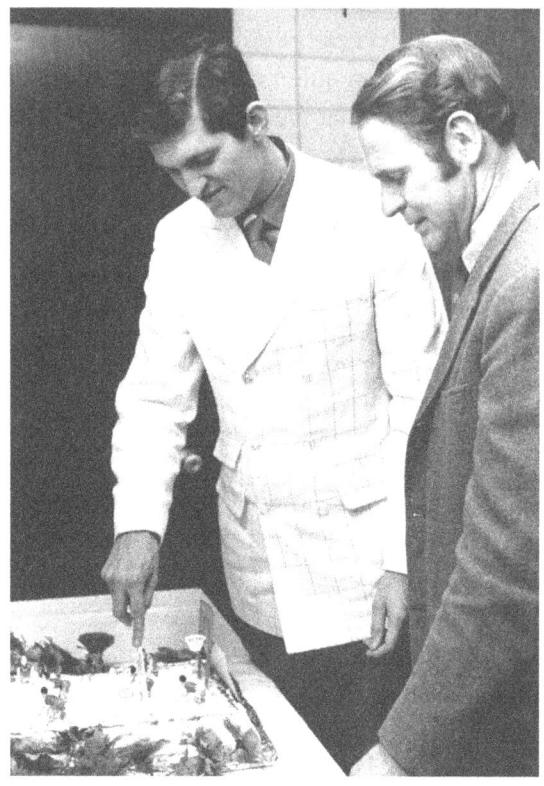

Joe Williams celebrating his birthday with Tom Wasdin, wearing the white sports coat that he got as a gift. He soon was wearing the sports coat at every game and event associated with the Jacksonville University basketball team.

But then, at exactly 9:45 a.m. on Tuesday, February 24, 1970, the telephone call came, providing an equal measure of relief and exhilaration. Jacksonville University, a school that only 15 years earlier was a junior college, was invited to play in the NCAA Tournament. In a season that started in 1969, in a year that saw so much history written, little JU had just written a few paragraphs of its own.

Chapter 10

ANSWERING THE QUESTION: JU WHO?

"I knew that we had arrived." – Tom Wasdin

Awards started trickling in. Artis Gilmore made the National Basketball Association Coach's All-American team, as well as Basketball Weekly's All-American team. Vaughn Wedeking made an All-American team for college players under six feet tall.

All of that was nice, but a tournament beckoned with more history waiting to be written.

The Dolphins were to play in the Mideast Regional, but they would not receive a first-round bye. Instead, they were to play a 22-2 Western Kentucky team in Dayton, Ohio, with the winner advancing to play a 19-4 Iowa squad in nearby Columbus. It was the first time in JU's school history that the Dolphins would play on national TV. Once in Dayton, the players couldn't help but notice that a hotel had emblazoned its marquee with the words "JU Who?" Said Burrows, "We suspected that it was the hotel where Western Kentucky was staying."

The Hilltoppers had their own 7-footer, an athletic junior named Jim McDaniels who would go on to play in the ABA, NBA and in Europe. McDaniels had averaged 28 points and 13 rebounds that season and he proved a formidable foe ... for a while. Late in the first half, the Dolphins shook off any tournament jitters they might've had and flexed their collective muscles to pull away from Western Kentucky for a 109-96 victory. Gilmore poured in 30 points while dominating the boards with 19 rebounds along with 8 blocked shots. Morgan shined, too, scoring 24 points with 7 assists. Wedeking added 19 points.

JU Who?

The Dolphins sure answered that question, and in so doing became the first team from the state of Florida to ever win an NCAA Tournament game. Years later, McDaniels recalled, "I don't think we were really aware of what we were running into. But when the game started, we realized we'd run into a buzz saw. When Artis Gilmore came out with that afro, it literally scared you to death."

The victory pushed JU to No.4 in the AP poll. It also earned them the right to face No.7 Iowa, the reigning Big Ten champion. In their undefeated Big Ten season, the Hawkeyes averaged better than 100 points per game in conference play. Like the Dolphins, they also played pressure defense. And they could run. It was going to be a challenge, and it didn't help that Morgan was battling an ear infection and Wedeking the flu. The two still had huge games, as if nothing was ailing them.

"You have to understand the environment I grew up in," Morgan said. "When I was a kid, my father had a milk route. One day, while loading his truck at four in the morning, he slipped and fell and shattered his right elbow. So he finished loading his truck with his left arm, drove 45 miles, did his route, and then called my mom to call a doctor because his right arm had swelled to three times the size. That's the work ethic I grew up with. And I'm going to tell my dad I couldn't play a basketball game because of an earache? That wasn't going to happen."

The Iowa game proved tight and tenacious; a seesaw battle with aggressive defensive play and lots of running. Gilmore played much of the game in foul trouble, but Williams couldn't afford to keep him on the bench very long. Sure enough, six minutes into the second half, the big center fouled out for the first time in his college career.

Would this be the end? Had Jacksonville's joyride hit a roadblock?

While he was disappointed, feeling he'd let his teammates down, Gilmore found himself also coaching and encouraging Burrows.

"Pembrook, listen man," Gilmore implored, "you've really gotta make things happen. You've gotta go."

Burrows looked at Gilmore as if he were stating the obvious.

"Well, I guess so," he replied.

It went down to the final minute, with Iowa's "Downtown" Freddie Brown and John "JJ" Johnson pouring in points, seemingly at will. For JU, Morgan nailed a jumper with 40 seconds remaining to unlock the score and give the Dolphins a tenuous 2-point lead. The Hawkeyes responded with a 3-point play to lead 103-102 with 16 seconds remaining. Wedeking fought the ball upcourt with Iowa swarming everywhere on defense. He got a pass off to Morgan, who was immediately double-teamed. Morgan fed the ball back to Wedeking at the right corner of the court, where he launched a shot that hit the rim and bounced back to the right. Seemingly from nowhere, Burrows leapt for the rebound, soaring high above everyone else, and tipped the ball into the basket with just two seconds remaining as the JU bench and Dolphin fans erupted with sheer joy.

Joe Dean, a colorful TV analyst and the man who coined the term "string music," happened to be a friend of Williams. Caught in the moment, Dean rushed the court after the final ticks evaporated, giving the Dolphins a 104-103 victory, and embraced Williams in a huge bear hug. Most everyone else, led by Gilmore, swarmed Burrows, who had played the game of his college career, hitting 11-of-12 field goals, scoring 23 points and grabbing 9 rebounds.

"I was so happy and proud for Pembrook, and so happy to see him get recognition," Gilmore said. "Pembrook was playing it down, though. To him, he was just doing what he was there to do."

Sure, Burrows understood the magnitude of the moment, but he still didn't understand what all the individual fuss over him was about. "That play was just me doing what I did every day in practice," he said. "It was nothing planned. I knew the clock was running out, so I just jumped up, got my hand on the ball, and tipped it back in. Looking back on it, though, it was probably the number one play of my career at JU."

Back in Jacksonville, students spilled from their dorm rooms and danced on University Boulevard as they sang *The Rooster*. Cinderella's shoe still fit. But two days later another Mideast Regional opponent waited, and this one was even more formidable. The opponent now was No.1-ranked Kentucky, under legendary coach Adolph Rupp, with the winner of this game getting their ticket punched to the Final Four.

On the off day between tournament games, Wasdin flew back to Jacksonville on a private plane with boosters. Florida's high school state basketball tournament for all the classifications was playing at the Jacksonville Coliseum and Wasdin's coaching class that he taught was hosting the JU hospitality room.

"I felt like I needed to be there," he said. "So I flew in on a Thursday night and was at the hospitality room the next day at 9 a.m. I felt like it would be good for recruiting to be there. It was amazing the reaction I got. People came up to me all day long and wanted to talk about the Iowa game."

Groups of coaches, coming at Wasdin in waves, kept approaching him, asking questions.

"I knew then," Wasdin said, "that we had arrived with high school coaches in the state."

Times were changing in Florida, and they were also changing in Kentucky, too. The 1969-70 season would prove to be the last that Kentucky would field without a black player. Still, Adolph Rupp's squad was ranked No.1 in the country, with 6-foot-8 All-American Dan Issel playing power forward.

The night before the game, Rex Morgan couldn't sleep. He'd gone to bed at 10 p.m., but found himself just tossing and turning. Finally, at 1:30 a.m., he got up, got dressed, and went down to the hotel coffee shop for a bite. Sitting there chatting were about a half-dozen sports writers, led by the *Jacksonville Journal's* Gene Pullen and legendary *Miami Herald* columnist Edwin Pope.

"Hey Morgan," Pullen said, catching sight of the JU guard, "are you just getting in?"

Morgan knew how the media felt about JU's renegade image, and like his coaches, he wasn't going to try and buck that image.

"Yeah," he replied to Pullen, smiling.

The next day against Kentucky, the Dolphins fell behind by 6 points early, but a 13-2 run gave them the lead. Dublin was playing inspired defense, and the energy he brought from the bench seeped into the offense. From there, the lead bounced back and forth before a Gilmore field goal with four minutes to play gave JU a lead they never relinquished.

Once again, though, Gilmore had gotten into foul trouble, which hamstrung the Dolphins. This time, however, JU had a way of responding. Early in the second half, Gilmore was called for a charge near midcourt when one of Kentucky's small guards maneuvered himself in the big man's path, giving Gilmore his fourth foul. At that point, Williams had little choice but to take his center out of the game, leaving Kentucky's All-American Dan Issel more room to maneuver beneath the bucket and inflict some serious damage on the Dolphins.

"Don't worry," Wedeking told Gilmore as the center took his seat on the bench. "I'll take care of Issel."

How Wedeking would do that, Gilmore didn't know. After all, Wedeking was only 5-foot-10, almost a foot shorter than Issel, and not as gifted as a player. But Wedeking was quick and fundamentally a very sound player with uncanny court vision. A savvy leader, who with Greg Nelson once led their Indiana high school team to 51 consecutive victories, Wedeking had a quiet confidence about him. He was also the team's most intelligent player, an academic All-American who would eventually become a dentist and a talented artist.

Gilmore watched from the bench when, with 10:16 left in the game, Wedeking somehow managed to maneuver himself directly in front of Issel as the Wildcats employed a fast break. Even better, Wedeking took a charge just as Coach Wasdin had taught him to, with Issel rolling over him, which made the violent collision look even worse.

"Vaughn put the exact same move on Issel as one of their guards put on me," Gilmore recalled. "At that time, Dan was playing extremely well. You could tell he was determined to take that Kentucky team on his shoulders and lead them to a win. But he plowed over Vaughn like an 18-wheeler."

Immediately, Greg Nelson recalled the practice a few months earlier when Coach Wasdin blew a whistle, gathered everyone around and then demonstrated how to take a charge, placing his body in harm's way as he and the rest of his teammates plowed into him. "After Vaughn took that charge against Issel, I helped him up and saw that same crazy determination in Vaughn's eyes that I'd seen in Coach Wasdin's."

It obviously sold well to the closest referee, who whistled Issel for his fifth foul, sending Kentucky's star player to the bench for the remainder of the game.

"It all goes back to that lesson we learned earlier in the season, in that practice," Nelson said. "Coach Wasdin insisted that we play as men, that we be tough."

The undersized Wedeking had to be tough to take Issel's violent impact. In fact, Nelson recalled how he actually *heard* Issel, a heavy breather, moments before the collision.

"Issel was this big, raw-boned player who was very intense," Nelson said. "His body size and temperament was very similar to FSU's Dave Cowens. The way he breathed, you could hear him coming. He was hell-bent on getting down the court, and he had a full head of steam when he plowed into Vaughn, and Vaughn just stood there and took the shot."

Aside from Issel's breathing, the other thing Nelson had no problem hearing was a profane Adolph Rupp bolting from Kentucky's bench and loudly complaining about the call. "He was screaming so much that he was spitting," Nelson recalled. "The assistant coach was Joe B. Hall, and he had to restrain him."

While it was good to have Issel out of the game, it only seemed to inspire the rest of the Wildcats, who actually narrowed JU's lead from then on. Thankfully for the Dolphins, Rex Morgan had what he called "the best game of my career." The senior guard finished 10-for-10 from the field and 8-for-8 from the free-throw line as Jacksonville held on for a 106-100 upset victory against the No.1-ranked team in the country. When the final buzzer sounded, Curtis Kruer, a forward on JU's team, noticed Dan Issel crying on the bench.

Afterward, Adolph Rupp continued to loudly complain, even maligning JU to the press in the process, contending that the charging call against Issel cost Kentucky the game. When he heard Rupp complaining moments after the game, Wasdin couldn't restrain himself. "Hey coach! If it was good enough for your guys, why isn't it good enough for us?!" Wasdin shouted at Rupp, referring to the earlier charge his guard had drawn on Gilmore in almost the exact same play at almost the exact same spot on the court.

Back in Jacksonville, students crowed *The Rooster* as never before. And when the Dolphins' flight landed at the airport, a mob of frenzied fans greeted them at the airport with a fervor that took them aback. Estimates put the number of people who were there at thirty thousand, jamming the roadways and eating up all of the airport's parking spaces. It put flight schedules back six hours that day. On the drive to campus, delivered via a police escort, fans lined the streets and stood on overpasses waving, holding signs and cheering as horns honked all along the way. Blacks and whites joined together, united by the common community bond that was the JU Dolphins, a source of tremendous civic pride. And for good reason.

Nobody, not anyone from a school this size, had ever made it to the Final Four.

Nobody has done it since.

"The unity of the city was extraordinary," Gilmore said. "There had been racial tension and division, and there had been that race riot earlier in the season. But as we kept winning, I saw a difference. I saw people really coming together. It was totally galvanizing for the community."

Added Morgan, "It gave us so much pride that the city cared. Jacksonville had always been such a football town. If somebody from the Florida Gator football team got a hangnail, it was front-page news. But now the city was behind us."

They believed in their Dolphins, even though many in the national media still had trouble doing so. *Sports Illustrated*, which had gone to press before JU's victory against Kentucky, showed four teams on its cover; the four teams the national magazine obviously thought would emerge from the regionals and vie for the 1970 National Championship. On that cover were New Mexico State, UCLA, St. Bonaventure and Kentucky.

Not Jacksonville.

But the Dolphins were indeed one of the four teams still standing, and it finally got people's attention.

Nobody was asking JU Who? anymore.

This little David of a school had dreamed the impossible dream, and made it a reality. They were now in the Final Four, where Goliath waited for them.

Chapter 11

THIS TIME, GOLIATH WON ... WITH SOME HELP

"I couldn't help but think about what we'd been told – that the bluebloods, the hierarchy, The Establishment, was against us."
–Tom Wasdin

Not everyone loves an underdog. And not everyone loved the Jacksonville Dolphins and the story they wrote on the pages of history during the 1969-70 college basketball season. Folks along Florida's First Coast fervently embraced the team, and JU's players found that when they played road games opposing student bodies were oddly enamored with them. They were hip, cool, fun, different ... reflecting the free spirit of the decade that had just ended and the new one that was just beginning. But there was a segment of folks who saw this tiny school that came from nowhere, and wanted them to go right back.

That segment was known as The Establishment.

By the time the Dolphins reached college basketball's Final Four, The Establishment was getting more and more nervous; its contempt for JU barely concealed. The late Paul Hemphill, a longtime sportswriter and author, picked up on The Establishment's disdain for the Dolphins and wrote about it for *Sport* magazine. He referred to it as the NCAA Establishment, writing:

*There was nothing particularly humorous to the NCAA Establishment about the arrival of Jacksonville University in College Park, Maryland for **their** finale. There is an Establishment in college basketball, just as there is in anything else. The NCAA Establishment includes people like Kentucky's Adolph Rupp, who thinks zone defenses and tall players are Communist threats; UCLA's*

John Wooden, who has all the sartorial and verbal flair of a funeral director; the anonymous coach who said that a national title for Jacksonville would "set college basketball coaching back 20 years," and even the sports writer who wrote from the University of Maryland campus that freewheeling, undisciplined, free-form play was "for playgrounds and Jacksonville University."

It was a common theme that other sportswriters also tapped into. Dwight Chapin of the *Los Angeles Times* wrote that the UCLA-Jacksonville University finals matchup pitted "discipline against devil-may-care, the Establishment against the Age of Aquarius."

Forty-four years later, in his authoritative biography of John Wooden, titled "Wooden: A Coach's Life", *Sports Illustrated* senior writer Seth Davis wrote: "The contest was instantly cast as a sixties-style culture clash writ small. UCLA was square, old school, establishment; Jacksonville was hip, rebellious, cool."

When the country's college coaches met for an annual meeting during the Final Four, it was Kentucky's Rupp, still stinging over his No.1-ranked team's loss to the Dolphins in the Mideast Regional, who sneered that JU must be cheating, citing a summer job Artis Gilmore had working for parks and recreation that had sparked an NCAA investigation. In the meeting, Rupp referred to the Dolphins as "that crooked team from Jacksonville." The comment elicited an immediate reaction from Abe Lemons, Joe Williams' friend, mentor and former college coach. Lemons snapped at Rupp, saying, "I don't know of any of them throwing a game." The room fell quiet. Lemons' pointed reference was to a point-shaving scandal unearthed in 1951 that rocked Kentucky and college basketball. An NCAA investigation also revealed that Kentucky had paid players and had ineligible players. It resulted in the Wildcats being forced to cancel their entire 1952-53 season. The Kentucky head coach when all that occurred was Adolph Rupp.

But Rupp, who was so locked into the established way of doing things that he had not yet signed a black player to his program though it was now 1970, wasn't the only one who was displeased to see Jacksonville on the Final Four dance floor. Hemphill, in his *Sport* magazine piece, went on to write:

The Establishment did not like it that the Jacksonville Dolphins were in the 1970 NCAA championships. "What is this, Rent-a-Goon?"

said a writer, pointing at JU's two giant black junior-college transfers, 7-foot-2 Artis Gilmore and 7-foot-0 Pembrook Burrows III. "Just look at them, would you?" said the wife of an NCAA official, nodding toward the entrance to Cole Field House as Joe Williams and his team came to work, smacking gum and horsing around and wearing bell-bottoms and zippered racing jackets, and what she was really saying was, "How tacky, the very idea." *Williams, they had read, had no curfew for his players, scribbled his game plans on the backs of cocktail napkins and wore this God-awful "lucky" outfit to every game; white six-button blazer, blue bell-bottoms, psychedelic tie and watermelon-red shirt.*

And their followers: route salesmen and hardware-store owners and small-town doctors, many of them still trying to straighten out the difference between charging and hooking, self conscious and still suspicious about any game that's played indoors. And the players: good old boys from places like Chipley and Jacksonville, who gorged themselves at the "training" table, drank beer in public, pulled pranks like hiding each other's shorts, and had painted green and gold stripes on their shoes when they found out they were going to be on color television at College Park.

"Basketball is supposed to be fun," Williams had been quoted, and that was especially disturbing to the Establishment when they realized that Jacksonville University had lost only one of its 27 games and was ranked fourth in the nation."

Little did The Establishment know that UCLA wasn't quite the button-down program it appeared to be. Rick Betchley, a backup guard-forward on the team, noted that there was a simmering uneasiness surrounding the Bruins that season, indicative of the turbulent times of that era. Betchley said that one of UCLA's star black players, guard Henry Bibby, received frequent lectures from head coach John Wooden. "Wooden did not want Bibby dating white women," Betchley said, adding that there were other things Wooden was doing, and not doing, that had Bruins players viewing him differently than the media and public, which had practically bestowed sainthood on him.

It all boiled over at the team's year-end banquet, when backup forward Bill Seibert stood at the podium and for almost 10 minutes attacked the Bruins' system, decrying "double standards" and "unequal treatment" between starters and substitutes. Some alumni, and even

Seibert's father, tried to shout the player down. Afterward, Seibert's teammates gave him a standing ovation.

Wooden might have been a throwback to the '50s, but as Bob Dylan's '60s anthem had signaled, the times were indeed a-changin'.

Even still, for a country still rooted in conventional ways of doing things, John Wooden and the UCLA Bruins represented a tether– thin and threadbare, for sure – to the simpler decade of the '50s. Meanwhile, the Establishment didn't know what to make of the unconventional Jacksonville Dolphins. They just knew they didn't like them. Even the playful sing-along song that forward Pembrook Burrows III would lead them in, *The Rooster*, must have befuddled them.

No, The Establishment sure didn't like Jacksonville University being there at their party, and they wanted them gone as soon as possible. They almost got their wish in the semifinal game, when the Dolphins played St. Bonaventure, another small school that entered the game with its own Cinderella story and a 25-1 record. But the Bonnies had lost their star player, future Naismith Memorial Basketball Hall of Famer Bob Lanier, to a torn knee ligament, suffered in the East Regional against Villanova.

The game was closer than most expected. In fact, the Bonnies exploded to a 13-3 lead, which finally got JU's attention. The Dolphins battled back, chipping away at the margin before taking their first lead, 26-24, late in the first half. At halftime, they had a 42-34 advantage. Still, Joe Williams implored his players in the locker room, particularly Artis Gilmore.

"You gotta do it for me, baby!" he beseeched his big center.

It didn't take Gilmore long to respond. In the first 10 minutes of the second half, he single-handedly commandeered the game, pouring in 12 points. JU cruised to a 91-83 victory.

But the closeness of the game, and especially how St. Bonaventure owned the lead for much of the first half, prompted people to wonder what might have been for the Bonnies had Lanier not missed the contest with a knee injury. In fact, a quarter of a century later, the what-might-have-been question led to a documentary on that team called: "Unfinished Dreams: The 1969-70 St. Bonaventure Basketball Season."

From the Dolphins' perspective, when they look back on the game through a lens forty-plus years long, they see things differently. Without

Bob Lanier playing, they admit they probably took the Bonnies for granted.

"I think you play to the level of your competition," said Rex Morgan, a senior guard on the team. "Yeah, it was a close game, but it was never in doubt. It was just a matter of time. I was never worried that game. Besides, we had just played three great games, beating No. 1 Kentucky and Iowa in two of them, so we were due for a little bit of a letdown."

Said Artis Gilmore, "The level of intensity wasn't the same for the St. Bonaventure game as it had been for our other games in the tournament. For the first time, we were not considered the underdogs. We played like we'd already won the game."

"Had Lanier played, we still would've beaten them," forward Greg Nelson said flatly. "I always believed we were a team of destiny. Whenever I watch March Madness, I always look for the team that has that juice. We were that team. I never doubted that we would play in the finals. I didn't go into the Final Four thinking we were the underdogs. We rode that horse earlier in the tournament. All that *Jacksonville Who?* stuff. We got there after beating Iowa and Kentucky in the regional, and they were both great teams."

"I wish Bob Lanier had played," Pembrook Burrows III said. "I think we all wished he hadn't gotten injured so we could've played their best with our best. As athletes, that's what you want. But now there'll always be that question: if Bob Lanier had played, would they have won? He was their big man. He was their Artis Gilmore. I wish he would've played so that question wouldn't be hanging over that game. I'll say this, too, without him playing there was probably a little bit of a letup on our part. I understand, though, that people will always wonder."

It would not be the only question hanging over that 1970 Final Four. Another question would emerge, one rooted in corruption rather than curiosity.

JU's coaches and players knew what the perception was of their team, and they mostly laughed it off. Sometimes, they even fed it. It didn't hurt Tom Wasdin's pedal-to-the-metal recruiting efforts to tell prospective players that JU was not only a great place to get an education, but also a fun place to play basketball. Wasdin was still working tirelessly behind the scenes, recruiting as if the Dolphins hadn't had any success at all. His reputation for spotting talent and doggedly pursuing it was starting to get noticed.

"What's writing all about?" John Crittenden of the *Miami News* wrote. "It's sticking around and asking one more question and not getting your feelings hurt, and that's Wasdin as a recruiter."

As usual, Williams deflected praise to Wasdin and his assistant coach's relentless recruiting efforts, saying: "I called practice one day and they all showed up."

Still, there were suspicious minds, especially with The Establishment, reasoning that small schools seemingly coming from nowhere must be cheating. But if there was anything scandalous, it was the shamefully small shoestring budget that Joe Williams and Tom Wasdin had to operate with. The joke during the tournament was that JU's coaches didn't even have a university-issued credit card and that only six years earlier the Dolphins' recruiting budget was a pitiful pittance of $250. Said one sportswriter, "Hell, Jacksonville was so broke it couldn't *afford* to cheat."

Instead, it was hard work and a lot of it – the kind of around-the-clock efforts that ruined health and wrecked marriages. Said Williams, "When I left in the morning nobody was awake and when I got home at night nobody was awake."

The Establishment, though, didn't want to acknowledge Jacksonville's hard work. As far as The Establishment was concerned, Wasdin noted, "We were this outlaw team because we were from the South, had blacks and we had fun playing. They made a big deal of guys drinking beer. Rex Morgan was 21. Why couldn't he have a beer if he wanted to? What exactly was the problem?"

Mostly, the Dolphins let people think what they wanted, enjoying the ride and feeding the myth when they could.

"We let the story get bigger than what it was," Morgan said. "Joe supposedly didn't have training rules and all that other stuff. We just let people run with it. Did we have a curfew? No. Did we need a curfew? No, because we knew what we needed to do to win. I think Joe Williams and Tom Wasdin were ahead of their time as coaches. They were definitely ahead of the time in the South with having black players on the roster. But they also allowed players to make decisions. Doing that gave us ownership over those decisions. Letting us play

Sweet Georgia Brown during warm-ups not only created ownership, but it also kept us loose. You could dunk in warm-ups but not in games, so they let us dunk in warm-ups. Back then, nobody knew about us, but when they saw us dunking during warm-ups, it was like, 'Oh my gosh, this is an athletic team.' We needed attention, and it got us attention."

Morgan, who later made his career coaching basketball, recalls fondly how fun it was playing for Williams and Wasdin.

"My high school coach was very strict. But Joe and Tom were always promoting you. They diverted all the praise to the players. Yeah, they let us drink beer and show them that we could be responsible. So we drank a little beer in public. We didn't do drugs. But that was still frowned on by The Establishment. We were 21 and Joe and Tom treated us like men. They treated us like men until we proved that we shouldn't be treated that way. But all of us responded to it positively. We never wanted to disappoint Joe and Tom. They were like your parents. You didn't want to embarrass or disappoint them."

None of the noise in the background fazed Morgan. Again, they often found themselves feeding the myth instead of fighting it. The one thing, however, that did bother Morgan and others is the notion that the team was made of misfits – or "goons" as one sportswriter called them. Years later, Morgan reflected on the special group of young men who had come from the sticks of Northeast Florida and rocked college basketball.

"All 12 guys on that team graduated from college, and that's another tribute to Joe and Tom," Morgan noted. "It's not like we were these 12 outlaws that people made us out to be. We all graduated and we all did well in life."

Morgan's observation is an understatement. Starting with Morgan, this is what those 12 players did with their lives:

- Rex Morgan went on to own a private school in Jacksonville and become a nationally recognized high school basketball coach.
- Artis Gilmore became a star in the ABA, NBA and an inductee into the Naismith Memorial Basketball Hall of Fame.
- Greg Nelson became the owner of a chain of nursing homes and a member of Jacksonville University's Board of Trustees.
- Vaughn Wedeking became a dentist.
- Rod McIntyre became an attorney.

- Mike Blevins became a commercial banker.
- Pembrook Burrows III became a Captain in the Florida Highway Patrol.
- Dan Hawkins became a salesman in heavy machinery.
- Rusty Baldwin became a dentist.
- Ken Selke became a doctor, specializing in cardiology.
- Curtis Kruer became a marine biologist.
- Chip Dublin went into education.

"We had a lot of charisma on that team, leaders," Morgan said. "We had two 7-footers. We also were the first team to average more than 100 points for a season. I've always been real proud of that team and what we accomplished then, and also what we accomplished later with our lives."

The team had drawn together a city and a region unlike anything seen in America at the time, especially in the South. Like most Southern cities Jacksonville had its share of ugly racial strife, including riots. But at a time when teams like Kentucky still didn't dress any black players, the Dolphins had three – Artis Gilmore, Pembrook Burrows III and Chip Dublin – galvanizing a fan base of all colors, creeds and economic strata. To be sure, some of those fans were late to the bandwagon. Frank Casey, the team's de facto sports information director and traveling secretary who became the first person known to statistically track and record blocked shots, recalled getting a message from athletic director Dr. Judson Harris. Dr. Harris told Casey that Jacksonville's mayor, Hans Tanzler, a former center on the Florida Gators basketball team who later made an unsuccessful run for governor of Florida, wanted tickets to the Final Four.

"He wanted *eight* tickets, and we didn't have them," Casey recalled. "This is a guy who had little interest in us all season. And now here we were in the Final Four and he wanted *eight* tickets."

Casey told Dr. Harris that there were no tickets to be had.

"What am I going to tell the mayor?" the athletic director asked.

"Tell him, 'Where have you been all season?'" Casey replied. "We played 15 games in Jacksonville and I never saw him there."

The fans who *were* there, with or without tickets, were rabid, wearing straw boaters and round green-and-white stickers that said JU CAN DO. Back home, Jacksonville felt like it suddenly became

Once a Coach, Always a Coach

the center of the universe. Frank Frangie, 11 at the time, grew up to become a Jacksonville sports journalist and radio and TV personality. He recalled his cousins from Pittsburgh calling and asking, "Is that *your* Jacksonville?"

"Yeah, that's us," he replied proudly.

All of it provided the kind of backstory that usually made the narrative appealing to just about anyone. Small school. Underfunded and underappreciated. Hard-working, forward-thinking young coaches. Success built on sweat.

But this is not what The Establishment saw. And it certainly was not what they wanted as national champions, especially if the Dolphins supplanted The Establishment's most established program – UCLA.

The Bruins arrived at College Park trying to win their fourth straight title. Their team captain, guard John Vallely, remembered getting ready to practice right after JU had the court, and watching them with astonishment. "There was a boom box right there on the table next to the court, and their practice seemed more like chaos compared to how structured our practices were. Guys were having fun, jiving. I thought, 'Geez, are you kidding me? We'd never get away with that.'"

Perhaps some of his teammates might've felt jealous, but not Vallely.

"It was just a different way of doing things," he said. "It wasn't the way we did things. Actually, I thought what we were doing was the coolest thing, because we were so organized."

Rick Betchley recalled how Coach Wooden had 3x5 index cards at practice, meticulously keeping to a schedule. "Practices were timed to the minute," Betchley said. "There were no timeouts, either. We went from one drill to another. Everything was game-action related. For example, we only shot free throws after running hard."

After seeing the Dolphins practice briefly, Vallely didn't give them another thought. Not even after both teams made it to the finals did he spend much time ruminating on the Dolphin players. "We were taught by Coach Wooden not to think a lot about other people, as well as never to compare yourself to another human being," he said. "The focus was on things we can control. It wasn't our job to think about them. We knew they were huge. But we were taught to play our game."

There was, however, undeniably one thing on the mind of Bruins players all season. It wasn't just that they were going for their fourth consecutive National Championship. They were trying to quiet a chorus of critics who didn't think they could win a title without Lew Alcindor. The Bruins' dominating center had moved on to the NBA, where he later changed his name to Kareem Abdul-Jabbar en route to fame and championships with the Los Angeles Lakers and eventually a spot in the Naismith Memorial Basketball Hall of Fame. Thus, the question shadowed them all season: could the UCLA Bruins win without Lew Alcindor? Their answer was: why not? After all, they won prior to him. Not only were the Bruins going after their fourth straight championship, they were vying for their sixth in seven years.

Of course, there also was the professorial, though sartorially challenged, John Wooden – aka The Wizard of Westwood – who was well on his way toward establishing himself as college basketball's greatest coach ever.

UCLA was a dynasty in every definition of the word. The Bruins were college basketball's brutes, a monolithic machine that mowed down anyone in their way. Meanwhile, with its student body of just 2,700, Jacksonville was – and still is – the smallest school to ever make it to the NCAA Championship Game. Not only that, but just five years earlier the Dolphins' were an NAIA school, and 15 years earlier they were a junior college. The school had also only been in existence since 1934, a mere 36 years.

It was the classic David versus Goliath showdown ... only this time it appeared Goliath would be the one getting some extra help.

The comment, cold and clinical, came to Wasdin the day before the title game, and it came from a prominent college coach in the inner circle, though himself not a card carrying member of The Establishment. The prominent coach's words disturbed Wasdin, as it would anyone in sports who believes, perhaps naively, in level playing fields.

"We were told that we didn't have a chance, that The Establishment wasn't going to let us win," Wasdin said. "That was the message we got, that they weren't going to let us win and our options were that we could take it like gentlemen and not complain or come across like sour grapes."

The normally feel-good Cinderella story that college basketball often thrives on during its tournament didn't cut it with The

Establishment. Neither did it cut it with any cosmic connection to destiny. The superstitious types noted that the last time the NCAA Finals were held at College Park was in 1966, and that was when a little known independent, Texas Western (now known as UTEP), defeated powerhouse Kentucky. It was a milestone game in the Civil Rights movement because Texas Western started five black players and Kentucky was an all-white team. Four years later, the NCAA assigned Jacksonville the same hotel where Texas Western slept.

It didn't matter. None of it mattered.

"The message we got was that we weren't going to win because the officials weren't going to let us," Wasdin said. "The Establishment didn't want it. Our chances of winning were very slim. Joe accepted that fate. He knew it going in. If it happened, it happened, and he wasn't going to cause a stink. That was the mindset. Don't cause a scene. Be a gracious loser. That's what he did and that's what we have done."

Until now.

Whatever it was that The Establishment was afraid of was on display even before the game started, when JU emerged wearing not the standard Chuck Taylor Converse canvas shoes, but rather a nascent German brand known as adidas, spelled with all lower-case letters, and which the Dolphins' cheerleaders had painted green and gold stripes onto in deference to the game being televised on color TV.

As the Jacksonville players warmed up to their favorite pregame song, *Sweet Georgia Brown*, the jazz standard popularized by the Harlem Globetrotters, while also dunking basketballs, the difference between the two schools again couldn't have been more blatant. UCLA center Steve Patterson turned to the stoic John Wooden and asked: "Coach, why can't *we* warm up like that?" To The Establishment it must've seemed like when their teenage daughters first saw Elvis Presley on TV, his hips gyrating with sexual innuendo.

Jacksonville was confident, but stopped short of being cocky.

"There wasn't a person on that team who didn't think we could beat UCLA," Frank Casey said.

"It's a game we fully expected to win," Rex Morgan said. "But then again, as players, you're a little naive that the game was going to be called straight up."

But was it?

Jacksonville was off and running at the opening tipoff, when Gilmore slapped the ball to Morgan who zipped in for a quick layup. From there, the Dolphins steadily built an early first-half lead. "Going in we recognized that UCLA was the powerhouse, the most successful college team during that time," Gilmore said. "But at the start of that game, we were playing extremely well." Even still, the lack of respect for the Dolphins couldn't have been more apparent than when NBC announcer Curt Gowdy twice referred to Jacksonville University as "Jacksonville State." But JU's quick start got everyone's attention and, as usual, it was Gilmore who was leading the way, scoring several buckets on passes that were lobbed over UCLA's 6-foot-8 Sidney Wicks, who gave up six inches in height to the 7-foot-2 center. Midway through the first half, Jacksonville had a 9-point lead, with Gilmore on his way to scoring 14 of JU's first 31 points.

A couple of key events followed:

- During a TV timeout, Wicks went to John Wooden and assistant coach Denny Crum, who normally made the defensive adjustments, and implored them to let him play *behind* Gilmore instead of fronting him. They made the switch.
- Midway through the first half, Rex Morgan came down on Greg Nelson's foot and turned his ankle.

Playing Wicks behind Gilmore produced immediate results, and it made so much sense that today Morgan, who made his career coaching basketball, wonders why, if UCLA had such brilliant and legendary coaching, they didn't start the game that way. Still, what followed was unexpected. Blocking an Artis Gilmore shot just did not happen. But there was Sidney Wicks blocking not one, not two, but several of Gilmore's hook shots. What made this odder, if not impossible, is that Gilmore didn't have a conventional hook shot. It certainly wasn't like the skyhook Lew Alcindor later perfected in the NBA, when he became Kareem Abdul-Jabbar and lofted rainbows that found their pot of gold at the bottom of the net. When Gilmore leapt and extended his arm for a hook shot, he'd get such elevation that he'd shoot *down* at the basket.

"People don't realize what a physical specimen Artis Gilmore was," said Frank Frangie, the 11-year-old Jacksonville boy who grew up to become a sports media personality in the city. "Artis was as tall as

Kareem Abdul-Jabbar, as strong as Wilt Chamberlain and could jump like 'Dr. J' Julius Erving. He could jump like a 6-foot-6 forward. You just didn't see people blocking his shots."

Evidently, the officials didn't see what everybody else could clearly see.

"It was goaltending," Morgan said. "Artis was shooting down at the basket. There's no way that can be a blocked shot. But they were letting it happen, and as we were getting back on defense we were looking at the official like, 'Why aren't you calling that?' And they'd be looking back at us and then at the other official, as if to say, 'It's not my call.'"

"From courtside, it even looked to me like they knocked one of Artis' shots off the rim," Wasdin said, "and they still didn't call goaltending."

Dr. Duane Bork, JU's team physician, wished that NCAA rules allowed dunking. "The goaltending was just absolutely gross," he said. "It was so obvious. It's a shame Artis couldn't let one go and slam it home, because he would've broken Sidney Wicks' hand. That's how close Wicks' hand was to the rim. There were times when the back of his wrist was in contact with the rim."

Gilmore, a proud man who measures his words carefully, knew the type of player he was. "I was always the intimidator, the guy blocking shots," he said. "My elevation was extraordinary. My hook shot was a straight downward motion. I was shooting *down* at an angle. It should've been goaltending. But what are you going to do, argue with the officials? I never argued with the officials. Instead, my thinking was, 'What do I need to do? I need to adjust my game.' I wasn't frustrated, but I was probably out of sync."

Twenty three years after that game, Artis Gilmore and his teammate Vaughn Wedeking were asked to help with a cancer fundraiser for former Bruins shooting guard John Vallely, who in 1991 lost his daughter to pediatric cancer at the age of 12. While in Los Angeles for the fundraiser, Gilmore and Wedeking, who died in 2009 of frontotemporal dementia, were invited to dinner at the home of Andy Hill, another former guard on that UCLA team who later co-wrote a book with John Wooden. In fact, Wooden was at the dinner that night along with other luminaries like the Hall of Fame former baseball player Rod Carew.

"Right at the start of dinner," Gilmore recalled, "John Vallely told us, 'We looked at the film and those were not blocked shots. We just wanted to say that right off.'"

The casual admission, delivered as if it were a punch line with accompanying chuckles, caught Gilmore and Wedeking by surprise, even though *they* knew that *everybody* knew that there was no way Sidney Wicks had blocked all those shots.

"I said nothing," Gilmore recalled. "I kind of laughed it off. I looked at John Wooden and he didn't say anything, either. He just sort of smiled."

The blunt admission to goaltending, and getting away with it from the officials, only added credence to the other question marks hovering over that game; question marks that might yet turn into exclamation points.

Years after the dinner, Vallely again acknowledged the obvious. "Some of those blocks were goaltending," he said. "I remember thinking at the time that some of the blocks were clearly goaltending. I'm sure Artis got thrown off balance by some of the calls that weren't made."

In 2003, Frank Pace, a JU graduate who later became a TV producer for such shows as "Murphy Brown", "Suddenly Susan" and "George Lopez", wrote about the dinner for Jacksonville's *Florida Times-Union* newspaper. According to Pace's eyewitness account, Vallely spoke up just as the dinner began, saying:

"Let's get this out of the way now so we can get on with the evening – Sidney goaltended Artis."

"At least four times," Hill added.

Not to take away from the game Sidney Wicks played. From the get-go, Wicks was determined and locked in. "Sidney was the type of player who rose to every challenge," said Denny Crum, one of Coach Wooden's assistants that season who later became an iconic head coach at the University of Louisville, where he won two National Championships. "Whatever it took, that's what Sidney did."

Rick Betchley recalled how even from the opening tipoff, Wicks was in a zone. "When our center, Steve Patterson, went to jump ball with Artis Gilmore, he pulled Patterson by the back of the jersey and got in there to jump ball, shaking his finger at Gilmore, as if to say, 'No, no, no.' Artis was an imposing guy, the biggest guy we'd seen, especially with that afro. But Sidney was always a showman. Not a showboater. A showman. He recognized the national stage. He had a flair for the dramatic and that was live theater to him. That was his moment. He was in a zone."

Recalling how Wicks was that rare player who could match the moment confronting him, Crum said, "Nobody intimidated Sidney. He was big, strong, quick, agile, could run the floor and he could block shots. He was 6-foot-8 and he could jump. It wasn't uncommon to see him block shots on players bigger than him. If Sidney Wicks was on you in the low post it was no picnic, I can tell you that."

Crum said he never thought, or even heard it suggested, that any of Wicks' blocked shots on Gilmore were goaltending.

"I'm not saying it couldn't have been," he said. "There were only two officials on a game back then, so some things could've gotten by them, or they might not have had a good angle. But I never even thought about them being anything but blocked shots. What I do know is that it turned the game around."

In his landmark biography of John Wooden, Seth Davis wrote: "Wicks admitted later that several of those blocks should have been called goaltends, but Gilmore was visibly shaken."

There is no known full audio film that exists from the 1970 NCAA Championship Game. There is only a highlight reel and some choppy black-and-white footage with spotty sound. Not only does it show that Gilmore's hook shots could not have been blocked, but also that UCLA's Curtis Rowe clearly dunked the ball early in the first half and was not called for it. Dunking in college basketball was illegal at the time. After Rowe dunked on him, Gilmore stood there stunned for several seconds, looking around as if to ask: *What's going on?*

"Not only didn't they take the basket away," Rex Morgan noted, "he didn't get called for unsportsmanlike conduct, which was the rule at the time if you dunked the ball."

All of it was enough to throw the Dolphins out of sync. But there was more; something so obvious that even an 11-year-old boy, a diehard JU fan, could see even though he wasn't there at the game. Instead, Frank Frangie was playing for the Jacksonville Hornets on March 21, 1970, when the Dolphins were playing the Bruins for the national championship. The Hornets were a traveling youth basketball team, and on that day they were playing an away game a couple of hours west of

Jacksonville at the Florida Sheriff's Boy's Ranch in Live Oak. Though just a young boy, Frangie could see how JU had galvanized the city.

"We didn't have a pro team back then," Frangie said. In fact, the only pro team in the state of Florida was the Miami Dolphins. "The JU basketball players were our idols. I was a 5-foot-6 power forward and I wore number 42 because that was Pembrook Burrows' number. Our center wore number 53 because that was Artis Gilmore's number. Our guard wore number 10 because that was Vaughn Wedeking's number. Even our first guy off the bench wore number 55, because that was Greg Nelson's number. That song the players sung, *The Rooster*; to a bunch of 11-year-olds that was called songwriting. We all sang it."

And on that afternoon of the National Championship game, the boys all crowded to the back window of a yellow school bus as they motored to Live Oak. Following behind was the car of one of their parents, where inside they were listening to the radio broadcast of the JU-UCLA game and relaying the play-by-play to the boys in the school bus.

"If they flashed the headlights twice, it meant JU scored," Frangie said. "One headlight flashed meant UCLA scored. A right blinker meant UCLA hit a free throw. A left blinker meant JU made a free throw ... and there were not many of those, by the way."

No, there weren't.

"There were lots of whistles, and none of them were going for us," recalled Dr. Duane Bork, JU's team physician. "We were the new kid on the block and UCLA was The Establishment, so something extraordinary was going to have to happen for us to win. Coach Wooden had a lot of influence. He was a great student of the game, but he also was very influential. He'd have that program wrapped up in his hand, and he'd hammer it on his thigh if he was upset with the officials. He'd slap his thigh very loudly until the official got the message. He was a manipulator, and he had power over those officials. It was obvious that we weren't getting any calls and they were getting all the calls. They were going to the foul line regularly. Meanwhile, we'd get knocked to the floor and there would be no whistle."

There were other problems, too. Midway through the first half, shortly after the TV timeout that the Bruins used to regroup, down as they were by 9 points, Morgan turned his ankle and couldn't get back in time in transition, allowing some quick points and the momentum

Once a Coach, Always a Coach

to swing over to the Bruins. That Morgan was slowed by a throbbing ankle wasn't immediately apparent. During a timeout, Wasdin recalled Morgan trying to lace his shoe tighter and hearing him mutter, "Aw, shit." Turning, he saw that Morgan had torn his shoelace.

Becoming increasingly apparent, however, was that the number of fouls being called by the two officials, Bobby Scott and Lenny Wirtz, were disproportionately against Jacksonville. Just before UCLA took a 41-36 lead into halftime, Wasdin, agitated and sitting on the edge of his seat, his body in a pugnacious pose leaning forward, yelled at an official on the court, "Mr. Scott, we haven't shot one yet. We haven't shot a foul."

The thought Wasdin couldn't get out of his head was what he had heard the day before – that The Establishment wasn't going to let them win; that the calls were going to go against them.

"We had the taller team and got the ball in closest to the basket, and yet we weren't getting fouled and they were," he said. "We were not getting any calls and every time I turned around they were going to the foul line. They were getting points and we were getting in foul trouble, and both of those things are bad. It didn't seem like we were getting a fair shake with the officiating with the fouls and the goaltending. It seemed to me like the officials weren't going to do anything unless they had to. Early in the game, it looked like a very well-officiated game. But once we got that big lead, things changed. I couldn't help but think about what we'd been told – that the bluebloods, the hierarchy, The Establishment, was against us."

Curtis Kruer, a sophomore forward on that JU squad, also ruminates about that game, even 40-plus years later.

"We were ahead and we were rolling early in that game," he said. "And then we were taken out of our rhythm. There's no doubt in my mind that we were up against The Establishment. You can imagine what Adolph Rupp was saying behind the scenes. Rupp was a racist, and here we were, this team from Jacksonville, with black players, a team with swagger doing things like playing the Jackson 5 in the locker room. We were his worst nightmare."

But for the Dolphins at the time, there were pressing matters to contend with other than the officiating or the perceived Establishment. And that was the condition of Rex Morgan's ankle. In the locker room during halftime, Morgan had his ankle taped tightly, and although he couldn't even walk the next day, he was able to play the second half relatively pain free, perhaps because he was feeding off adrenaline.

It wouldn't prove to be enough, though, because the second half produced more of the same. Gilmore, out of rhythm because of goaltending calls that never came, as well as the growing number of whistles blown against him, could never find his groove. Morgan couldn't seem to get in sync, either. Chip Dublin's shoulder was barking at him, the result of taking a hard charge in the St. Bonaventure game, and he missed shot after shot from the floor. "Chipper was just a shadow of himself," Williams said. On top of that, a couple of questionable charges were called against Dublin, adding to the growing disparity of fouls cited against each team.

"They were calling touch fouls on us, and none on them," Wasdin said. "With everything going against us – the fouls, the officials, the calls, the breaks – the guys started pressing. They started doubting."

Thus the second half proved more of the same bad results for the Dolphins, with UCLA cruising to an 80-69 victory. This small David of a school, the smallest school to ever make it to the NCAA Finals, would be denied. This time, Goliath won ... but not without what looked like some extra help.

"The referees changed the tenor of that game, especially in the second half," Greg Nelson said. "You do things the way you'd done them all season, and now it results in fouls. When that happens, you start questioning yourself. The referees will take you out of sync. I remember right after the game, when they brought in the stat sheet, noticing how disproportionate it was. It was off. But what are you going to do? It's always spilt milk to complain that the referees screwed you."

The game's final statistics, which were perhaps looked upon as an aberration in 1970, look more like an abomination forty-plus years later.

In the entire history of the NCAA Championship Game – from 1939 through 2014, which covers 76 years – there has never been a larger margin between the numbers of foul shots taken by two teams as there were in that 1970 title game.

The final tally had UCLA shooting 35 free throws and Jacksonville just 8. No finals game before or since has eclipsed that 27-foul shot differential.

Did it make a difference?

Twenty-four of UCLA's 80 points, or 30 percent of their scoring, came at the free throw line – in other words almost one out of every three of their points came after a whistle against JU. Conversely, only seven of Jacksonville's 69 points came from free throws, or just one out of every 10 points the Dolphins scored.

JU's two star players – Artis Gilmore and Rex Morgan – shot exactly one free throw between the two of them. Gilmore was 1-for-1 from the free throw line, and that was it. According to the officials, Morgan never once was fouled.

Yet, both Gilmore and Morgan fouled out.

After the game, Morgan's father told him that from youth basketball through high school basketball and now through his entire college career, it was the only game where he never – not once – went to the free throw line.

Frank Casey, who was Morgan's friend since infancy, still can't comprehend what happened in that game. "When one team makes four times as many points from the foul line, something isn't right," he said. "I watched Rex his whole career. Rex made his living taking the ball, going to the basket and getting fouled. To look at the box score, even after all these years, and see that he never took a foul shot and Artis took just one ... it's astounding. It's so absurd that the facts stand on their own. UCLA pressed us a third of the game. Usually that produces fouls."

It didn't.

Gilmore took 29 shots with Sidney Wicks, who was six inches shorter, guarding him. Yet he drew only one foul.

"It defies logic," Casey said.

"Artis shot the ball 29 times and only got fouled once?" Morgan asked rhetorically, his words laced with incredulity. "That's absurd. That's all I can say about that. It's absurd. Either Sidney Wicks and UCLA are the greatest defensive team in the history of college basketball, or there was something not level on that floor."

All these years later, Morgan still dwells on the figures from the box score, and the message they sent. "The stats hit you in the face," he said. "I guess we would've had to have been 15 points better than them if we were going to beat them."

UCLA's starting five of Curtis Rowe, Sidney Wicks, Steve Patterson, John Vallely and Henry Bibby attempted 30 foul shots, making 22. Meanwhile, Jacksonville's starting five of Artis Gilmore, Rex Morgan, Vaughn Wedeking, Pembrook Burrows III and Mike Blevins attempted only three free throws, making two. The differential, then, shows that UCLA's starters shot 27 more free throws than Jacksonville's starters, and scored 20 more points from it.

It was also the first time since 1944, when Dartmouth shot just five free throws in a 42-40 loss to Utah, in which a team didn't go to the free throw line double-digit times. And even back then, in that game from a quarter of a century earlier, Utah shot 14 free throws, making it a nine shot differential between the two teams.

The other stat that screams some sort of behind-the-scenes conspiracy is that Jacksonville was a scoring power that season, unlike anything college basketball had ever seen before. The Dolphins were the first team to average more than 100 points in a season. They scored *a lot*. And they were fouled *a lot*. For the season, the Dolphins averaged 29.3 foul shots a game, or a staggering 21.3 more foul shots than they were allowed against UCLA.

"It sounds like sour grapes and I know that," Morgan said. "But when you see the stats, it doesn't look all that straight and level."

Bruins players, when told more than 40 years later of the foul shot discrepancy, were surprised; but they didn't react with indignation.

"I'd be shocked if something was done to change the course of that game, but I'm not ruling it out," Vallely said. "In the area of goaltending on Artis Gilmore, there were two that probably were pretty sure. I remember Artis shooting the ball down. So not getting those goaltending calls looked questionable, and I think any Bruin would tell him that."

From the bench, Betchley didn't notice anything unusual about the officiating. When told of the foul-shot differential, he was nonplussed. "I don't rule out anything anymore," he said, regarding any conspiracy theories. "But I will say this. We were not a team that fouled a lot. We were very disciplined. Very well-coached. We didn't reach in a lot. We didn't foul a lot in general."

That's true. But still, the discrepancy is staggering even by UCLA's standards that season. The Bruins had played 27 games prior to the title game. In those 27 games, they averaged going to the foul line 30 times, while their opponents averaged 20 trips to the stripe. That's a 10 foul shot differential; hardly close to the 27 that came in the championship game.

Denny Crum pointed out that basketball – and particularly college basketball during that era without dunking – was "a different game in those days. It was a finesse game and not brute strength. We were very good at getting the ball to the right player where they wanted it, at their comfort level, where they were at their best. It's hard to guard players when you're doing that. You either have to foul or give up a lot of easy baskets. I also think that, aside from Gilmore, we were more athletic than Jacksonville."

Even still, the numbers from that game are somewhat staggering. Through 2014, the Top 10 National Championship games with the largest differential in free throw attempts reads like this:

1. 1970 UCLA-**Jacksonville** – 27
2. 1997 Arizona-Kentucky – 24
3. 1966 Texas Western-Kentucky – 21
4. (tie) 1954 La Salle-Bradley – 20
    1991 Duke-Kansas – 20
5. 1985 Villanova-Georgetown – 19
6. 2004 UConn-Georgia Tech – 18
7. 1969 UCLA-Purdue – 17
8. (tie) 1965 UCLA-Michigan – 16
    1993 UNC-Michigan – 16

Not surprisingly, in all ten of those games, the team that shot the most free throws won.

Through 2014, there have been only 10 teams who failed to shoot double-digit free throws in the NCAA Championship Game. That list reads like this:

1. 1944 Dartmouth – 5
2. (tie) 1942 Dartmouth – 6
    2005 Illinois – 6
3. (tie) 1993 Michigan – 7
    2002 Indiana – 7

4. (tie) 1942 Stanford – 8
   1970 **Jacksonville** – 8
   1985 Georgetown – 8
   1991 Kansas – 8
5. 1982 Georgetown – 9

Not surprisingly, all 10 of those teams lost, save for Stanford in 1942, which shot eight free throws to Dartmouth's six in that championship game, and won 42-40.

Finally, through 2014 these were the most free throws attempted in the NCAA Championship Game.

1. 1954 Bradley – 44
2. (tie) 1969 UCLA – 41
   1997 Arizona – 41
3. 2009 UNC – 40
4. 2004 UConn – 39
5. 1958 Kentucky 36
6. (tie) 1950 CCNY – 35
   1970 **UCLA** – 35
   1952 Kansas – 35
7. (tie) 1966 Texas Western – 34
   1974 NC State – 34
   1978 Drake – 34

Not surprisingly, 10 of 11 of those teams won their championship games. The only team to fall short was Drake in 1978, which lost 94-88 to a Kentucky team that shot 25 free throws to its 34.

Of all that history, however, the one that matters most to JU is that 1970 game, which still is the largest differential in free throw shots attempted (27) in the history of an NCAA finals. It's a game that saw UCLA's starters attempt 30 free throws and JU's starters just three; a game with several questionable non-goaltending calls and a non-dunking call; a game that saw not one UCLA player foul out while JU's two best players, Gilmore and Morgan, both fouled out – Gilmore for only the second time that season and Morgan for the first time.

While cross-examining history can reveal a lot, Gilmore emphasized that it remains exactly that.

"It's *history*," he said. "It's still *history*, and nothing now is going to change the outcome of that game, or the statistics."

Whether it was because they were out of sync, frustrated, pressing or whatever, the statistics will also show that Jacksonville's players didn't perform at their best, which they will be the first to admit to.

"I've relived that game a thousand times, and I've always felt that if we played them again, we'd beat them," Morgan said. "I have a lot of respect for UCLA. That was a great team. All five of their starters played in the NBA. But we could've played better. Artis and I didn't play our best games (Gilmore was 9 for 29 and Morgan 5 for 11) and we didn't get much from the bench like we normally did (Dublin was 0 for 5, Nelson 3 for 9 and McIntyre 1 for 3; in all the bench shot just 39 percent). And there's a lot to be said about being there before, which was obviously the case for UCLA."

It is that part, not knowing what to expect, that Joe Williams wonders about whenever he allows his mind to wander into the what-ifs?

"We weren't prepared for the onslaught of attention – all the writers, the media, the cameras," he said. "It was such a wild ride. I had never experienced anything like that before. It all seems like a big blur to me now. It happened so fast, and there was so much confusion. It was almost like we were there, and not there."

Soon, very soon, Williams would literally not be there any longer with JU.

Pembrook Burrow's what-if? is whether he could've done more. He shot 6 for 9 from the field, but he believes he should've done something when he saw Gilmore struggling. "It was not our best game, and it wasn't Artis' best game, either," he said. "Our timing was off the whole game. I probably should've gone to the low post and asked for the ball more, until Artis got back on track. I'll always wonder if there was something more I could've done?"

As for Morgan, his what-if? is what might've been had he taken himself out midway through the first half, when JU was rolling and he also rolled his ankle. Unable to keep up, Morgan saw UCLA convert several fast breaks and the momentum begin to shift.

"I couldn't get back in time on defense," he said. "I was fine the second half, when I got my ankle taped. But it still haunts me to this day: what would've happened had I not turned my ankle? I should have been smart enough to tell Joe and Tom to take me out. But I know how I am. You'd have had to cut my leg off to get me out. Did I hurt the team? I'll never know. If I had have taken myself out and we still lost, that would have haunted me even more."

Joe Williams wishes he'd have known just how much Chip Dublin's shoulder was bothering him from the charge he took in the semifinal game against St. Bonaventure. "In the whirlwind of everything that was going on, I didn't have as much time with the players as I wanted," he said. "Had I been there before, I would've known what to expect, and I would've done a much better job. I had no idea the amount of noise and distraction I'd encounter. It was like a tsunami, and you get caught up in it. Our doctor traveled with us on all those trips, and I think he gave Chipper a shot. But I don't know. In all the whirlwind of everything that was going on, I don't know. What I do know is that when we played UCLA, he wasn't very effective."

In the postgame locker room, Burrows recalled how Morgan, the only starting senior on the team, made the rounds, saying goodbye to everyone. "I enjoyed playing with you guys," Morgan told his teammates.

"He was giving us handshakes and hugs, and that's when it hit me," Burrows said. "This was it. This was the last game, the last time we'd ever play together. It was not like we were going back to Jacksonville to practice and get ready for another game."

Joe Williams not only knew that there wasn't another game, but also that he would likely be leaving Jacksonville. Furman, where he had coached as an assistant in 1963-64, wanted him back as its head coach, and he was ready to leave. But he had a message to deliver to his team first. Knowing what was said prior to the game, about how The Establishment would not allow them to win, he measured his words carefully.

"I was prepared for the game in the sense that if anything happened, I wasn't going to let it bother me," he said. "I wasn't going to complain or make an issue of anything. That's not me. I told our players to be positive and that I was really proud of what they'd accomplished and I wanted them to enjoy the accomplishment. I told them that there'd be no sour grapes; that we got here and we had a great year. So don't hang your head, don't complain about the officiating, and don't complain about anything else."

Williams gave the same speech to the media, taking the high road even while he'd just taken it on the chin. His reward was an editorial four days later in the *Louisville Courier-Journal* newspaper, the largest circulation newspaper in basketball-crazy Kentucky. Beneath an editorial about the Cambodian coup that ousted Premier Norodom Sihanouk was another editorial entitled: Impressive Show of Sportsmanship. After perfunctory praise for Kentucky and Louisville, the editorial focused on Jacksonville and their young head coach, Joe Williams. It said:

The season should not end without notice of the conduct of Coach Joe Williams, whose Cinderella Jacksonville team almost scaled the NCAA pinnacle before losing to UCLA. After what must have been a heartbreaking loss, Coach Williams refused to blame the officials or his players or the tactics of his opponents, as so many coaches seem to do these days. Instead, he had nothing but praise for his players, for winning coach John Wooden and the splendid players of UCLA.

It is this sort of thing that sends everyone away with a good feeling about the event, the game, and sports in general. And it offers an example we wish more coaches and school officials would emulate. It would do a great deal, we imagine, to keep down the resentment and ill-feeling that so often erupts in postgame violence. Few people like to lose. And angry recriminations from coaches and school officials, blaming their team's losses on the referee or the dirty play of opponents, are often the spark needed to turn the hurt pride and raw tempers of disappointed fans into violent action against opposing fans or team members, or against casual bystanders.

Perhaps a little more sportsmanship of the type displayed by Coach Williams would help set the tone for students and fans, and make unnecessary the elaborate security precautions that are so often required at sports events.

Though not one for memories or memorabilia, Williams cut out the article and saved it. "I tend to look forward, not back," he said.

Even before the UCLA game, he was looking forward, negotiating a job offer from Furman to be the university's next head basketball coach. But there were still a few things for Williams to wrap up with Jacksonville – specifically, a conversation with Artis Gilmore, who still had his senior season left to play.

"I encouraged you to come here to JU," Williams told Gilmore a few days later, confiding in him. "I have an opportunity to go to Furman. But if you want, I'll stay."

"Take it," Gilmore told him. "I know what you're going through here. Take the Furman job."

In a lot of respects, given how cheaply JU operated, it was easy for Williams to do so; but in other respects, it wasn't easy. Williams had grown close to his players, especially Gilmore, whom he remembered recruiting in Chipley and seeing Gilmore living in such impoverished conditions that he didn't even own a pair of shoes.

"Furman was doubling my salary, but if Artis had told me to stay, I would've stayed," Williams said. "I was that close to him. When Artis got pneumonia once, I fixed a tent in my house and took care of him like a son. We had an unreal bond."

Part of the thousands who waited to greet Jacksonville University at the airport when the team returned from the Final Four.

Williams obviously sensed the bond with the Jacksonville community, too. When the Dolphins returned from the Final Four, the mob of people waiting for them was unlike anything they'd ever seen. People lined the streets as a police escort brought them back to campus.

"It was like a parade," Gilmore recalled.

The team was then taken to the Gator Bowl, where it was estimated that somewhere around 30,000 to 40,000 people arrived for a celebration.

"It seemed like the whole city was there," Frank Frangie said. "Everybody came. I was with my dad and he must've seen the look on my face, because I remember him clearly saying to me, 'You're going to remember this for the rest of your life.' My dad died two years later, and to this day I remember the clothes he had on, and the clothes I had on. For an 11-year-old it was the biggest thing in the world to me. I remember it like yesterday."

Jacksonville tried to counter Furman's offer, but it was too little and way too late. From the time he got there in 1964, Williams endured year after year of almost obscene frugality.

"The administration there were the most ridiculous people in the world," he said. "I remember when we didn't even have laundry money and the players had to sweep and clean the gym as part of their scholarship."

One day, in a conversation with a physics professor, Williams asked:

"Your students who are here on a physics scholarship, do they have to clean the lab every day?"

"No," the professor replied.

"Then how come my players who are here on a basketball scholarship have to clean the gym?"

Williams was coaching the basketball team *and* teaching five classes until Wasdin got there, and took the school workload off him.

Williams was making $9,000 that final year. Wasdin was making $10,000 because he had a master's degree. Williams was happy that his friend was making more. "It didn't matter to me," he said, "and I needed the help."

Furman's offer was for $18,000 plus the use of two cars, gas, all his clothes provided, laundry and dry cleaning, medical coverage for doctors and druggists, an entertainment budget, help for his basketball camp and a lucrative TV show that had Texaco as one of its sponsors.

Jacksonville's offer was $12,000 a year, a mere $3,000 pay raise for making the NCAA Championship Game, and a free week at the school president's cabin in Lake Lure, N.C.

All things considered, it was a no-brainer. Still, Williams cared about the players he was leaving behind. And he knew that critics would accuse him of bolting because of the ongoing investigation that was looking into Gilmore's summer job at parks and recreation that paid him $75 a day, a nice chunk of change in 1970's America.

"As far as Artis' situation was concerned, I was worried about it only because with the NCAA if you're innocent you still have to prove it," he said. "I knew that we had done nothing wrong, but you never know what the NCAA is going to do. I even had a letter from New York City Mayor John Lindsay that showed that Lew Alcindor was making $125 a day for his work there in the city. He'd visit five playgrounds a day and make $25 from each one."

The New York City program and the Jacksonville one, as well as many similar ones that universities around the country were using for its players, were designed to help inner-city kids, providing them a role model who was in college.

"The program we had Artis in was legal," Williams said. "We had it checked out. Twenty other schools around the country were doing the same thing. But with the NCAA, you never know what they're going to do. They eventually reprimanded JU and brought an end to schools being able to do that. But that's not why I left. Again, if Artis wanted me to stay, I would've stayed. I left because of how I'd been treated since I'd been there. The season before we were 17-7, beat Florida, which went to the NIT, and then added Artis and Pembrook. If they were serious about keeping me, they would've done something then. But they didn't."

So Williams left for Furman, and he obviously wanted Wasdin to go with him.

"I would've loved for Tom to have come; that would have been logical," Williams said. "There probably have never been two coaches who worked as closely together as Tom and me. I also knew it was logical for him to become JU's next head coach, and he deserved that opportunity. I had Furman offer him $15,000 to come be my assistant. That was my way of making sure JU paid him enough. I really took care of Tom."

Wasdin did consider following his friend to Furman. But he also thought that his time to be a college head coach had arrived. He also recalled how, when he left Paxon High School in 1964, that the following year the team he left behind won the state championship.

"I wasn't going to make the same mistake twice," he said.

He knew what he had coming back at JU. The Dolphins were returning everybody but Rex Morgan, Rod McIntyre, Dan Hawkins and Ken Selke. That meant that four of the starters – Artis Gilmore, Pembrook Burrows III, Vaughn Wedeking and Mike Blevins – were returning. And JU would also be adding Ernie Fleming, who'd sat out the previous year to get academically eligible, and the highly touted Harold Fox, a future NBA player, who was coming from Brevard Junior College.

The future looked bright. Little did Wasdin know, though, that when he returned to Cocoa Beach a few weeks later to help manage the Canaveral Pier over spring break, that the presence he maintained there would also be a part of the future.

While back in Brevard County, Wasdin touched base with Harold Fox. Pembrook Burrows III, who had been at BJC a year before, and had played a season together with Fox, stopped in for a visit. Meanwhile, Rex Morgan had driven to Fort Lauderdale for spring break, and on his way back he stopped to see Wasdin.

"We were out on the Pier, and I remember that's when Tom told me what they'd heard the night before the championship game, that The Establishment wasn't going to let us win."

It was hard for him to take. It's still hard now, and the questions still linger. Why was the officiating so lopsided? Whatever rationale the two referees, Bobby Scott and Lenny Wirtz, may have had, they both took to their graves. Scott died in 2010 and Wirtz in 2013. Wooden died in 2010.

Even still, the memory of that 1970 NCAA Championship Game lingers, as do the thoughts of what could have been. It would have made a great story; the smallest school in NCAA Finals history beating the most dominant program in NCAA history.

But it wasn't to be.

This time, Goliath won ... with some help.

Chapter 12

THE SPOTLIGHT AND THE SHADOW OF SUCCESS

"We're here to win a national championship." – Tom Wasdin

How do you top finishing second in the nation? There is only one way – to finish first.

Tom Wasdin knew that, so when he succeeded his friend Joe Williams and was introduced as the fourth basketball coach in Jacksonville University's history, this is what he confidently declared at his first news conference:

"We're here to win a national championship."

Adding an exclamation point to that statement was Jacksonville University President Bob Spiro, who said, "You don't have to do anything like last year ... just move up one place in the ratings."

The collective reaction from JU's growing fan base – bandwagon fans or not – was to take what Coach Wasdin and President Spiro had uttered as a no-brainer. *Of course winning the national championship was the mission. Why wouldn't it be?* In fact, not only was winning the national championship logical, Wasdin would find out that anything less than that was unacceptable.

He soon learned, though, that he and Dolphin fans had been spoiled by the enormous success of making it all the way to the NCAA National Championship game. Throughout college basketball's history, there have been many outstanding coaches and top-tier programs that have never even played for a national title, much less won one. It isn't easy. The road to a national championship is wrought with unpredictable potholes and unexpected accidents that can – and often do – wreck a season.

Wasdin quickly discovered something else, too.

Not only was he now the central actor on the stage, which placed the spotlight and all its heat squarely on him, but the actor who had just left the stage cast a heavy shadow.

Joe Williams was beloved at JU, and unless Tom Wasdin won a national championship, he'd always be perceived as *not* Joe Williams. Never mind that Williams consistently and profusely credited Wasdin for spearheading the recruiting efforts that brought players talented enough to even play for a national championship. That was all well and good with JU fans. Nobody dared deny that Wasdin was a great recruiter. That had become a given. But would he be a great coach? The pressure was on, not only from JU's administration and its fans, but also from the media who had suddenly discovered Dolphins basketball and ratcheted up the expectations and hype. Yes, the pressure was on, and the only way to relieve it was to win one more game – i.e. *the* game – than they did the year before.

So in retrospect, announcing that "we're here to win a national championship" wasn't the smartest thing for Wasdin to say just as he was settling into the starting blocks of what would be a three-year sprint as a head coach. It only intensified the unreal and, indeed, unrealistic pressure. As Wasdin would admit years later, "I caused some of my own problems." By his third season at JU, there were actually boos heard, directed at him, even though Wasdin's body of work saw him take Jacksonville to two NCAA tournaments and an NIT tournament in his three seasons with the university, while also winning at least 20 games in each of those three seasons. He also compiled one of the best college coaching records in the country during his three years as head coach. The list of winningest college basketball coaches from 1970-73 reads like this:

1. John Wooden, UCLA, 89-1
2. Al McGuire, Marquette, 78-9
3. Jerry Tarkanian, Long Beach State, 75-12
4. Dean Smith, North Carolina, 74-17
5. Frank McGuire, South Carolina, 69-18
6. Dave Gavitt, Providence, 68-18
7. Guy Lewis, Houston, 65-18
8. Tom Wasdin, Jacksonville University, 63-18

"Tom was a great coach. Don't let anybody say he wasn't," said Pat Williams, who was a prominent JU booster at the time and instrumental in establishing the Century Club. "The program didn't suffer any after Joe Williams left. Even when Joe was there, Tom had a lot to do with the coaching of the team. Tom was young, passionate, personable, and like Joe, he was a very hard worker. What he didn't have that Joe had was that Joe had Tom Wasdin as his recruiter."

One of the things Tom Wasdin sold recruits on was that Jacksonville University was just minutes from the Atlantic Ocean and its beautiful beach.

One of the players Wasdin had worked so diligently to recruit was, of course, Artis Gilmore, who was by now bringing the program unprecedented national exposure. In fact, that offseason before Gilmore's senior year, Wasdin and Gilmore went to a banquet together at New York City's famed Toots Shor's Restaurant, where the country's top sports stars were honored. There they sat with such luminaries as Roger Maris, Arthur Ashe, Johnny Unitas, Willie Shoemaker and

Tom Dempsey. It was there that Wasdin struck up a conversation and eventually a friendship with Maris, who lived in nearby Gainesville, Fla., where he ran a beer distributorship. Maris soon became a regular at JU basketball games, where he and Wasdin would often go out afterward for a bite to eat and good conversation.

It was an exhilarating yet busy time. In addition to being the head coach, Wasdin remained very much involved in recruiting, even though he hired Art Tolis to be his assistant coach and head recruiter. It helped that Wasdin's relentless efforts from his days as an assistant had built momentum that carried over, as evidenced by the fact that during that first season, they recruited six former high school All-Americans – Ricky Coleman, Henry Williams, Shawn Leftwich, Jimmie Clark, Dave Stowers and Mike Denney.

Don Rutledge, who had joined JU as the freshmen team's coach, was immediately taken by Wasdin's adaptability.

"He did a tremendous job of putting together a system for the people involved," Rutledge said. "He adapted to his players and he didn't restrict them so much that they didn't have a certain measure of freedom. At the same time, he had a basic philosophy. He believed in getting the ball into the hands of his best players, and he believed in constantly keeping pressure on the ball and on the other team. If the other team missed a shot or a free throw, that ball was at midcourt and in the other basket in seconds. Our players were already sprinting, forcing a 3-on-2 or 2-on-1 situation. He always kept the pressure on the other team.

"I remember when Pete Maravich was a rookie with the Atlanta Hawks and they were conducting preseason practices at Bolles High School in Jacksonville. Tom went to watch them practice to see how they communicated on the fastbreak. He brought a lot of what he learned back to our practices to help make us quicker and better."

Others, too, could see that after the baton was passed from Williams to Wasdin, the program was still in good hands.

"Tom had such drive," said John Harrison, a former Dolphins player who became a prominent booster in the Century Club and later sat on Jacksonville University's Board of Trustees. "He helped put the university and the city on the map with his drive. Tom had so many good qualities. He was personable, energetic, dedicated and likable; someone who cared about people. He was so focused, too. Always thinking. Sometimes he didn't even hear you because he was so focused, thinking about something, thinking about ways to make the team and the program better. Sometimes I reflect back to what he and Joe Williams accomplished and it's really remarkable. These were two young guys who produced remarkable seasons even though they weren't seasoned coaches. They had a dream and a vision and they worked extremely hard and worked so well together."

Curtis Kruer was going into his junior year as a forward when Wasdin took over the program. He chaffed a bit under Joe Williams because Williams would make him run wind sprints whenever Artis Gilmore messed up. "Joe thought he was being funny and I just kind of rolled with it," Kruer said. "He gave me this nickname, Freddy Freshman, and it kind of stuck. Whenever Artis screwed up, he obviously didn't want to punish him, so he made me run. Again, Joe thought it was funny, and it bothered me a bit. But for the most part, I was just happy to be there."

Kruer was even happier when Wasdin got the head coaching job.

"Maybe I'm a bit biased because of the way Coach Wasdin treated me. Joe Williams sort of took my confidence away from me and Tom gave it back," Kruer said. "But I always thought Tom was a better coach than Joe. I thought he was more into the game, more into the nuances of the game. He was more intense, more into the game of basketball."

Wasdin wasn't just *into* the game of basketball; he was also looking for ways to *innovate* it. George Scholz, a point guard who later became a college basketball coach, which included a four-year stint in the mid-90s as JU's head coach, saw right away what others saw – Wasdin's intensity and fiery style along with a relentless push to always be better. What Scholz also saw, and what he didn't fully appreciate until years later when he was running college programs, was how forward thinking Wasdin and his staff were.

"They were way ahead of their time," Scholz said. "They were doing things like offensive efficiency ratings before anyone else. At the end of practice, instead of having us run wind sprints and yelling at us to run faster, like all coaches do, he had us play tag. And not just any tag, but dribble tag. So it would be a situation where I'd be dribbling a basketball and Vaughn Wedeking would be dribbling a basketball chasing me. It was great conditioning while improving your skills at the same time. We had a lot of variations of dribble tag."

By the time he left JU, Wasdin had forged a burgeoning career as a college basketball head coach. But to some people in Jacksonville, it wasn't enough. And, of course, he'd never have that same team that went to the 1970 NCAA Championship Game. Besides, it wasn't as if JU and its administration had changed much in terms of support and funding. It was still a small school trying to slay Goliaths, and still trying to do so with old-fashioned slingshots and a shoestring budget.

But there was cause for optimism and perhaps even bold talk. On March 27, 1970, when Tom Wasdin was introduced as Jacksonville University's new basketball coach, it was duly noted that the Dolphins were returning practically their entire starting lineup, minus Rex Morgan. To be sure, losing Morgan to graduation left a huge hole.

The 1970-71 Jacksonville University team. Standing from left to right: Assistant Coach Jim "Slick" Watson, Ernie Fleming, Pembrook Burrows III, Artis Gilmore, Greg Nelson, Mike Blevins, Head Coach Tom Wasdin. Kneeling left to right: Chipper Dublin, Rusty Baldwin, Vaughn Wedeking, Phil Carter, Curtis Kruer, Harold Fox.

"Rex wasn't our best player," Wasdin said. "Obviously that was Artis Gilmore. But I would say that Rex was our most important player."

Morgan was not only the undisputed team leader; he was a quarterback on the court and a tenacious and relentless competitor who exuded confidence, thus setting the tone for the team.

"I think Rex was missed tremendously," said Frank Casey, Morgan's childhood friend who was also JU's Sports Information Director. "I know it's a cliché, but he was a coach on the floor. He made sure his teammates knew what they needed to do, and if he got on them they accepted it. He was clutch, too. The bigger the moment, the bigger the game, the bigger Rex played. I once broke down the statistics, and in games that were close or against tougher opponents, Rex averaged twice as many points as he did in other games. He was the one who kept things going. He stirred the drink."

Still, the Dolphins were not only returning Artis Gilmore, a year older and wiser and more developed, they were also returning Pembrook Burrows III, Vaughn Wedeking, Chip Dublin, Greg Nelson, Mike Blevins, Rusty Baldwin and Curtis Kruer. Adding to the roster's solid lineup were dazzling recruits Harold Fox, who was another Brevard Junior College import, and Ernie Fleming, who had spent the previous season practicing with the team while getting eligible. The starting five were solid and experienced. There was depth, too, and lots of it.

Gilmore knew instinctively, though, that this team would have a different chemistry. He was impressed with Harold Fox's talent, and he knew what his good friend Ernie Fleming could do, since they had played together at Gardner-Webb Junior College. "But they played different roles than Rex Morgan had," he said. "It was really a major key not having the leadership Rex provided at the guard position. With Rex on the court, it allowed the head coach to focus on other things. It provided him with a special luxury in that way. We were lacking that. There were adjustments without Rex, and they were challenging."

At least the transition from Joe Williams to Tom Wasdin was a smooth one, and a source of comfort to the players. If Coach Williams was no longer their coach, the players couldn't think of anyone better to take over the program than Coach Wasdin.

Said Greg Nelson, "It's like if your mom and dad got divorced, and at least you still know that you'll be living with one or the other."

"I could not tell the difference," Pembrook Burrows III said. "It was the same after Coach Wasdin took over. Everything was the same. Nothing changed. Coach Wasdin was a little more intense than Coach Williams, but that was the same as before. As an assistant he was more intense, and he just kept that same intensity."

Wasdin's intensity was borne from an overwhelming desire to win, and it was something the players fed off of.

"Coach Wasdin was such a fierce competitor and I loved that about him," said Rusty Baldwin, a guard on the team. "We had great practices. Coach Wasdin had moxie, a feel for things. He knew the strengths and weaknesses and the psyche of his players, and he could process that. He'd get so excited at practices when things were cranking. He'd really get into it. He'd clasp both his hands together as if to say, *That's it! That's what I'm talking about!* He'd have such a smile. He couldn't contain himself. He really enjoyed seeing us improve and succeed."

Baldwin was a workout guy, a fitness fanatic, so he thrived under Wasdin's work ethic.

"Coach understood that to give us our best chance to win we had to be in the best shape," he said. "When it comes down to the last five minutes, it's all about who has the most guts, who's in the best shape. I always felt that was us. Our practices were hard, but they were not work. They were total joy. That was the highlight of our day, when we got together. Coach was demanding, but fun. He treated us very well."

Dr. Duane Bork, the team's physician, appreciated that Wasdin was consistently positive with his players. "I remember how, when we needed a basket, Tom would yell to Vaughn Wedeking, 'Score!' It wouldn't be, 'Shoot!' It was, 'Score!' The assumption was that if he shot the ball he was going to score. That was part of his positive reinforcement."

There was such a national buzz surrounding the team going into that season that those practices drew the attention of the great Boston Celtic center Bill Russell, who at the time was perhaps the most famous basketball player in the world. Russell came to Jacksonville and went to dinner a few times with Wasdin. Later, he even met the team when they were playing a regular-season game at Madison Square Garden.

"I remember that Russell wouldn't sign autographs and I asked him about it," Wasdin said. "He was a very humble guy and he didn't want to create the perception that he was being worshipped."

When Russell came to watch some of JU's preseason practices, the players weren't necessarily interested in autographs, but they naturally wanted to put on a show for the NBA legend.

"The guys were going all out for him," Wasdin recalled. "They were playing above the rim. On one play, Chipper Dublin was way up there, but then he accidentally got his knees cut out from underneath him and came down hard on his head. He suffered a concussion and I think the effects of it bothered him a lot that season."

The Dolphins now had a prominent spot on the national radar. Not only were the expectations high from Coach Wasdin, President Spiro and the JU fan base, but the country expected big things from the little school along Florida's First Coast. Jacksonville entered the season ranked No. 4, but their own expectations were reflected in the slogan they adopted for themselves – No.1 in '71.

Realistically, Wasdin had three goals:

1) Attempt to graduate all his players.

2) Take the team to a postseason tournament.

3) Stay out of the crosshairs of the NCAA, which continually kept looking for any violations.

But the expectations from the fan base were unrealistic, and he saw that even before the season started, when he spoke to a roomful of attorneys at a Bar Association meeting. After he got done speaking, Wasdin fielded questions.

"Coach Wasdin," one attorney asked, "where is the Final Four this season? I want to make sure we get hotel rooms."

The question and its obvious implication struck Wasdin.

"It was already a foregone conclusion that we were going back to the Final Four and to the championship game, where we would beat UCLA," he said.

It wasn't just external pressure. The Dolphins practiced that season game to game – or, as coaches and players often like to recite, one game at a time. But honest coaches will also admit that even while they prepare their team for the next game, they often insert drills or plays into practices in preparation for a team scheduled down the road. Or in

JU's case that season, for a team they *hoped* to play down the road – the UCLA Bruins.

"One of my assistant coaches, Jim 'Slick' Watson, had an idea to prepare Artis Gilmore for Sidney Wicks should we play UCLA again in the Finals," Wasdin said. "In practice, Slick would do a drill where he'd guard Artis and hold a stick over him. It was about three-feet long and maybe an inch or two in a diameter. We called it the 'Wicks Stick'. Whether or not Wicks' had goaltended Artis or actually blocked his shots, we didn't want that to happen again. Artis would either have to shoot around or over that stick. That also shows that we'd set our goals very high. We were practicing and preparing to do one thing – win a national championship."

If there were any questions about Tom Wasdin's coaching ability, they didn't reside in John Harrison. The former JU player had grown up in Jacksonville, attending Robert E. Lee High School at the same time Wasdin coached at Paxon High. "Those Paxon teams were well-coached and Tom worked very, very hard," Harrison said. "When he came to JU he was that same high energy guy. I could see from my conversations with him that he had a plan and knew how he was going to carry out that plan. He had already upgraded JU's talent level. I knew he'd be a great coach, too. He had a feel for basketball and he was constantly learning, going to clinics. He had an ability to pick people's brains and make people feel very comfortable talking to him."

The start of the season looked sunny, but a rain cloud quickly formed over it – both literally and figuratively. Just before the first practice, Harold Fox and Ernie Fleming were playing pickup basketball at a recreation park in a poorer section of Jacksonville, honing their games. A sudden afternoon thunderstorm, common in Florida, had the two players running to a nearby store for shelter. Hitting the sidewalk, Fox hit a slick spot and skidded toward the store. Bracing himself, he placed his hand against the store window, which unbeknownst to him already had a crack in it. The window shattered, with shards of glass slicing into Fox's shooting hand and tendons, causing a gash that required more than 150 stitches to close as Wasdin stood at his side, offering support and comfort. Though the freak injury theoretically healed in time for the season opener, Fox was never quite the same; his wrist action on his shot never quite as silky and smooth. One thing that didn't change, though, were expectations.

The Dolphins' opener saw 9,000-plus people file into the Jacksonville Coliseum. They wanted to see domination, and they got it against overmatched Biscayne College. Gilmore scored 50 points, leading the team to a 132-88 victory. Next was Madison Square Garden, where the Dolphins let the nation know that they once again meant business, beating St. Peter's College by a whopping 152-106 margin. On top of that, JU set an NCAA record by scoring 86 points in the second half. Gilmore's 34 rebounds that game also set a JU and Madison Square Garden record. The Dolphins' 126 field goal attempts also were both a JU and NCAA record. And they did it all while the great Boston Celtic, Bill Russell, watched. The message to Russell and the rest of the country was clear: Not only had the Dolphins picked up right where they had left off the previous season, they were shifting into overdrive. The combined 258 points in their first two games was second most in NCAA history.

Next was the Civitan Classic at the Jacksonville Coliseum, where the Dolphins promptly beat George Washington, 110-85, in an opener that saw five JU players score in double figures, setting the stage for a championship game against Coach Hugh Durham's Florida State Seminoles. Interest in the JU-FSU matchup was overwhelming, with 10,112 fans cramming into the Coliseum, setting a record for the largest crowd in Florida basketball history. It was a furiously competitive game, with Artis Gilmore again showing why he was one of the nation's best players. Not only did Gilmore score 31 points, he also grabbed 26 rebounds, which happened to be only one fewer than the entire FSU team combined. JU won, 114-108, pushing its record to 5-0 and thus adding to its national prominence.

Afterward, FSU head coach Hugh Durham said, "It's the only basketball game I've ever seen that I'd pay to see again."

But reality was waiting. Not only reality, but as JU would later learn, a harbinger at how the season would eventually end. The No.3-ranked Dolphins traveled to Louisville to play No.10 Western Kentucky, another school not known as a traditional power in the early '70s, but which was making the nation notice that it, too, was producing some quality basketball. Coming off the largest attendance ever in a game in the state of Florida, JU now played in front of nearly twice as many fans in Louisville. Almost 17,500 people came to see the game and the matchup between the Dolphins' 7-foot-2 Artis Gilmore and the Hilltoppers' 6-foot-11 Jim McDaniels, both of whom were destined to play in the NBA. They weren't disappointed ... well, at least the Western Kentucky fans weren't disappointed. McDaniels made his first 10 baskets and finished with 46 points. A 13-4 Hilltopper run at the end of the first half gave them a 12-point lead at intermission; and from there JU could never get any closer than seven points, eventually losing, 97-84.

It was a disappointing loss; one that bothered Artis Gilmore.

"The game was in Kentucky and we didn't have the intensity we needed to have in that type of environment," he said. "It was cold, pouring down snow, and the fans were jam-packed in Freedom Hall. I remember one guy saying that he was willing to pay $100 for a ticket. It was a very intense environment, and we just didn't have what we needed. There were games where we did a great job of elevating our intensity to match the situation. But in that game and in that environment, we didn't have the frame of mind that we needed to have."

Wasdin bluntly assessed the loss afterward, saying, "We got outshot, outrebounded, outscored, outcoached and just plain got beat." Wasdin also knew that he and his team had encountered a matchup zone – a hybrid between zone and man-to-man defense – that they hadn't seen before "and we didn't adjust well to it." The victory pushed Western Kentucky to No. 5 in the polls, while JU fell to No. 8.

Back in Jacksonville, people couldn't believe that their Dolphins had actually lost. But two games later, against Wake Forest, which also employed a matchup zone defense, JU lost again, dropping its record to 6-2. Coming off a season where Jacksonville had only lost one regular-season game before losing to UCLA for the NCAA Championship, fans found it hard to fathom that only eight games into this season, their team had already lost twice.

Later, when his team traveled to the Virgin Islands for games, Wasdin had them work diligently on the matchup zone. "I wasn't going to let that happen again," he said, "and we never had any problems with it after that."

As the team physician Dr. Duane Bork watched the games, he

could see what a discerning basketball eye could notice. This team was talented. Very talented. "But what they were lacking was a coach on the floor, and that was Rex Morgan," Dr. Bork said. "Rex was very savvy. Without him, we didn't have the same chemistry and balance. Without him, we sometimes got in our own away. Rex had great court vision. He could get the ball where it needed to be. He could get it to Artis in the right place at the right time. He was a playmaker."

Most people, however, weren't talking about Rex Morgan, who had moved on to the NBA's Boston Celtics. They were talking about how JU had already lost twice as many regular-season games as the season before. The spotlight grew hotter, and the shadow of last season's accomplishments fell heavier.

"The fans were great until we lost to Western Kentucky and Wake Forest," Wasdin said. "That's when I started developing a tough skin, and it served me well. I had the attitude that I was coaching for the team, and not the crowd."

If the fans were disappointed, and they were, it would be a long time before they would be disappointed again. After the loss to Wake Forest, the Dolphins went on the kind of run that, while impressive, most fans in Jacksonville expected, winning a record 15 consecutive games to improve to 21-2. Along the way, they beat Joe Williams' Furman team, 94-60. It would be the first of five times Wasdin and Williams would face each other during the three years Wasdin was JU's coach, with the Dolphins winning all five of those games.

"Tom always had very good, tough defenses," Williams noted. "He also had really good, athletic players who could score. Tom could coach. I knew that going back to when we were junior high school coaches. The reason I brought him into JU was because I believed he was one of the best coaches around. I wanted someone who would work as hard as I would, and who would be an excellent coach. That was Tom."

Williams was also appreciative that Wasdin had offered Furman enough guarantee money that Williams could then take the team down to the Virgin Islands.

"It was a friendly rivalry we had," Wasdin said. "At the time, Joe was building a program at Furman. He was a great coach who had some good players and ran a very good program. He was always very hard to beat."

After that first meeting as college coaches, which came at the Jacksonville Coliseum, Williams was complimentary following the game, telling the media that he enjoyed being back in Jacksonville "right up to tipoff," adding that as far as he was concerned, the Dolphins were "better than last year."

They certainly appeared to be. The 15-game winning streak, still the longest ever in JU history, signaled that. In addition, the Dolphins beat Florida State three times that season, including for the first time ever in Tallahassee. As exciting as the 1969-70 season had been, this team was equally, if not more, impressive.

"It was a good group of players, guys who worked hard and gave everything they had," Wasdin said. "They were a pleasure to coach and to be around."

But there were growing outside distractions surrounding the team. Throughout all of Jacksonville's success, starting late in the Joe Williams' era and into the Tom Wasdin years, the NCAA was always sniffing around, trying to find some type of illegal activity. The prevailing thought, fair or not, was that such a small school could not be winning so big without something underhanded occurring. Though the NCAA never found anything, it was an ongoing distraction and added pressure to the program.

"What was helpful, and what I always appreciated, is that Joe Williams, even though he was now at Furman, came down and helped us with the NCAA," Wasdin said. "Like me, he knew we had done nothing wrong. He stayed in Jacksonville to assist us in refuting any charges. He didn't have to do that. But that's the kind of guy Joe is."

Williams had also directed a recruit named Butch Taylor to Jacksonville, and Taylor eventually became a solid player for the Dolphins.

Despite the distractions, the Dolphins motored to that impressive 21-2 record, with Artis Gilmore leading the nation in rebounding and Pembrook Burrows III in field goal percentage. It was a special team that did many special things, including establishing some all-time Jacksonville University records.

With the end of the season approaching, and JU obviously ensured another ticket to the NCAA tournament, adversity hit. While practicing for the team's penultimate regular-season game, a road trip at Houston, where the tough-at-home 19-5 Cougars awaited, Vaughn Wedeking suffered a severe right ankle injury, tearing ligaments. The game against Houston would be nationally televised from the new 10,000-seat Hofheinz Pavilion. Per usual protocol, the contract called for officials from two different conferences to work the game – in this case a Southeastern Conference official (who normally worked the independent JU games) with a Missouri Valley Conference official (who normally worked the independent Houston games). But an hour before the game, Wasdin learned that *both* officials were from the Missouri Valley Conference. Under those circumstances, Wasdin could have refused to play. It reminded him, too, of what Oklahoma City head coach Abe Lemons told him before the season started, when he looked at JU's schedule. Lemons knew that Houston, which had moved into Hofheinz Pavilion on December 1, 1969, had yet to lose a game at home.

"Make sure you get a split officiating crew," Lemons told Wasdin. "And even then, you might as well chalk it up as a loss."

Knowing, however, that it was a nationally televised game and that it would be one of his team's last tune-ups before the NCAA Tournament, Wasdin relented.

In retrospect, Wasdin probably never should have allowed his team to take the court – and not just because of the officiating. After taking a 45-40 halftime lead, a bizarre event occurred when the Dolphins emerged for the second half. As they took the court to warm up, a fan ran out, kicked Harold Fox hard in the ankle, and then disappeared back into the crowd. Fox tried to play on the badly bruised ankle, but it was clear his mobility was affected.

Sports Illustrated writer Joe Jares reported the episode this way:

Shortly before the second half started, Wasdin came over to the press table. "You know what happened?" he said in a strangled voice. "Some fan tripped Fox when he was coming out and he sprained his ankle." (After the game, Fox said a spectator kicked him in the left ankle and then ran into the stands. Another version had Fox tripping over his own feet.) Wasdin went over to Houston head coach Guy Lewis to complain. "Tom," said Lewis, "I didn't put anybody over there to trip him."

However it happened, Jares noted that it hurt JU's efforts, especially on defense. Houston guard Poo Welch, one of the team's best scorers, was held to just four first-half points by a healthy Fox. But in the second half, with Fox hobbled, Welch erupted for 16 points.

For the Dolphins, it seemed as if they were cursed with ankle injuries that season. In addition to Wedeking and Fox, Greg Nelson and Mike Blevins were also hobbled with ankle injuries. But the immediate concern now was Fox, and the crowd's behavior, which had grown worse, punctuated by their throwing coins and debris onto the court.

"We had a lot of problems with Houston, just a lot of little things that they were doing to try and disrupt us in addition to not having an SEC official," said Frank Casey, the team's Sports Information Director. "The lights didn't work in our locker room. They didn't have towels for us to take showers. They didn't keep the stats correctly and tried to shortchange Artis with his rebounding. They only had him with eight rebounds and, heck, he had that many in the first half. There were just a lot of those chippy things with Houston, stuff that we didn't have with anyone else, not even Florida State, and they became our hated rival. And then, during that game, things really got nasty and ugly."

It was unbelievable to Wasdin and JU at how the officials lost control of the game and particularly the crowd, allowing debris to be thrown on the court. At one point, late in the game, he walked over to show the officials a penny on the court as an example of how things had gotten out of hand. But instead of calling a technical foul on the crowd, the official rang up Wasdin with a technical for leaving the bench and walking onto the court. Houston converted the foul shot. A few minutes later, as the clock wound down, Harold Fox missed an uncontested, wide-open 20-foot jumper with two seconds remaining, giving Houston an 83-82 victory.

Wasdin had gone into the game thinking that it was what coaches call a "trap" game. In this case, it meant a road game that a better team could lose if it wasn't careful, especially in a hostile environment. Houston proved to be exactly that. It didn't help, either, that injuries were surfacing at an inopportune time. Greg Nelson had suffered a severely sprained ankle in JU's last home game against East Carolina, and didn't play against Houston. Neither did Vaughn Wedeking.

"I had gone up for a layup," Nelson said, "and when I came down I bent my ankle to the right, got hit, and bent it the other way to the left. It was severely sprained. It tore ligaments."

All the injuries exacerbated the bitter loss, but the Dolphins quickly got back in the win column with a resounding 94-75 victory at Miami to end the regular season in a game that turned out to be historic, what with the Hurricanes shutting down their basketball program afterward.

It was not a surprise that the 22-3 Dolphins got another invite to the 25-team NCAA Tournament. What was surprising, however, is that the NCAA paired Jacksonville against Western Kentucky in the first round. Both were top 10 teams. Wasdin, who was particularly suspicious of the NCAA basketball establishment, considering what had happened the previous year in the finals, had a conspiracy theory.

"We were ranked seventh and Western Kentucky was fifth or sixth," he said. "Now why would you pair two top 10 teams against each other in the first round? They knew Western Kentucky was loaded, and they knew we were loaded. I think they were worried that we'd both make it to the Final Four. Since they didn't want that, then how do you prevent it? You pair those two teams together in the first round."

As it turned out, the team that did win that opening-round game did make it to the Final Four. JU's fans automatically assumed that it would be their Dolphins who would advance.

Said Pembrook Burrows III: "Where we had gotten to at that point in the season was expected, and we were expected to go farther."

The rematch against Western Kentucky was slated for South Bend, Indiana, and the Dolphins' flight went through Chicago, where Wasdin crossed paths with Notre Dame football coach Ara Parseghian, who wished him good luck. However, what followed the Dolphins to South Bend was bad luck – or, more specifically, what *didn't* follow them. Several JU boosters were scheduled to fly into South Bend via a charter flight that also carried the Dolphins' team physician, Dr. Duane Bork. But because of bad weather, the charter flight and Dr. Bork never left Jacksonville.

"We ended up watching the game on a TV at the airport," Dr. Bork said.

Just returning from his severe ankle injury that had torn ligaments, JU guard Vaughn Wedeking, who was still not full speed, asked for a pain killer, and Notre Dame's physician administered a shot just prior to the game. It helped, but Wedeking and Greg Nelson were both still hobbled by their ankles. In fact, neither had practiced nor played in the final two regular-season games leading up to the tournament game. Both were smart, veteran players, and valuable on the floor for that reason. At the guard position, Wedeking was the closest player JU had to Rex Morgan, in terms of being an on-court coach.

They both played, Nelson more than Wedeking, who sat out most of the second half. But they were hardly themselves.

"I was ineffective," Nelson said. "I could run, but I couldn't feel my ankle. It was my last shot to play college ball, so you would've had to strap me to the side of a bridge to keep me from playing."

In spite of all that, the Dolphins roared out against Western Kentucky, determined not only to advance in the tournament, but to avenge their early, regular-season loss to the Hilltoppers. With two minutes remaining before halftime, the JU held an 18-point lead, 44-26. Early in the second half, Jacksonville maintained a double-digit lead, and a victory definitely seemed in sight. Disgusted with their starters, the Hilltoppers went to their bench, and it was then that the game also got physical. As it did, Wasdin remembered something he'd heard at a coaches clinic – that the more physical the game, the more it hurts a highly skilled team. That's exactly what he saw with his players. It became a backyard, street-ball game and it took the Dolphins out of their rhythm.

Gradually, Western Kentucky closed the gap, pulling to within less than 10 points. That's when the Hilltoppers reinserted their starters, who were now fresh and energized by what the bench had just accomplished. JU was losing its poise, and it didn't help that at halftime Wedeking asked for another pain killer, but was denied by the Notre Dame doctor, who erred on the side of caution. Had JU's team physician, Dr. Bork, been there, he'd have administered the shot, comfortable as he was in knowing the full extent of Wedeking's injury.

"Dr. Bork knew the injury and knew it wasn't serious," Wasdin said.

Dr. Bork concurred. "As I recall, the physician who was there was a pediatrician, so it was out of his turf," he said. "I'd have had no problem giving Vaughn a shot at halftime. He had a sprained ankle. Nothing more. Had he been able play that second half, I think it would've made a big difference. I think we would've won the game handily."

Hobbling, Wedeking tried to play through the pain, but it was clear he couldn't, and he spent the most of the second half on the bench. Not having his leadership and his heads-up court play hurt Jacksonville.

The injuries also meant that Coach Wasdin had to stick with players longer in the game, unable to give them a rest. When Western Kentucky reinserted its starters, they had fresh legs. Meanwhile, JU's players were showing rare signs of fatigue. Pembrook Burrows III, who was used to being substituted for, only had one point. Trying to play on his sprained ankle, Greg Nelson had only four points.

The game furiously hurled toward the final buzzer, with JU always maintaining the lead until Western Kentucky knotted the game at 72-72 with less than half a minute remaining. After calling a timeout, Wasdin set up an inbounds play designed to immediately get the ball to Harold Fox, and if Fox wasn't open, then the ball was to go to Ernie Fleming, who was then to work it to Fox. Had Wedeking been in the game, the play would have gone through him. Sure enough, Fox was double-teamed on the inbounds pass and the ball went to Fleming. He dribbled, stopped, and then went to pass it to Fox. But suddenly, Fleming saw a Hilltopper cutting to intercept the ball. So Fleming stopped, but then made the mistake of dribbling again.

With Jacksonville out of timeouts, the double dribble gave the Hilltoppers an inbounds pass near half-court with the Dolphins scrambling to set up on defense. Fleming had been guarding Jim McDaniels most of the game, and Arts Gilmore had been guarding Clarence Glover. Anticipating that with one play remaining Western Kentucky was going to try and go to McDaniels, Gilmore told Fleming to switch. "I'll take McDaniels and you take Glover," he said. Wasdin knew nothing of the switch until after the game. What he did know is that while "Fleming was a great player, he was not very good at freelancing."

His teammates, for the most part, knew that about Fleming, too.

"A great player. A great physical talent," said Curtis Kruer, a forward on the team. "But changing things up on him at the last minute was bad timing. You could do that with a Rex Morgan or a Vaughn Wedeking. But Fleming wasn't that type of player."

The analogy is akin to musical bands. Some perform great live, but struggle in a studio environment when trying to record an album. Some are great in the studio, but struggle live.

"In pickup basketball, Ernie Fleming was unstoppable, just a great, great player," Casey said. "But when you put a jersey on him under the lights with officials and more structure and having to decipher defenses under pressure and tense situations, then it could become a deer-in-the-headlights situation. Sometimes those situations would overwhelm him."

The closing seconds of the Western Kentucky game was exactly that type of situation.

Not that anybody on the team blamed Fleming, who suffered the indignity the following season of having opposing fans chant at him during games: "DOU-BLE DRIB-BLE!!! DOU-BLE DRIB-BLE!!!"

"As far as the double dribble was concerned, anybody could have done it – anybody," Pembrook Burrows III said. "That's part of the game. How could we get mad at Ernie? He helped us get to that point. We got that far as a team. There were a lot of things each of us could have done differently to have made the outcome different."

To this day, Gilmore fiercely protects the memory of Fleming, who was his closest friend on the team. "Ernie made a mistake and it haunted him his entire life. We never talked about it, but I knew," Gilmore said. "But as far as we as a team blaming Ernie for the loss, that didn't happen. No, no. We lost that game as a team. All of us could've made different decisions that could've affected the outcome differently."

Even still, years later, Gilmore couldn't help but think of what might have been had Rex Morgan been at the guard position, assuming that Robin role to his Batman, as they had enjoyed the season before.

"Rex felt very comfortable in critical situations," he said. "I'd like to think that it probably would've been different."

There were others, like former JU player John Harrison, who held that same opinion and who knew how much the team missed Morgan from the year before. "That team that went back to the NCAA Tournament the second year was *not* the same," Harrison said. "They were missing a *huge* part of that team, and that was Rex Morgan. It was also a team that wasn't going to sneak up on anybody. The year before, we snuck up on everybody."

And then there was the more immediate possibility; the fact that had it not been for his severely sprained ankle, Vaughn Wedeking would've been on the court. After all, Morgan was in the NBA; but Wedeking was on the bench, and the team sorely missed his smarts and savvy, not to mention his leadership.

Noted Wasdin, "Had Wedeking been in the game, he'd have been handling the ball."

Flustered by the switch that Gilmore called, where he was to take Clarence Glover and Gilmore was to take Jim McDaniels, Fleming couldn't find his man. And Glover, sensing that nobody was guarding him, crouched at the corner of the court and then practically crawled toward the basket, undetected. A quick inbounds pass found him with five seconds remaining, and Glover scored on an easy layup, giving Western Kentucky its only lead of the game, 74-72.

It would prove to be the final score, and it would prove to be a devastating blow for Jacksonville.

Anybody who walked into the postgame locker room probably felt as if they had walked into a morgue.

"We were shocked, just in a state of shock," Gilmore said. "We were at a loss for words. There was nothing anybody could say."

"I've run that game back in my mind many times, thinking of ways I could've helped Jacksonville University to win," Greg Nelson said. "I can't stand to watch it. It hurts more than the loss to UCLA the year before. We had a legitimate shot to win the whole thing. We missed a moment. We could've put JU on the map."

Postgame, Wasdin didn't temper his words, saying, "I don't know what to say. I'm embarrassed at how we let this game get away when we had the game to win." Years later, the loss still haunts him, and he ranks it as one of the two most distressing losses in his coaching career – the other being the one-point loss to Pensacola High School when Wasdin was at Paxon High School, and Pensacola advanced to the state championship and won by 20 points. Obviously, though, the loss to Western Kentucky was worse, if not simply because of the bigger stage.

"I still think about Western Kentucky today," Wasdin said. "Without some bad luck and some injuries, I think we could've won the national championship that year. And when you win a national championship, it becomes a life-changing event. Who knows what would've happened had we had Vaughn Wedeking and Greg Nelson in that game in the closing minutes. We certainly were not nearly as good as we would've been with them. I'd like to think that we would have won that game, made it back to the Final Four, and then won the National Championship."

As it was, Western Kentucky advanced all the way to the Final Four, where the Hilltoppers lost to Villanova, which then lost to John Wooden's undefeated UCLA Bruins for the national title.

"Losing to Western Kentucky was tough," said Rusty Baldwin, a guard on the team. "It had nothing to do with coaching. Coach Wasdin was very knowledgeable. He had a great knack for bringing out the talent in a player. We had tremendous chemistry. Everybody was for the team. We practiced hard, but practices were fun. Coach made them fun. We won a lot of games Monday through Thursday in practice. We had a tremendous belief in ourselves. That's why it was such a tough loss. Nobody worked harder than our team. I thought that team was as good or better as the previous year."

The previous year.

It shadowed that 1970-71 Jacksonville Dolphins team. Still does.

"Had we not had the season we had the year before, then making it to the NCAA Tournament and losing in the first round wouldn't have felt so bad. But it did feel bad," said Greg Nelson, who went on to become a multimillionaire businessman and a JU Board of Trustee member. "Personally, I felt like we let everybody down. That loss has stayed with me the rest of my life. Whenever you lose or fail, you over-prepare yourself for the next time, for the next opportunity. It's a motivation. That loss still motivates me. In all aspects of my life, it still motivates me."

Back in Jacksonville, it was like a funeral. The fans were, of course, spoiled by the sudden success of the previous season's team and, just like the coaches and players, they wanted desperately for the 1970-71 team to not only repeat that success, but exceed it with a national championship.

"Those were magical years," Casey said. "The hype and the excitement at the end of the 1969-70 season carried over into the 1970-71 season. All of a sudden, *Sports Illustrated* was writing about us, the *New York Times* was covering our games. We were playing in the largest arena in the state, and filling it. We were not only setting home attendance records, but attendance records on the road. What those teams accomplished was really overwhelmingly good."

Said Harrison: "If you look at the body of work of the whole season, it was very successful. If you take away the fact that JU played in the championship game the year before, people would have been ecstatic. And people forget that we had lost our floor leader from the year before in Rex Morgan. You don't just replace that. Sure we had talent coming in, but they were coming in from junior college or they hadn't played with the varsity the year before. I understand that when you have high expectations you're naturally going to be disappointed when you don't meet those expectations. But I thought the season was very successful."

The fans, however, wanted more from that 1970-71 team. They wanted a national title. When that didn't happen, it was a letdown for them.

"People loved that team so much they were mourning," Wasdin said.

Unlike the season before, when a parade of people waited for them upon their return, nobody was lining up along the streets from the airport back to campus, celebrating the team's season.

And now the team was gone.

Artis Gilmore moved on to the ABA and eventually to the NBA and a spot in the Naismith Memorial Basketball Hall of Fame. Pembrook Burrows III, Vaughn Wedeking, Greg Nelson, Chip Dublin and Mike Blevins also moved on.

It was a great two-year run, with back-to-back trips to the NCAA Tournament and a combined 49-6 record. To be sure, there was a lot about the 1970-71 season that JU could be immensely proud of. Gilmore had a sensational senior year, finishing his career with 1,312 point and a 24.3 points per game average, as well as grabbing 1,224 rebounds, good for a 22.7 average per game. Wedeking's 356 career assists moved him to seventh place all-time. Burrows became the school's most accurate shooter, making 64.6 percent of his field goal attempts during his JU career.

As a team, Jacksonville led the nation in scoring, averaging 99.9 points per game. The 152 points against St. Peter's College and the 15-game winning streak are both still the best in school history. The Dolphins practically revolutionized the college game, setting scoring records without the benefit of the dunk, 3-point baskets or the shot clock. In addition, the 82 rebounds the team grabbed against St. Peter's College still stands as the best rebounding game in school history. And the 33 assists against Miami is still a JU record, as well.

The Dolphins also beat their rival Florida State Seminoles three times that season – in the Civitan Classic, at home and on the road at Tully Gym; the latter marking the first time a JU team had beaten FSU on their home court. "FSU had always laid claim to the basketball throne in the state of Florida," Greg Nelson said. "We were the new kid trying to usurp them. Beating them three times was special."

Yes, looking back, there was a lot to be proud of with this team. "We had a very good year," Wasdin said, "and if we could've gone back to the Finals, it would've been a great year. All things considered, I was extremely proud of what our team accomplished that season."

At the time, however, nobody cared to reflect on what a great season it was. Things were still moving forward, with winning and tournament bids now considered the norm at Jacksonville University. Tom Wasdin was certainly known as a great recruiter and those who knew basketball were also clearly seeing that he was an outstanding X's and O's coach. Sure, nobody expected him to recruit another Artis Gilmore. Even for the now-spoiled JU fan base, that would be asking a bit much. But Wasdin, through his tireless efforts, was bringing in another stellar recruiting class, which was once again better than a small school like JU deserved. Even better, he definitely hadn't lost his unquenchable thirst for winning.

But Wasdin also had a bug in his ear, from his old friend Rick Stottler back in Cocoa Beach. Wasdin no longer spent the summers working the pier, but he still returned to work special events. He helped establish some iconic events and businesses along the Space Coast. With legendary surfer and promoter Dick Catri, Wasdin helped start and establish the Easter Surfing Festival, a contest that saw a youngster named Kelly Slater, who later became the Babe Ruth and Michael Jordan of the sport, first cut his competitive teeth. And when Catri moved his surf shop to another locale, it was Wasdin who leased the space to a guy named Ron DiMenna, who had a fledgling store called Ron Jon Surf Shop. Wasdin also developed relationships with a small group of surfers – Mike Tabeling, Gary Propper, Bruce Valluzzi, Claude

Codgen, and Joe and Betsy Twombly, all of whom became legends in the sport.

"I had taught them at Cocoa Beach High School," he said. "At that time, surfers were considered outcasts, so I think they liked it that I accepted them and had good relationships with them."

Stottler was proud of what his friend had accomplished as a basketball coach, but he could also clearly see the pressure cooker he was in. Even more, he saw a smart, savvy businessman in Wasdin. Stottler didn't want to add any more pressure on his friend, but he did leave him with a thought and an invitation after that first season.

"Tom," he said, "any time you want to get out of coaching, why don't you come down here to Cocoa Beach and we'll make some real money? This coaching ... you've got a real high-pressure job, and it's not good for your health. Besides, you're not making a lot of money."

"I've got two more years on my contract," Wasdin replied. "I don't want to do anything yet, Rick."

The offer was there, and the thought sat in the back of Wasdin's mind. Eventually, it would be a thought that would push itself to the fore. But not yet. There was still more basketball to coach.

Chapter 13

LIFE AFTER ARTIS

"There was an attitude where people reasoned that because we'd been second in the nation, why can't we do that every year? It was not realistic." – Tom Wasdin

As the 1971-72 season approached, any story written about the Jacksonville University basketball team had one common theme – the Dolphins no longer had Artis Gilmore. It was obviously the most notable difference between JU's last two NCAA Tournament seasons and the upcoming season. Gilmore had undeniably put Jacksonville University on the map, and his presence in college basketball, much less in Jacksonville, had been huge.

But it went beyond no longer having Gilmore and his imposing 7-foot-2 presence. Also gone were Pembrook Burrows III, Vaughn Wedeking, Greg Nelson, Chip Dublin and Mike Blevins. In fact, the only meaningful players who had been on that 1970 Final Four team were Rusty Baldwin and Curtis Kruer. And even then, both were career backup players. Still, anybody who decided to sell JU's chances short because it no longer had Gilmore and other key players neglected to take into account Tom Wasdin's recruiting ability, coaching skills and tireless work ethic.

So while the rest of the country focused on what was missing, the optimist and positive thinker that is Tom Wasdin focused on what he had, and he liked what he saw.

"I thought we had the nucleus of a darn good team," he said. "Ernie Fleming and Harold Fox were both returning, and both were potential All-Americans. In fact, both Fleming and Fox were later drafted into the NBA – Fleming with the Boston Celtics and Fox with the Buffalo

Braves. I had some real good players coming up from the freshmen team. One of them was David Brent, who was a 7-footer that one of my assistants, Art Tolis, had done a good job of recruiting. Another was George Scholz, a point guard. We had Leon Benbow, a 6-foot-5 kid who could really jump and play some of the best defense of any player I ever had, and who was later drafted by the Chicago Bulls. Rusty Baldwin and Curtis Kruer were coming back. I liked our chances."

The 1971-72 Jacksonville University team. Standing from left to right: Head Coach Tom Wasdin, Assistant Coach Art Tolis, Curtis Kruer, Abe Steward, Bob Nylin, David Brent, Kevin O'Riordan, Ernie Fleming, Mike Drasites, Assistant Coach Jim "Slick" Watson, Assistant Coach Drayton Miller. Kneeling first row left to right: A team manager, Phil Carter, Glenn Dockery, Harold Fox, Rusty Baldwin, Lindsay Huth, Leon Benbow, George Scholz, Paul Molinaro.

There were other newcomers, too, like 6-foot-6 Abe Steward, an All-American transfer from Wyoming's Casper Junior College; 6-foot-7 Kevin O'Riordan; and 6-foot-8 junior Bob Nylin, who had transferred from University of Miami after the Hurricanes dropped their basketball program.

"There was a lot of talent, but I knew that it would be a different team and that I would have to coach them differently, too," Wasdin said. "I knew this team wouldn't have the same height that we'd had the previous two years, especially without Artis and Pembrook, but it was a very quick team. David Brent was tall, but he was not physically dominating like Artis was. I knew I had to build this team more on quickness."

The incoming freshmen team, thanks to the recruiting tandem of Wasdin and Art Tolis, had brought in six former high school All-Americans – Ricky Coleman, Henry Williams, Shawn Leftwich, Jimmie Clark, Dave Stowers and Mike Denney.

"Imagine what it was like for me," said Dr. Drayton Miller, the freshmen team's coach. "I had *six* former high school All-Americans to coach. That meant every time we played I had to sit one of them out of my starting lineup. Kentucky also had a very good freshmen team that year and we tried to get them to play us. We even agreed to play them at their place and donate the money to charity of their choosing. But they wouldn't."

Not only was JU's varsity gathering national attention, even its JV team was getting ink. A *Sports Illustrated* writer attended one of Jacksonville's freshmen games and heard, and then wrote about, this exchange between Miller and a booster who missed the first half of a game that saw the JV team score a staggering 93 points:

> *Dr. Drayton Miller was coaching the Jacksonville University freshmen team when he was approached by a member of the school's Century Club. The Super Six as the freshmen team was called – on it were six high school All-Americans – was on its way to the lockers and the man was upset that he missed seeing them play.*
>
> *"Why did you start early?" he asked Miller.*
>
> *"We began on time," was the reply. "Stick around and watch the second half."*
>
> *The Baby Dolphins finished with 153 points and by the time the season was over had broken every school record for a 25-game schedule. The freshmen team received so much publicity that a 10-minute film clip was shown on a major television network."*

Whenever Wasdin checked what the polls and prognosticators were saying, he noticed that even without Artis Gilmore, he and the program had still established a healthy measure of respect around the country. Various polls all had the Dolphins ranked in the Top 20, even though JU's schedule was continuing to get tougher.

To be sure, Wasdin had nothing but good thoughts about the team as the season approached. But he soon had another thought. He found himself occasionally reflecting on that magical 1969-70 season, when he was his friend Joe Williams' assistant, and all the breaks they'd gotten en route to reaching the NCAA Championship game.

"It seemed like we used up all our good luck that season," he said, "because the next season and in 1971-72, we had a lot of bad luck."

The bad breaks arrived early. Before the season even began, Rusty Baldwin tore ankle ligaments, Curtis Kruer had knee surgery and sophomore George Scholz broke his nose.

Still, JU manhandled Biscayne College, 110-75, in the opener. Then the Dolphins went on the road to play East Carolina in another game that they won. But in that game, David Brent was accidentally kicked and he suffered a small broken bone in his leg, knocking him out of action until the end of the calendar year. It was a big blow. No, David Brent wasn't Artis Gilmore, but he was an extremely talented 7-footer who had just led the freshmen team by averaging 25 points and 20 rebounds per game.

"It wasn't weight bearing, but it was very painful," Wasdin said. "Even after he returned, he never completely recovered. I always felt sad about that, because he had the potential to be as good of a big man of any who ever played at JU, including Artis Gilmore."

Wasdin's assessment was hardly hyperbole. Others around the program saw the enormous athleticism and potential in David Brent.

"Here you had a guy who was 7-foot and in high school he set the Missouri state record for the 440 and the high jump," said Dr. Drayton Miller, the freshmen team's coach. "He was an unbelievable athlete and basketball player. As tall as he was, he could handle the ball like Magic Johnson. He was tremendous, but he was also young and naive. It's a shame his career never panned out, because I believe he could've had as much impact on the game as Michael Jordan."

Even without Brent, the Dolphins raced to a 14-2 record. Their only losses came against Santa Clara and a powerhouse Florida State team that went all the way to the Final Four that season before losing to eventual champion (and no surprise here) UCLA.

"We really had it rolling," Wasdin said.

Nylin, the University of Miami transfer, found himself deeply impressed with how Coach Wasdin ran his program.

"We were always prepared," Nylin said. "I remember in practice once, I told Coach Don Beasley, one of our assistant coaches, that we were running drills until we were running grooves into the court. And he replied, 'Yes, and we'll continue to do it until you can do it in your sleep.' We saw how it paid off. Against teams, especially in big games, we knew everywhere they were going to go. Coach made sure we had everything we needed to win those ballgames. As far as X's and O's were concerned, Coach Wasdin was excellent."

And another thing Nylin appreciated was the way Wasdin related to players; his people skills.

"When I got to JU, I had long hair and a goatee," said Nylin, who later became a high school coach and then principal. "Before my senior year, Coach Wasdin came to me and said, 'Can you do me a favor? Can you shave your goatee? It would help the image of the program.' He never *told* me. He *asked* me. Coach Wasdin had such a good way of handling his players. If he had told me what to do, I probably wouldn't have done it. But because he asked me, and the way he asked me, I was happy to do it."

It helped that even while Coach Wasdin worked the team hard in practice, the players could see that he was an incredibly hard worker himself. And while he demanded his team to be physically fit, he was in shape, too.

"He could do one-handed pushups" Nylin said. So when Wasdin worked them to fatigue and then had the shooting free throws, they knew it was for a good reason. "He believed in the importance in making free throws at the end of the game. That's why he had us shooting them in practice when we were tired. When it came time to step to the free-throw line at the end of the game, we knew we were going to make those shots."

It was a good group, a hard-working group, one determined not to fall off college basketball's radar even though they no longer had

Artis Gilmore. Steadily, they motored through the season, taking on all comers and more often than not coming out on top; and sometimes more than once against the same opponent.

One of those teams that Jacksonville beat twice that season was South Alabama, a squad they had beaten twice the year before and would beat twice again the following season. While disappointed, South Alabama head coach Jimmy Taylor wasn't surprised. Taylor had first been impressed with Tom Wasdin when Wasdin became Joe Williams' assistant coach.

"He was the perfect assistant coach; he really complemented Joe Williams," Taylor said. "I could see then that he was definitely head coaching material."

Taylor, who like Wasdin later became a successful and wealthy businessman, saw something else in Wasdin.

"I've made my living dealing with people and reading people," said Taylor, who later became the CEO of 31 banks. "The first time I looked into Tom Wasdin's eyes, they told me he was destined to be great in anything he did. His face and especially his eyes told you everything. He had life in his eyes. He was a person you wouldn't forget soon."

The two would talk as head coaches, and through the years Taylor continued to see that special persona in Wasdin.

"It was amazing to me the look he would have no matter what," he said. "It was just a look he had when he listened to you, when he talked to you. I knew he had something special, and I've been around a lot of important people in my life."

Taylor could always expect a solidly prepared team whenever he faced Wasdin's JU Dolphins.

"We ran a match-up zone at South Alabama, and as far as I knew we were the only team in the country that did," he said. "We ran it all the time and it gave people fits. But Tom had a great ability to adapt his team to what was going on in a game. He was a good technician. He had the whole package. Some guys are great recruiters but only so-so coaches, and some guys are great coaches but only average recruiters. He could do both, and more.

"He had a determination and an ability to relate to people, to handle people, to get them to do what he wanted them to do. There was a magnetism and charisma about him that was unbelievable. I would've hated to have been a woman around him back then. It's very unusual to find someone proficient in all aspects of what it takes to be a coach. It's nearly impossible to find. I'm convinced that had he stayed in the game he would have been one of the all-time greats."

It wasn't just Jimmy Taylor's South Alabama team that Jacksonville was beating, the Dolphins ran off nine consecutive victories. During that streak they beat Texas Tech, North Texas State, East Tennessee State, South Alabama, Stetson, Florida State, St. Peter's and also Joe Williams' Furman squad twice in back-to-back games.

It was the first time Wasdin had coached a game against Stetson, which always fielded a well-coached team under the stately and gentlemanly Glenn Wilkes, who was in the middle of a legendary career, coaching the Hatters from 1957-1993. The two coaches knew each other going back to Wasdin's days as Paxon High's head coach.

"I had a good first impression of Tom, and that never changed," Wilkes said. "He was really dedicated to the profession. A lot of coaches, when the season is over, they don't do much with the team until the next season starts. But Tom was involved with his players year-round. He impressed me as a coach and a person."

For years, Wilkes ran a camp at Stetson and at times Wasdin would help work it.

"He was always one of the better coaches to have in camp," Wilkes said. "A lot of coaches are going out at night rather than helping the kids. Tom was one of those guys who was all about the kids. At Jacksonville, he was a players' coach. And what I mean by that is that Tom let players play to their strengths. He didn't put a tight rein on them. Basketball is supposed to be fun. A lot of coaches defeat players by putting in such strict rules and offensive patterns that players can't show what they can do. Tom adjusted to his personnel rather than making them adjust to him."

But sometimes all the coaching acumen in the world can't prevent the inexplicable from happening. After rattling off that nine-game winning streak and threatening to close in on the school record of 15-consecutive victories that they strung together a season before, the Dolphins went on an uncharacteristic three-game losing streak, and then went 3-5 in their last eight games. The losses didn't come to slouches – Creighton, Cincinnati, Marquette, all on the road, and then FSU and Providence at home.

Before the season, Wasdin had noticed the brutal late-season schedule and mentioned his concern – as well as his dismay – that their athletic director hadn't taken better care of them. "After that, I got very involved in our schedule," he said. "When you look at that stretch from February 3rd through the 16th, we had Furman, Creighton, Marquette and South Alabama all on the road with no home games in between. Then we returned home to play Florida State. It was a killer. Very difficult."

Not that the Dolphins got any sympathy from the selection committee when it came time to assemble an NCAA Tournament field. Wasdin knew what was coming.

"You can't lose games that late in the season and expect to get an NCAA Tournament bid," he said.

What you can get a bid to, though, is the National Invitation Tournament. Once upon a time, just a few years earlier, a tiny school with no basketball history like Jacksonville would have been thrilled with an NIT bid. But some JU fans, many of whom didn't follow the team during all the lean years, viewed it as a failure.

During the NIT, David Brent finally seemed to be healed from the broken bone in his leg, erupting for 28 points in one of the tournament games.

"Toward the end of the year, Brent became our leading scorer," Wasdin said. "Had he been healthy all year, we would've been in the NCAA Tournament – easily."

As it was in those days, before the NCAA dramatically expanded its field, the NIT was considered a much more prestigious and competitive tournament. That year, Jacksonville's road to the NIT's Final Four saw the Dolphins beat Fordham and Lafayette before losing to a Lefty Driesell-coached Maryland squad that featured All-American Tom McMillen, along with Len Elmore, Jim O'Brien and Mark Cartwright. Not only were the Terrapins the ACC's regular-season champions, they eventually won the NIT. In the consolation game, Jacksonville beat St. John's to take third. It was a strong finish, and the Dolphins had overcome a lot to win at least 20 games again (20-8), beating a lot of solid teams along the way, including a Florida State Seminoles squad that made it to the Final Four.

The NIT trip, and finishing third, was rewarding for the team.

Bob Nylin recalled how, back then, the entire tournament was in New York City, at Madison Square Garden, and what a thrill that was.

"We were there for 10 days, and we really had a good time," he said. "We went to the 'Johnny Carson Show' and the cast of 'The Godfather' was staying at the same hotel – the St. Regis Hotel – where we were at. I remember riding in the elevator with James Caan. I met Jack Nicholson, too, and talked to him about a movie he had coming up. It was exciting times."

But something else happened at the hotel. Agents had gotten to David Brent and talked him into turning pro early. Brent eventually signed with the ABA's Memphis Pros for a reported $300,000.

"It was ridiculous," Dr. Drayton Miller recalled. "The contract was structured so that he would get $100,000 if he led the league in rebounds. Well, Artis Gilmore was going to do that. He would get $100,000 if he led the league in scoring. Well, Billy Cunningham was playing in the ABA. He would get $100,000 if he was the league MVP. But the league had Dr. J, Julius Erving. That damn contract wasn't worth two cents."

A story in Jacksonville's *Florida Times-Union* newspaper all but confirmed that. Sports writer Maynard Eller wrote that Brent's contract was for a 1972 Lincoln Mark IV, $10,000 cash and annual contracts scaled from $45,000 in 1972-73 to $75,000 in 1976-77.

"I gave up my college eligibility because I felt I had a duty to my family for the years they have helped me," Brent was quoted as saying. "I didn't consider the money as much as that I wanted to play in Memphis, which is only 200 miles from my home in St. Louis."

The article quoted sports agent Herb Rudoy, who represented Artis Gilmore, as saying that Brent might have cost himself $700,000 by signing with the ABA so quickly instead of waiting to see what happened with the NBA draft. Rudoy, who had planned to represent Brent, said he had contacted five NBA teams, all of which were willing to sign Brent for more than a million dollars.

"It was all about that Lincoln Mark IV," said Rusty Baldwin, a backup guard on the team. Baldwin recalled a conversation with Brent at their hotel room in New York City after the team had lost their NIT game.

"I'm going to sign with the ABA," Brent told Baldwin.

"What?" Baldwin replied, incredulous.

"Yeah, man. I'm going to sign. They're giving me a Mark IV."

"Are you crazy?"

Baldwin tried to talk sense into Brent, a 7-footer with such a promising future.

"He wasn't ready," Baldwin said. "He wasn't tough enough and I told him that. I was always telling him that. I really believe that he had more talent than anybody I'd seen at JU. Even more than Artis Gilmore. But he wasn't nearly as tough as Artis. He couldn't carry Artis' jock. But, boy, did he have some serious talent. He was the fastest man on the team and he had one of the sweetest shots. I thought he needed another two years in college. But he left for a Lincoln Mark IV."

Brent never made it in professional ball, eventually drifting back to St. Louis and into anonymity.

Brent's departure disappointed Wasdin, but it didn't dampen his thoughts about that team and what they had accomplished.

"As a coach, it was one of the most satisfying seasons I ever had," he said.

But Wasdin detected a different vibe from some JU fans, who were turning out at the Jacksonville Coliseum in half the numbers than they'd done the previous two seasons. Not only were the home crowds smaller, but he could sense that there was not as much enthusiasm around the program, and that saddened him, given how much they were winning and how much they had accomplished.

It was then that Wasdin seriously started to think about getting out of coaching. His good friend Rick Stottler from his Cocoa Beach days would often come to his games, and cheer the Dolphins. Stottler wouldn't pressure Wasdin to get out of coaching and go into business with him. But Wasdin knew the offer was always there, and just seeing Stottler at games was a constant reminder.

It wasn't just the pressure Wasdin was feeling, it was the unfair expectations and how a growing segment of the fan base didn't know and appreciate just how difficult it was to be as successful as Jacksonville had been. "There was an attitude where people reasoned that because we'd been second in the nation, why can't we do that every year?" Wasdin said. "It was not realistic."

Wasdin had a close friend, John Gehrig, who ran Atlantic National Bank in Jacksonville, and the two men occasionally had lunch together.

After the Dolphins returned from the NIT, Wasdin got a phone call from Gehrig.

"Coach, let's do lunch," he said.

"Okay, where?" Wasdin replied.

"Same place."

They met at their usual eating establishment.

"Coach, listen to me," Gehrig began. "I know you feel bad about this season. But don't worry about it. We won't be this bad anymore."

Gehrig's words stunned Wasdin.

"He thought we were bad," Wasdin recalled years later, still shaking his head at the memory. "My best friend thought we were *bad*. We didn't have a bad year. We won 20 games. It hurt me that that team didn't get the respect it deserved. I thought the players played hard and were great to coach. We had lost Brent for two-fifths of the season with a broken leg, and we still finished third in a very tough NIT field. The players and coaches thought we had a great season, and we couldn't wait for the next season, when we were going to benefit from what was coming up from an outstanding freshmen team. It hurt me that we weren't getting the respect I thought we deserved. And I knew I wasn't getting respect. I'd never coached anywhere where I wasn't well-respected, but I could see that I wasn't getting that kind of respect at Jacksonville."

On top of not feeling respected – knowing that some still viewed him as a great recruiter, but not a great coach – Wasdin also didn't quite feel accepted. He'd grown up in nearby Waldo, on a farm. He understood the small-town, folksy mentality of Jacksonville. He understood the people. But a part of him didn't feel like the people there understood him.

"I dressed like I was from Fifth Avenue in New York City because I felt it gave us an edge in recruiting," he said. "I dressed very, very well. Some of the locals didn't like that. But they didn't know me."

Others, though, like freshmen coach Dr. Drayton Miller, saw things through different lenses. Yeah, Wasdin dressed differently and carried himself differently. But as far as Dr. Miller was concerned, he did so in a way that was both impressive and prescient.

"Tom was on the cutting edge of a lot of things – on and off the court," he said. "He was a forward thinking guy, ahead of his time in a lot of ways. He was getting his nails buffed, which back then was unheard for a man. He was the first guy I knew who was getting razor cuts when the rest of us were still going to a barber. He was the first guy I knew of who wore silk underwear. And he had a wardrobe that was impressive. I remember this one suit he had that everybody was in awe of. He had style and he had his own inimitable style. It set him apart. He was always out front of everybody, doing things years in advance of the rest of us. He was always going for the best of the best. And then there was that personality. Like a magnet. A magnetic personality. When he went places, he drew a crowd."

But Wasdin was wise enough to know that the crowd he often drew could be one way in his presence, and another way behind his back. If the thought of leaving had been an open-ended sentence with ellipses dots, he could now feel a period forming; perhaps even an exclamation point.

"I started to develop the philosophy that only you are responsible for your happiness," he said. "If you don't like your boss, fire him and go get another job. It also made me realize that life in the fast lane and being famous doesn't have a lot to do with your happiness. Happiness comes from within. All along, I never thought I'd make my entire career in coaching, spending my whole working life wearing gym shorts with a whistle around my neck. Not that there is anything wrong with that. But I had other thoughts. I knew there was something else in the world besides coaching."

And there would be, but not before Tom Wasdin took one more team back to the NCAA Tournament.

Chapter 14

A Last Hurrah And A Long Goodbye To Coaching

"Don't they understand what they have here? Don't they see the level of success you're having with this program?" – Dick Vitale

Few doubted anymore that Joe Williams and Tom Wasdin had built a legitimate basketball power at Jacksonville University, and that as long as Wasdin was running the program the Dolphins would not be receding back into the mire of mediocrity. In the past three seasons, the Dolphins had produced two NCAA Tournament teams and one NIT squad, all while playing a progressively tougher and tougher schedule. Not playing beyond the regular season was no longer an option. But each season brought with it its own set of circumstances and challenges. This would be the first year since the 1968-69 season that JU didn't have a 7-footer on its roster. Still, they had a talented core group of athletic players that had most prognosticators ranking them in the Top 20.

Arriving with their recent success was what Tom Wasdin quickly pointed out to reporters before the season started; that players now wanted to come to JU and that it didn't take much explanation to fill prospects in on who the Dolphins were and what they had accomplished.

"We run and we try to play a pro-type game," Wasdin said, stating the obvious fact that JU employed an uptempo style of basketball that was popular with players. "We've had nine players drafted in the pros the last three years. We've never had a junior college player who hasn't started and who hasn't been drafted."

It wasn't just players who wanted to come to JU. It was coaches, too. Don Beasley was an assistant coach at Middle Tennessee State when he received an unexpected phone call from Tom Wasdin, inquiring to see if he'd be interested in coming to Jacksonville University as an assistant.

"I thought it was a prank," he said. "Tom Wasdin was interested in *me*, at a program like what JU had at the time? It was a pretty easy decision."

Beasley quickly discovered that even though Wasdin ran a big-time program, he didn't big-time his assistants. "It was so surprising and refreshing that Coach Wasdin gave his assistants a lot of autonomy and he asked our opinions. I had never worked for anybody like that. That's the one thing I took away from Tom, which was that you hire good people and allow them to get involved. He'd ask you what you think, and if he liked your idea he'd say, 'Okay, you're in charge of that now. Get it done.'"

There was a lot to try and get done that third season. With all of JU's big-time success came a big-time schedule. This meant increasingly tougher opponents. During the 1969-70 season, critics continually pointed to JU's schedule, saying it was soft and therefore the regular-season record, as sterling as it was with only one loss, needed to be tempered. But nobody was criticizing JU's schedule anymore. Sure, like all programs, there were some cupcakes, but the 1972-73 season had 14 opponents scheduled who were either ranked or who had been traditional powers.

"We had turned the corner," Wasdin said. "But even with all our success and consistent seasons winning 20-or-more games against tougher opponents, attendance was declining. So here I was, not only still trying to sell our program to the community, but actually having to oversell our team."

The pressure was on, more than ever. And it would've been enough if it was just winning basketball games that Wasdin had to contend with. But it wasn't. The nonstop schedule had taken its toll on his marriage to Glenda. She worried about her husband and the pressure she could see that he put on himself. The two still cared deeply about each other. But they had drifted apart. Their divergent religious beliefs became a growing issue, too. She was Mormon and he was Baptist, and that wasn't going to change. Tom had attended some of the Mormon religious services. He had given it a chance. But he found himself chafing at how the faith seemed more focused on criticizing other religious beliefs rather than promoting itself. He'd also learned enough, too, to know that Glenda not being married to a Mormon man carried with it serious consequences in her religious beliefs.

"There were a lot of factors," Tom said. "To say we drifted apart is probably an oversimplification. But that's what happened. We had different interests and our different faiths became a bigger issue. We were no longer attending church together and we were no longer spending time together. But the pressures and requirements of coaching became an issue, too – working long hours, always being on the road, either playing games or recruiting."

Tom and Glenda parted friends, with their amicable divorce finalized in January of 1973.

"Glenda was one of the nicest and most wonderful mothers that there's ever been, so I knew my children would be in good hands with her," he said. "But not having Steve and Lori with me was sad. It was really hard."

There were other pressures, too. For some reason, JU's administration started micromanaging his program in the same manner that used to drive Joe Williams nuts and eventually drove Williams to Furman. "They started clamping down on expenses and I couldn't figure out why," Wasdin said. "Here we were, bringing the university national exposure, and they were making it more and more difficult for us to be successful. All of a sudden, every expense had to be pre-approved by the Dean, Dan Thomas. That actually started my second season there, but in that third season it got really bad and it was just a lot of aggravation I didn't need."

It didn't help, too, that the NCAA kept snooping around, kept investigating. "They never found a single violation," Wasdin said. "But even still, nobody likes to have the NCAA digging into your program all the time. It just added to the pressure I was feeling, and it also put pressure on our players."

For a lot of reasons, then, things just didn't feel right. And there was always that nagging undercurrent where Wasdin knew he wasn't fully appreciated by a segment of fans who didn't understand how enormously difficult it was to take a small school with a small-minded administration and go up against the big boys of Division

I college basketball. But they did, and once again the Dolphins had great success.

After opening-season victories against William & Mary and Florida Tech, the Dolphins played in three tournaments – the Steel Bowl Tournament; the Nassau Classic, where they lost to a great Long Beach State squad coached by Jerry Tarkanian; and the Gator Bowl Tournament. Interspersed between tournament play were games against St. Peter's College and Furman. It was a tough stretch and JU emerged from it 5-2.

The tournaments toughened the team and solidified a new unit that was still learning how to play together. It also provided the players with some rest. Wasdin had promised the squad that if they won the Gator Bowl Tournament, he'd give them three days off. They did, and he did. It was a good bonding experience, which Wasdin was happy to see, because he knew that if this team was going to accomplish some great things, then they did indeed have to be a team.

But something else happened during that Gator Bowl Tournament that stuck with Wasdin for the rest of the season and also the rest of his life. He was booed. It came before the game against Rutgers, during the pregame announcements – a smattering of boos when his name was announced. Later that evening, Wasdin ran into one of Rutgers' assistant coaches, a young fellow by the name of Dick Vitale who later became an iconic college basketball TV analyst.

"Tom," Vitale said to Wasdin, "I couldn't help but notice that they booed you when you got introduced. I can't believe that."

Wasdin tried to shrug it off, but Vitale was incredulous.

"Don't they understand what they have here?" Vitale continued. "Don't they see the level of success you're having with this program?"

Obviously not.

Not all of JU's fans felt that way. It was definitely a minority. But it was a minority that Wasdin was going to make sure weren't heard from again. After the game he told the public address announcer that, for the rest of the season, not to introduce him or any of the other coaches pregame.

"I didn't know who was doing it, but I was going to make sure they didn't have that opportunity again," Wasdin said. "I didn't like it, and neither did the players. Suppose I have a recruit at the game, and they introduce the coach and the coach gets booed. What's that recruit going to think? He's going to think that he's not going to want to go somewhere where they're booing the coach."

But make no mistake, it was personal, too. It was bad enough that the crowds at the Jacksonville Coliseum were steadily shrinking, in spite of the program consistently fielding postseason tournament teams and winning 20-or-more games each season. But to hear boos...

"You try not to let it bother you, but of course it hurts your feelings," Wasdin said. "To work as hard as we did and to have the success that we were having at a small school like Jacksonville, where we weren't getting much support from the administration, and then to hear boos ... it was hard to accept."

Later, he heard support from coaching colleagues who had enormous respect for the job Wasdin was doing with JU, and it mitigated the hurt he felt. One of those coaches was Marquette's Al McGuire. Like Dick Vitale, McGuire was incredulous that fans had actually booed Wasdin, and he told Wasdin so. McGuire also couldn't believe how tight JU was with money, considering all the goodwill and publicity and, yes, money that the basketball program was bringing in. In the early '70s, top coaches in the country were earning about $40,000 a year, but at $16,000 a year Wasdin wasn't even making half that much. Again, McGuire was incredulous.

"You should be making as much as anyone in the country," he told Wasdin.

All of it practically forced Wasdin to again seriously think about getting out of coaching. His good friend Rick Stottler from his Cocoa Beach days would often come to home games and cheer the Dolphins. Stottler wouldn't pressure Wasdin to get out of coaching and go into business with him. But Wasdin knew that the offer was always there, and just seeing Stottler at JU's home games was a constant reminder. Hearing boos when his name was announced made him think more and more about life after coaching.

For the time being, though, most of his thoughts remained immersed on the task ahead; on how best to attack this season, and how to get the most out of his personnel.

As everyone was quick to note, with David Brent leaving for the ABA just before the season, the Dolphins didn't have a 7-footer. But

The 1972-73 Jacksonville University team. Top row from left to right: Assistant Coach Don Beasley, Head Coach Tom Wasdin, David Stowers, Ron Stevens, Butch Taylor, Bob Nylin, Tim Wisnewski, Shawn Leftwich, Abe Steward, Assistant Coach Drayton Miller, Assistant Coach Rusty Baldwin. Bottom row kneeling: Jimmie Clark, Andy Denny, Paul Molinaro, Leon Benbow, Henry Williams, George Scholz, Lindsay Huth, Ricky Coleman.

they did have another junior college transfer in 6-foot-10 Butch Taylor, who'd been a JUCO All-American and who was directed to the school by former coach Joe Williams. Coming up from the freshmen squad were 6-foot-6 Henry Williams; 6-foot-2 Ricky Coleman; 6-foot-8 Shawn Leftwich; 6-foot-2 Jimmie Clark; 6-foot-7 Dave Stowers; and 6-foot-4 Mike Denney. Of course, there were some key returning lettermen, too – Leon Benbow, Abe Steward, George Scholz, Bob Nylin and Lindsay Huth. JU never got the benefit of Coleman, though. A former high school All-American who averaged 22 points per game as a guard on the Dolphins' freshmen team, Coleman tore his anterior cruciate ligament in his knee and never completely recovered that season.

As the team grew more comfortable with each other, they not only beat a very good Furman team and then won the Gator Bowl tournament; they also used those three victories as a springboard to a nine-game winning streak. Along the way, the Dolphins beat a Florida State team that was coming off a Final Four appearance the previous season.

By now, FSU head coach Hugh Durham was accustomed to fiercely contested games against Jacksonville, something he appreciated more years later when he became the Dolphins' head coach and experienced firsthand just how difficult it was to achieve the type of success Wasdin and Williams had without getting the full support of the university's administration.

"Tom didn't just do a phenomenal recruiting job at Jacksonville, he was a strong X's and O's coach, too," Durham said. "Both are important at that level. In high school, you don't recruit. So when he had success as a high school coach he had to take what he had and develop it. You can't have success at that level without knowing what to do on the court. At the college level, you can't just be an X's and O's guy. You also have to go get good players, because they're not just going to show up. Tom was very competitive and successful both as a coach and a recruiter. To be successful as a coach, you have to get good people and give them an opportunity to use their skills while helping them develop. Tom had those skills."

After a narrow 87-84 loss to Providence, JU streaked to another four consecutive victories, which was enough to keep the Dolphins on the national radar and hopefully keep intact their goal of getting back to the prestigious NCAA Tournament.

Other schools and coaches were noticing that, even without a 7-footer, these Dolphins were still a team to be taken seriously. One of those victories during their nine-game winning streak came against Southwestern Louisiana, which was ranked No.8 in the nation. The Dolphins, unranked going into the game, had already beaten No.16-ranked Oral Roberts and their All-American guard Richie Fuqua. But a Top 10 team was a better challenge – and it was a challenge that JU met. The Dolphins didn't just beat the Ragin' Cajuns, they smoked them, 120-78. The game was so lopsided that Jacksonville led 67-36 at the half. The running and pro-style offense that Wasdin had told reporters about before the season was on full display. Afterward, Southwestern Louisiana head coach Beryl Shipley summed up his team's loss by saying, "They outshot us, outrebounded us, outhustled us, out-defensed us ... whatever it was, they outed us."

John Harrison, a former JU player who was now an active booster in the Century Club, marveled at the coaching job he saw Wasdin do. It was like a clinic.

"I knew from watching Tom's practices how good they practiced and how well-organized they were," Harrison said. "He ran very good practices. Tom always had the team well-prepared. So I can't say that the game against Southwestern Louisiana surprised me. But I will say this: that game was one of the best games I've ever seen. We were about as perfect as we could've been in the execution of a game plan. I'll never forget it. It was about as near-perfect of a basketball game as I've ever seen."

Afterward, the enthusiasm surrounding JU's program was sky high – both in the press and in public opinion. But in the press there had been a newspaper article about being booed, reminding Wasdin of how hurtful that was. So when he saw fans jumping on the bandwagon again, he couldn't get too excited. "As far as I was concerned, the damage had been done," he said. "By then, my attitude was: we are giving this all that we can. We are working as hard as we can. And if that wasn't enough ..."

Gradually, JU climbed the polls, reaching No. 13 after beating East Carolina to go 13-2. Then came a loss to a Providence team that had two future NBA stars in Ernie DiGregorio and Marvin Barnes. In fact, Providence eventually would make it all the way to the Final Four.

Later in the season, after beating Creighton, Bluejays head coach Eddie Sutton said about JU: "Quick? Man, they're super-quick. And they're physical along with it. We've got a big, strong team but they pushed us around as much as anybody we've played. They are going to go a long way in the NCAAs."

The season-ender was a huge disappointment, and one that lingered with the Dolphins. Jacksonville traveled to Houston to play the Cougars at the Hofheinz Pavilion, where two years earlier they had run into so much trouble that seemed deliberate – lights not working in the locker room, no shower towels, Harold Fox getting kicked by a fan, no Southeastern Conference official, fans throwing debris on the court, etc. It was again another tight, fiercely competitive game, with neither team leading by more than six points the entire evening. When JU's Butch Taylor hit a free throw with 24 seconds remaining, it gave the Dolphins a 75-74 lead. Houston answered with Jerry Bonney's jumper from the corner that found the bottom of the net with only six seconds remaining. With no time to waste, JU's Abe Steward hurled a pass the length of the court to Leon Benbow, who laid in a bucket just before the buzzer sounded.

Or did he?

A few minutes after the game seemingly ended, an official approached Wasdin.

"Coach," he asked, "can we talk to you? I'm afraid you're not going to like what you hear."

They went over to the official scorer's desk.

"Mr. Timer," the official asked the timekeeper, "did the shot get off before time expired?"

The timekeeper's response was both swift and scandalous.

"No! Disallowed!"

Pandemonium followed. Amidst all the confusion, an unbelievable scene caught the corner of Wasdin's eye. Butch Taylor, his All-American JUCO transfer, was choking the timekeeper. Wasdin pulled him off, but Taylor couldn't understand why.

"Coach, I ain't gonna hurt him," he said. "I'm just gonna choke him until he tells the truth."

Once again, it was a bitter loss to Houston, and not because the Dolphins thought they'd been beaten, but because they knew they hadn't been treated fairly. Whereas two years earlier it was the two Missouri Valley Conference officials who had cost the Dolphins the game, this time it was the scorekeeper who did them in.

Their 21-5 record was again one of the best in the country, and again the Dolphins got another invite to the NCAA Tournament – their third in four seasons. Not only that, but Wasdin also felt a measure of pride when he later heard that he received votes from colleagues like Hugh Durham and Joe Williams, who voted for him to be coach of the year.

The first-round game was against Austin Peay State University, who had the nation's fourth-leading scorer in a rail-thin, 6-foot-6 freshman named James "Fly" Williams. Williams was a city smart kid from Brooklyn, NY, where he played blacktop basketball with urban legends like World B. Free and Earl "The Goat" Manigault. Leonard Hamilton, who later coached the Miami Hurricanes and Florida State Seminoles, was at the time a young assistant at Austin Peay, and he convinced the street wizard to bring his talents to the small school in Tennessee.

After falling behind 47-32 at halftime, the Dolphins mounted a steady comeback. It took awhile, but late buckets from Leon Benbow, Bob Nylin and a 20-footer from Jimmy Clark knotted the game at 75-75 with 26 seconds remaining.

As was expected, Austin Peay got the ball into "Fly" Williams' hands and he found a gap in the lane, where he pulled up for a five-footer that gave the Governors a stunning 77-75 victory.

Once again, even though the Dolphins won 20-plus games and had led the nation in free throw accuracy and were top 10 in field goal percentage, it was nonetheless bitter to be bounced from the NCAA Tournament in the first round.

Wasdin still went to St. Louis for the Final Four, where he learned that JU had played more games that season against teams that made the NCAA Tournament than any other tournament entrant. It was also there that he ran into Georgia Southern head coach J.E. Rowe, who'd become a friend.

"Coach," Wasdin told Rowe in confidence, "chances are high that I'm not going to be back at Jacksonville University next season."

Rowe was stunned.

"Tom, you have such a great program," he said. "Why would you leave?"

"I'm putting more into the program than I'm getting out of it," he said.

The season, with everything on and off the court, had been extremely difficult for Wasdin. He tried to tell JU's president, Robert Spiro, how the increasing restraints the administration was putting on the program were not only difficult, but that he felt it would eventually derail all the success and progress they had made.

"I told him they were going to kill big-time basketball at JU," Wasdin said. "He didn't say anything. He just listened. Never said a word."

It made Wasdin think about a conversation that Joe Williams had told him about, back when Williams brought him in as an assistant coach. One day, Williams was talking to the university's vice president, O.D. Barksdale.

"Barksdale told Joe that they didn't want to have a big-time college basketball program at JU, and that if that's what we wanted, then we needed to go somewhere else. I guess I didn't really want to believe that at the time. But by my third year there I was thinking that maybe that was true. Maybe they don't really want big-time basketball."

Tommy Hazouri, a 1966 graduate of Jacksonville who became the school's Alumni Director in 1968 and later the Mayor of Jacksonville from 1987-1991, could clearly sense Wasdin's frustration. It didn't surprise Hazouri, either.

"I was frustrated, too," he said. "As Alumni Director, I saw it as a huge opportunity to get people excited about the university and the city. But the university missed the opportunity to capitalize on that spotlight. The administration dropped the ball – literally and figuratively."

Again, not that it surprised Hazouri, knowing what he knew about the administration.

"O.D. Barksdale was no fan of the program," he said. "I think there was some jealousy there because of all the attention it was getting. They really didn't understand what we had going. The basketball program was our brand. We were the Dolphins before there was even the Miami Dolphins. They had an opportunity to take that and take a giant step forward. But they didn't. Bob Spiro, the president, was a big ego guy. It was always more about him than the university. To let someone like Tom Wasdin go, who was a better salesman for the university than the president, was a big mistake."

Hazouri's opinion of JU's administration was not unique. Pat Williams was a prominent booster at the time, and like Hazouri he could see that the meddling and the indifference as well as the outsized egos involved was an unhealthy mix.

"Bob Spiro was not my favorite person," Williams said. "He had a big ego. He thought he was the guy who made all of this come to pass. But he wasn't. All he did was jump on the bandwagon after it had gotten started. He tried to ride the coattails of the basketball program to his advantage. I remember when he was made rear admiral in the Navy reserves. It went to his head like everything else. I told him that

I didn't know whether to call him rear or admiral. Several times I just called him rear."

Harrison added that years later, when Spiro left, it made a lot of people happy.

"He was not very popular around Jacksonville because he was always promoting himself. And in my opinion, he was not even a very good president."

When Wasdin's coaching friend, Jimmy Taylor at South Alabama, learned about the extra pressure and lack of appreciation Wasdin and Williams had gotten at JU, he was incredulous.

"They should have statues of Joe Williams and Tom Wasdin at Jacksonville University," Taylor said. "All I can say about how they treated him is: where is Tom Wasdin today and where is JU basketball today? Ever since he's been gone, the program hasn't been the same."

One of the guys who later tried to return the Dolphins to their glory years was Wasdin's assistant that season – Don Beasley. After a three-year stint as Glenn Wilkes' assistant coach at Stetson University, Beasley returned to JU in 1975 as the Dolphins' head coach.

"What Coach Williams and Coach Wasdin accomplished at Jacksonville was unbelievable," Beasley said. "I didn't realize all the hard work and all that they did until I tried to do it and was a miserable failure at it, and got fired. I have giant respect for them, for what they were able to do in spite of that administration there. When you have an administration that wants to drink champagne on a beer budget ... well, that's not going to work."

After his three-year stint as JU's head coach, Beasley went back into the assistant coaching ranks and then eventually into a successful business career.

"The business world is like stealing after you've been through what we've been through as coaches," he said. "Especially with how tough it was, and how much you had to do at JU. That's the one thing I came to appreciate about Tom, that he was tough, just a tough son of a bitch. He had this attitude that, 'Hey, we're going to get it done one way or another.' He had a lot of mental toughness. And he wasn't saying, 'You guys go get 'em.' He was right in the middle of it, too. Undermanned, understaffed, underfunded ... it doesn't matter. Tom Wasdin will find a way to get it done. And where someone else is just trying to figure out what to do, he's already taken 10 steps. He doesn't run his life in neutral. He runs his life in gear."

That doesn't mean, though, that the pressure won't eventually exact its toll. The full enormity of just how much stress Wasdin was under didn't fully hit him until he had his annual postseason physical with Dr. Duane Bork, the team physician.

"I knew I was anxious, always worrying, and that I had problems sleeping," he said. "I just couldn't relax. Dr. Bork also found that, amongst other things, I had hypertension and high blood pressure."

He was only 37.

"Tom," Dr. Bork told him, "there are a lot of warnings on the checkup showing that long-term you're going to have medical problems. And when I say long-term, what I mean is that you won't have to worry about retirement, because you're not going to live that long unless you make changes in your life. Fact is, you have a tough job and you're not handling it very well. You have to make changes in your life."

Changes in your life.

The words resonated with Wasdin. But instead of making changes in his life, maybe what he needed instead was a change in his lifestyle. And only another job could do that.

While analyzing his options, he called his friend Rick Stottler.

"Rick," he asked, "are there still business opportunities for me and you down in Cocoa Beach?"

Stottler couldn't say "yes" fast enough, adding that he would match Wasdin's JU salary while assuring him there would be lucrative side projects they could do together.

It would be a switch, from coaching basketball to becoming a developer, but Wasdin was ready for a change. "My decision boiled down to three things – my health, the pressure at JU, and a good business opportunity. At the time, Stottler Stagg & Associates was an architectural, engineering, planning and surveying power in the Southeast."

Wasdin also knew he had done a lot of good work at Jacksonville, starting from his days as an assistant with his friend Joe Williams, and on through his three years as a head coach.

"When I left Paxon High School years earlier in Jacksonville, I left behind a team that won the state championship the following year," he said. "The same with Cocoa Beach High. That Bitty Basketball program I started produced some great players and that school became a state power for many years. When I left JU the team had only one senior graduating, and that was Abe Steward. After him, eight of the program's nine top players were returning. I felt satisfied that I left the program in great shape."

He also was deeply appreciative of the experience he had at Jacksonville. His years there shaped him for the decades ahead.

"It was a life-changing experience," he said. "I learned things that were valuable to me for the rest of my life. I will always be thankful to Joe Williams, to my players and to Jacksonville University for all that they gave me. Even though I had a successful college coaching career by most standards, by *my* standards I wasn't successful, simply because I wasn't happy. I don't think you can be successful unless you're happy. I firmly believe that only you are responsible for your happiness. I knew it was time to move on, and I was comfortable with that decision."

So Wasdin told Stottler he was coming, and he told Jacksonville University he was leaving.

"It was bittersweet," he recalled. "I was glad to get out from under the pressure and I knew that I was leaving the program better than when I came in as an assistant. We just had a great season, and the program had almost everyone coming back. That night, I had the best night's sleep I'd had in a long, long time."

If Jacksonville University's administrators and fans didn't know how good they had it, first with Joe Williams and then with Tom Wasdin, they soon found out. After an incredible run of one NIT bid and three NCAA Tournament bids in four years, the final one coming in Wasdin's 1972-73 season, the Dolphins have gone back to the NCAA Tournament only twice in the 40 years since. Wasdin also owns the best winning percentage of any basketball coach in JU history, which was eventually recognized in 2011, when he was inducted into Jacksonville University's Sports Hall of Fame.

Yes, if Jacksonville didn't know how good it had it, the university and the city would soon find out. Ever since that 1972-73 season ended, they've done a lot of reminiscing; looking back at those magical years that Joe Williams and Tom Wasdin put together.

But as for Tom Wasdin, he was looking ahead.

Chapter 15

A CLEAN BREAK FROM BASKETBALL AND A FAST BREAK INTO BUSINESS

"Nobody was writing in the newspaper that you had dropped a tray of dishes and broke them all. There was no external pressure. I did miss a lot of things about coaching, but the pressure and the toll on your life, I didn't miss." – Tom Wasdin

A lot happened along the Space Coast since Tom Wasdin left in 1966, first to go be Joe Williams' assistant coach and later the head coach at Jacksonville University. Man had not only gone to the moon, they were routinely going back, bringing ongoing exposure and growth to the area.

By the time Wasdin returned early in 1973, Brevard County was burgeoning, vibrant, spawning new schools like Astronaut High School in Titusville, which produced legendary athletes like Cris Collinsworth and Wilber Marshall. Eddie Feely, Wasdin's old athletic director at Cocoa Beach High, had moved to another new high school in the area, this one on Merritt Island, where he coached the Mustangs' football team to the 1972 State Championship. It was the same year that a boy named Kelly Slater was born, and he would grow up along Cocoa Beach to become the greatest surfer in the history of the sport. The Space Coast was in its prime, and so was Tom Wasdin, just 37, a man already with enough yesterdays to fill a lifetime, but with so many more tomorrows yet to live.

These were his old stomping grounds, but it was definitely a new beginning.

The years ahead would be busy, seeing him marry again, and

divorce again; become an influential mover and shaker both locally and statewide; involve himself in politics, policy and philanthropy; have a crippling disorder drive him to the brink of suicide; find and marry the love of his life; and become a multimillionaire developer and businessman.

It all started when he joined his old friend Rick Stottler and Stottler Stagg & Associates. Though he had a good entry level position, Tom Wasdin – just as with everything else in his life – started from the ground up, working his way to success.

When he returned to the Space Coast, there was some initial recognition, especially among the sports writers at the local *TODAY* newspaper. For a while, it was noted that a celebrity college basketball coach was back in Brevard County. To be sure, however, Wasdin was a *former* college coach; determined to keep it that way. Some schools – like Marquette and Southwest Louisiana – still nibbled at him, testing to see if he'd be interested in returning to the hardwood courts. But he wasn't. He had moved on, but occasionally he did look back. Wasdin couldn't help but notice how, now that he was no longer coaching, his lifestyle had changed, and changed dramatically.

"It's great to be famous," he ruminated. "It's a heck of an ego trip to have your own TV and radio show, to be able to go to the 21 Club in New York City for dinner and have people ask for your autograph. It was a change of pace. In Jacksonville, I was living at Bay Meadows, an exclusive community where they were paying me $10,000 a year just to use my name. When I moved back to Brevard County, I was living at the Plaza Apartments in Cape Canaveral, a one bedroom that I was paying $200 a month for."

It was better that way, living simply, streamlining his life for the long hours and hard work ahead.

And it was hard work. Building, constructing, developing ... it was like learning a new language. Wasdin was determined not only to make it, but to make a difference. He targeted the Canaveral Pier, which he was on track to own a third of once the debt was paid off.

"Rick Stottler and I developed a plan to create a landmark with the Pier," he said. "One of the things we eventually did was change the name, at the recommendation of Wendy Ellis, from Canaveral Pier to the Cocoa Beach Pier. Wendy, who at the time served with me on the Tourist Development Council, was handling our marketing and promotion for the Pier, Cocoa Expo and the Kennedy Point Yacht Club and Marina. Cocoa Beach had name recognition. People especially knew it because of the 'I Dream of Jeannie' television show. Besides, the Pier was *in* Cocoa Beach."

Wasdin was obviously familiar with the Pier due to all the summers he spent managing it. He had teamed with Dick Catri to promote and help build the Easter Surfing Festival at the Pier. After Catri moved his Shagg's Surf Shop off the Pier, it was Wasdin who negotiated the deal to bring Ron Jon Surf Shop onto it. Because of getting to know surfers as a high school teacher, he helped nurture the often misunderstood surfing community. In fact, it was those surfers he tapped into to shape the future of the Pier. First, though, he had to change the Pier's image and infrastructure.

"It takes a lot of money to maintain the Pier, so we knew we needed a revenue producer," Wasdin said. "We wanted to turn it into something more than a fishing pier."

He looked at the old teenage hangout he had started years earlier and had called the Asylum, and saw how it had gone through a lot of transformations, taking on the form of various retail stores. There was also the old Liar's Lounge, a small hangout that seated eight people at the bar with a pool table as its centerpiece. The nearby snack bar seated about another dozen people. None of it would be enough to ensure the long-term financial future of the Pier.

In addition to eventually changing the name to the Cocoa Beach Pier, Wasdin began marketing it as the East Coast Surfing Capital and as a landmark – a destination along the Space Coast.

They added a nice restaurant and lounge, calling it the Pier House Restaurant. They also built a walkway around it so people who were there for a nice evening didn't have to watch constant traffic trekking through. Instead, what diners saw were the surfers who came at night, thanks to Wasdin putting lights up high for them, along with showers down below. The surfers were the same crowd Wasdin had forged a friendly relationship with, whom he saw beyond their stereotype image – local legends like Garry Propper, Mike Tabeling, Bruce Valluzzi, Claude Codgen, and Joe and Betsy Twombly. And if anybody was noticing, there also was a little kid – an up-and-coming grommet –

named Kelly Slater, who would go on to become the sport's greatest surfer.

"We put in almost floor-to-ceiling windows so people could eat good food, have a drink, and watch the surfers," he said. "That was a big attraction, and the surfers also liked having an audience. We went from the Liar's Lounge and the snack bar with not many seats, to hundreds of seats with people waiting in line to get in."

Built in 1962, the Pier was gradually enjoying step-by-step renovations and remodeling.

"It was hard work, but I enjoyed it very much," Wasdin said. "We were able to take something that was not a good investment and turn it into something that was a very good investment."

Wasdin was smart enough – as well as experienced enough from his background in sports – to know that he needed a team around him. As other bigger and more involved projects and developments filled his plate, Wasdin looked for someone to manage what was then still called the Canaveral Pier. It had been Doc Kelley, the Cocoa Beach High track coach. But Kelley obviously could only do it part-time, around his teaching and coaching schedule. Wasdin now needed someone full-time. Billy Turner, a draftsman who was working for Wasdin at Stottler Stagg & Associates, had a suggestion.

"Billy knew I was looking for a manager to run the Cocoa Beach Pier and he came up to me one day and said, 'I've got the guy for you – my brother.'"

Thus, Wasdin hired Robin Turner, who had been working for a carnival company in Orlando, beginning a business and personal relationship that still endures, even while Robin Turner eventually moved on to become his own businessman and millionaire.

"My wife DeAnn and I had been traveling with the carnival and we were looking to get off the road," Turner said. "Tom was living at Chateau By The Sea at the time, unit 506. We went over one evening to talk with him, sometime in '81. He was a mesmerizing guy. Just super easy to talk to and communicate with. Very sincere. He wasn't painting a picture of something that couldn't be accomplished. It helped, too, that my brother spoke real highly of him."

That night, Wasdin hired Robin and DeAnn, who were boyfriend/

girlfriend at the time. Robin would manage the Pier and DeAnn would do the accounting and bookkeeping.

"We got hired as a team, and we were to each make $12,000 a year and we got to live rent-free in unit 505 at Chateau By The Sea. After living on a train, that was pretty romantic."

The Pier had improved, but it was still a rough place.

"You had to fight to get on it and fight to get off it," Turner recalled. "It wasn't too uncommon for a brawl to break out. Needless to say, it was far from its potential, but here was an opportunity and a challenge to take it and make it something special. Tom and Rick set goals and then they gave me the backing to reach those goals."

The year Turner arrived, the Pier had grossed $200,000. His second year there, working closely with Wasdin, Turner recalled that they grossed $2 million. His third year – $3 million. His fourth year – $4 million. It was in his third year that Turner hired Dennis Kolsch from the popular Mousetrap restaurant – another local landmark – to be the Pier's food and beverage manager. As a result, the Pier House Restaurant soon became a go-to destination along with the Hilton in Cape Canaveral, the Holiday Inn on Merritt Island, the Mousetrap, Bernard's Surf, Ramone's, Shakey's Pizza Parlor, the Carnival Club and Ramone's Rainbow Room above the Glass Bank in Cocoa Beach. Needless to say, they also cleaned up the Pier, making it a destination for families and tourists. Eventually, it became known as the landmark that it still is today.

Meanwhile, because of how the Pier became such an iconic landmark under his guidance, Wasdin was appointed to the Tourist Development Council by County Commissioner Theo York. His charge was to spearhead getting a tourism sales tax approved to benefit the local economy, which he helped accomplish.

It all seemed like a smooth ride ... but it wasn't. Early into his time with Stottler Stagg & Associates, Wasdin had a conversation with his friend Rick Stottler that wasn't too dissimilar to the one he had with his friend Joe Williams early in their time together at Jacksonville University.

Wasdin was running the Pier, the old *Surfside Slant* weekly Central Brevard newspaper that they had purchased and changed the name to *Surfside Sun*, and also the Camelot Inn restaurant, where his one perk was reduced rates on meals. Stottler was paying him the same $16,000 salary he made at Jacksonville University, but it wasn't the money that was most important. Wasdin was itching to do more. One day, he approached Stottler and asked him:

"Rick, are you sure this is going to work out?"

"Yes, no question," Stottler replied without hesitation. "Just be patient."

"Rick, I know I'm not an architect or an engineer," Wasdin said. "But I don't think I'm being utilized right, as to what I'm capable of doing."

It was shortly afterward when Wasdin finally got the Chateau By The Sea project – a 45-unit condominium project steps away from the Pier. He invested his own money into the project and became President and a 50 percent owner in the development. Rick Stottler and Charlie Moehle, his two partners with the Pier, each owned 25 percent.

"I couldn't wait to get started on it," he said. "It was the main lure for me leaving JU."

Dick Biery, who was hired as the builder for Chateau By The Sea, had known Wasdin from his coaching days. He and his friend Rick Stottler used to drive up a lot for Jacksonville University's home games.

"He was damn good at what he did as a coach," Biery recalled. "He was a tremendous recruiter and a people person. When he left coaching, I was shocked. When Rick put him in charge of Chateau By The Sea, he may as well have put Tom in charge of open heart surgery, because he knew nothing about it. But he learned fast, very fast, and he worked hard."

Biery saw then, as well as through the years, that Wasdin's people skills were a huge asset.

"What made him a great recruiter helped him in business," Biery said. "He was a great promoter and really good with people. He fit right in with anybody, whether it was the head of NASA or a guy on the construction crew."

Of course, it was only natural for Wasdin to tap into his sports background – particularly his experience as a coach. He hired Millie Aleguas to be his Vice President of Marketing, and together they became a formidable team. They even lived near each other in the same Plaza Apartment complex in Cape Canaveral. "We set out together to build the best condominium complex anywhere that would sell for the prices we were going to charge," he said. Toward that goal, Tom and Millie visited 20 condominium projects up and down Florida's East Coast, posing as a husband and wife who were interested in buying a condo, with Tom playing the role of an airline pilot.

"Everywhere we went, we made notes of what we liked and what we didn't like," Wasdin said. "It was just like coaching. I had a game plan, goals, and it was like I was scouting a team. Really, that's what we were doing – scouting. What I learned as a coach and a player, I've used my entire life. It has served me well. It served me well back then because I had invested all my cash – $10,000 into Chateau By The Sea. Since I was making $16,000, it was a big investment. But I saw it as my passport to financial success. This was a tryout."

Marketing and sales came natural to Wasdin, especially since he inherently had to do a lot of that when he was a college basketball coach and recruiter. In fact, through the years, people he came in contact with often raved about his marketing skills. For now, though, the immediate concern was this first project – Chateau By The Sea.

"I taught Millie what I knew and there were a lot of things we also learned together," he said. "We threw ourselves in Chateau By The Sea. Millie worked hard and she was good. She also liked it as much as I did."

Millie was an attractive woman, pretty and pert, a redhead with a dynamite smile and an outgoing personality that put potential buyers at ease. On January 1, 1974, they opened their first model. One problem. The economy was in trouble, with the Arab oil embargo affecting the U.S. economy, pushing interest rates to an all-time high.

"When we finished, we closed on only 23 units that first year," Wasdin said. "We still had 22 of 45 units vacant. The economy really impacted us. What we decided to do was turn the rest of the units into rentals – either furnished or unfurnished. If they were furnished, Millie decked them out with appliances, drapes, shades, linens ... everything. They became turnkey units for anyone who wanted to rent and move in. It also became attractive for investors, because they could buy a ready-to-rent unit. We also had some unfurnished units. It was a good lesson for me in adapting. We had a construction loan, and we had to pay taxes and insurance. Renting kept us above water until we sold all the units."

Impressed, Stottler approached Wasdin after Chateau By The Sea's completion.

"Tom," he said, "if you get your general contractor's license, I'll make you Senior Vice President of Construction Management for Stottler Stagg & Associates."

Wasdin went right to work on that, taking classes. He first passed his block test for Brevard County and then eventually took his state test ... but didn't pass. So he redoubled his efforts, studied hard, and took the test a second time two weeks later in Gainesville. When he did, he was able to review his first test and saw that there had been a mistake in grading. When he scanned his results, something didn't seem right, and he pointed out discrepancies to the test-giver.

"They had made a mistake on my score," he said. "It was a 20-point error. After they recalculated it and made the correction, it showed that I had passed the test. But since I was already in Gainesville, I retook the exam, just for fun. As Stottler had promised, when I passed the exam, he promoted me to Senior Vice President of Construction Management. It gave me credibility. Before, everyone thought I was only a coach."

Tom Wasdin's first construction project. The 45-unit Chateau By The Sea condominium complex on the Atlantic Ocean in Cocoa Beach, Florida.

Life was good, and most importantly Tom Wasdin was happy, enjoying what he was doing. Sure, there was stress. But it was a different stress. "Nobody knew about your mistakes but you and your accountant," he said. "Nobody was writing in the newspaper that you had dropped a tray of dishes and broke them all. There was no external pressure. I did miss a lot of things about coaching, but the pressure and the toll on your life, I didn't miss. I don't think I handled it well. But this new direction in my life, I really enjoyed. I was just enjoying life a lot. I was a single guy. I was playing sports again, mostly outfield on the Stottler Stagg softball team that became a state power, and also on their AAU basketball team. And when Chateau By The Sea was done, I moved into one of the oceanfront units in there. That was in the summer of 1974."

The first unit he sold was to Mac McLouth, the executive vice president at Stottler Stagg & Associates, who still lives at Chateau By The Sea. Right away, McLouth saw the skills that made Wasdin such a successful recruiter and college basketball coach. He also saw a guy who was still quite the athlete.

"He played basketball really well," said McLouth, who later served as Cape Canaveral's Port Commissioner for 32 years. "He was a hell of a competitor. A good athlete, but also a very smart and thoughtful competitor. He'd examine and analyze things, and he carried that through his entire life and in all aspects of his life. Whenever there was a problem, he approached it very thoroughly. Before he'd go after a job, he did his homework. He knew who the principal people involved were and who he needed to talk to. He was also very much a team player."

Several of the other Chateau By The Sea units Wasdin sold were to area coaches that he knew. One of them was Doc Kelley, a teacher and top-notch track and cross country coach at Cocoa Beach High.

"Tom would tell us that we all had to go running on the beach, at like 7 in the morning," Kelley said. "He was very competitive with running, just like everything else he does. One day, just the two of us were running, heading south. We must have run six, seven miles. Neither one of us was going to be the guy who said that it was time to turn around. We were letting testosterone do our thinking. Finally we cut over to Rick Stottler's house and had someone pick us up."

A friendship developed, and Wasdin talked Kelley into managing the Pier during the summer.

"I didn't know anything about the restaurant business, but Tom was a great motivator, the best, and he had a way of instilling confidence in you to do more than you thought you could do," Kelley said. "He was great. He always had a positive attitude, was always encouraging. If you screwed up, you screwed up. Now let's rise above it and move on. Everything he told me worked out."

Like many others, Kelley could see how Wasdin was the yin to Rick Stottler's yang.

"Tom was a great promoter and he could market," he said. "He was also great at getting people to look at things from a different viewpoint. If you had a strong opinion, he could take you all the way through and get you to see another side. He was tremendous at public relations. Rick Stottler was the antithesis of public relations. Rick would lose his temper and sever a relationship, and Tom was always coming in and fixing things."

One special relationship Wasdin developed was with Millie, as romantic feelings they had for each other continued to grow.

"She was very attractive, she took care of herself, and she was a hard worker, very smart," he said. "We worked so hard and so close together that we became best friends. She loved to work, and I loved to work. We'd often work until 8 or 9 o'clock and then go to the Mousetrap for dinner. Eventually, we fell in love and decided to get married. Rick Stottler had remodeled his house, and in 1975 we got married there."

Meanwhile, all over the country, the nation was ramping up for its bicentennial celebration. Although at the time he didn't yet have his general contractor's license, Wasdin became Stottler Stagg's construction manager for the critically important U.S. Bicentennial Exposition on Space & Technology project that they had secured from NASA, to be built at Kennedy Space Center and have President Gerald Ford as a visitor. Wasdin also oversaw the painting of the famous American flag that to this day still graces the side of the Vehicle Assembly Building, or VAB. Many government agencies had exhibits, housed under different domes, and Wasdin oversaw the construction.

"It was my first big construction project I did after Chateau By The Sea was done," he said. "It was new and because it was the bicentennial it was exciting. We were getting ready for President Ford to come down. I got thrown right into it and really enjoyed it. Rick gave me the entire Stottler Stagg company at my disposal to be able to use. It was exciting times."

Whenever there was a status update meeting, critical for a project like this, Stottler was amazed at how thorough Wasdin was. Nothing was left to chance and no loose ends left untied. Wasdin always had meticulous records of how every penny was spent while also staying on top of the subcontractors, consistently reporting in detail what they'd done the previous week and what was ahead for the upcoming week. He also all but memorized the American Institute of Architect documents. Eventually, he brought the project in on time and on budget. NASA presented Stottler Stagg & Associates with a special award, citing their work on the project.

Tom Wasdin wearing a hard hat at Kennedy Space Center.

"Tom," Stottler told him, "I'm so impressed with how well you've kept records and how you are always able to answer all their questions. We could not have done a better job."

He was rewarded with a month off, which he and Millie used to take a trip in a motor home, all the way to New England and eventually to Montreal, where they took in the 1976 Olympic Games.

Life was good.

But something had crept into Wasdin's life late in 1975 – something sinister and insidious. He had felt a twinge of pain near his jaw, similar to a bad toothache, but different. The pain would come ... and it would go. And it would get worse. Much worse. Tom Wasdin had never heard of Trigeminal Nueralgia. Most people haven't. Until they get it. Then their life changes. Sometimes, it even ends.

Just a year earlier, he learned another painful lesson about life ... and death. For the first time since the passing of his grandparents, Tom suffered the first loss of a close loved one – his father. Eddie Wasdin, only 65, was killed by a falling tree as it was cut for timber on land next to his farm. It stunned and saddened Tom, forcing him to contemplate how fleeting and fickle life can be. His relationship with his father was a bit conflicted, not so much because he was raised by his Uncle Wilbert and Auntie Estelle after his mother died during his infancy. It was more because his father did not want him to go to college, preferring that he stay and work on the family farm.

"I think he forgave me for that," Tom said. "But he did not contribute anything to help me go to college, except he loaned me gasoline from the farm gas tank to drive to UF, which totaled less than a $100. I had to sign for all the gas I used and he was going to take it out of anything I would get from my portion of his will."

Though he was self-educated, Eddie Wasdin became affluent. He was a good businessman and an extremely hard worker – two traits he wrote into his son's DNA.

But he was sparing in his compliments, and even more sparing in his affection.

"He once told me he was very proud of my success," Tom said. "But he was not the kind of person who showed his love very much. It was sad that I had now lost both my mother and father. I still had Auntie and Uncle and now they became even more important to me.

His funeral was very sad for me. He was the first person other than my grandmother and grandfather that was close to me to die. It gave me a better understanding that nothing was forever."

Uncle Wilbert and Auntie Estelle in their later years. They raised Tom and Dorothy Wasdin after their mother Faye died.

It also gave Wasdin insight into the money grab that can occur when someone dies and their wishes are not spelled out in legal detail. His father had amassed quite a bit of land and with it wealth. Eddie Wasdin had somewhat planned ahead for its dispersal, but not fully. Before his untimely death, all six kids – Tom and his sister Dorothy from Eddie's first marriage and four children from his second marriage – were shown their father's property and told how it would be divided. Even after Eddie Wasdin's death, Miss Edna, which was how Tom and Dorothy always addressed their stepmother, took Dorothy to 80 acres of land that butted up against their Auntie's and Uncle's property, and told her it would be hers and Tom's.

"We all felt that we knew exactly what we were going to get," Tom said. "Since my father hadn't contributed financially to my and Dorothy's upbringing, it seemed like a nice inheritance."

Not quite.

Tom Wasdin standing with his brother and sister, Jerry Wasdin and Dorothy Wasdin Prevatt.

"When we met with the attorney, he said we were not entitled to the land since it was in joint names, and the other name was my father's second wife – Miss Edna. Once she found out she didn't have to give us the land, she didn't. Her rationale was that her kids needed it more than we did. Dorothy and I ended up with only a couple of acres each."

Tom filed the experience away, and years later, when he was approaching retirement, he made sure all his wishes were legally binding and secure, with all the i's dotted and t's crossed.

While it was a painful lesson, there was a more serious pain he was experiencing, one that for a long time he kept hidden. Nobody, not even his close associates, would have suspected that Tom was suffering from the early stages of Trigeminal Neuralgia, and how it would practically consume him. What people saw was a young, charismatic leader who kept rising in prominence and power. Many attributed the success of Stottler Stagg & Associates to him. Wasdin was much more personable than Stottler, who didn't have near the social or people skills. Where

Stottler often drove wedges into relationships, Wasdin was a great negotiator, mediator and facilitator.

"Rick Stottler was not always enjoyable," recalled Andy Barber, who teamed with Wasdin with development projects from the mid-80's into the 90's. "Tom had an ability to calm and create consensus. He was able to repair the damage Stottler did and move things forward."

After bringing Chateau By The Sea to completion and ensuring that NASA's bicentennial celebration was a success, Wasdin moved on to Ocean Woods, a bustling and beautiful new community in Cape Canaveral. He, Stottler and Moehle each owned a third, with Stottler Stagg & Associates doing all of the architectural work, planning, surveying and engineering. It was a unique development in that it saved all the natural landscaping and built around the native vegetation. It was a departure from the normal scorched earth method of leveling everything, building homes, and then planting bushes and saplings.

"We called it Florida Natural Landscaping," Wasdin said.

Meanwhile, Millie was selling units faster than they could build them. It all seemed to be running smoothly until the Ocean Woods' Homeowners Association threatened a lawsuit because their maintenance fees were raised without their approval, as well as some disagreements about beachfront units and beach access.

"It was really a minor matter," Wasdin said. "All they basically wanted was control of the homeowner's association. We could have settled, but Stottler would not agree to it."

Stottler's attorney Curt Mosley, who later became Wasdin's attorney through the years, recalled a meeting with the homeowners and Stottler in his office at the old Glass Bank building in Cocoa Beach.

"The homeowners were threatening litigation and we were moving toward reaching an agreement, a settlement," Mosley said. "We would have had one, but at the last minute, Rick being Rick, he killed the settlement. He thought they were getting something for nothing. So he told them, 'I'm not paying you a damn penny!' Then he chewed them out and stormed out. That's when they got an attorney and we had a lawsuit."

Knowing Wasdin, Mosley knew that if he had been with him in the meeting, and not Stottler, there would have been an agreement.

"We'd have settled," Mosley said. "Tom's no pushover. He stands his ground. But he's also reasonable."

As it was, the lawsuit did not have a favorable outcome.

"We not only lost in court, but it cost us hundreds of thousands of dollars," Wasdin said. "What I learned from the experience is to settle all lawsuits, if possible. Usually, it's only attorneys who make money from lawsuits. I also learned that when money is involved, people lie."

Still, he looks back fondly – if not proudly – at the project and the way the development used existing nature. "Because of the way we saved the natural plants, we received a second-place award from the East Central Florida Planning District," Wasdin said. And first place? Well, first place went to a Walt Disney World project that came to be known as Epcot.

Work, like life, could have its ups and downs.

It was around this time when Wasdin was able to bring his son Steve and daughter Lori to spend the summers with him. Just as he had learned a work ethic as a boy, he instilled that into young Steve.

"I was landscaping, sweeping out houses, doing construction labor duties," Steve said. "I got to understand the importance of work. I remember those summers very fondly, getting to stay with my dad."

Lori also fondly recalls the summers with her father, and the lessons learned. Her father was always stressing the importance of physical fitness and eating correctly. And he didn't just stress it, he implemented it.

"My dad enjoyed exercise, running," Lori said. "He'd take my brother Steve and me to the beach and he'd have it marked off to where it was a mile, two miles, and he'd have us run with him. One time, we were running with him, and I cramped up. I was crying, begging, 'Please Dad, can we stop? I can't run anymore.' And he'd be saying, 'Come on. You can do it. Come on. We're almost there.'"

Still crying, Lori stopped. But her Dad and Steve kept going.

"I knew he was keeping an eye on me, but at the same time he wasn't going to stop," Lori said. "That's when I found out I could push myself a little more. It was either that or be left behind, and I didn't want to be left behind. I didn't want to disappoint him. I learned a life lesson from that. I learned not to quit, not to give up. I learned that you can push yourself a little more. Before that, I never really had to work hard for anything."

Years later, when Lori became a mother of four children, one of her daughters was diagnosed with diabetes in 2002.

"That's when it hit me," Lori said. "I could hear my dad's voice, preaching the importance of exercising and eating right."

For the first time since she was a young girl with her father, Lori started running ... and running and running and running. She found a group of girlfriends who wanted to do the same, and they trained for a marathon. In 2006, she ran and completed the Rock 'n' Roll Marathon in Phoenix, Ariz., and has competed in – and completed – numerous half marathons, as well.

"Now I run most every day," she said. "I've even run in blizzards. All of that translates to life. Keep going. Never give up. Work harder. Push yourself. I thank my father for that, and I admire him in so many ways."

At the same time when he was strengthening his relationship with his two children, Tom and Millie started hitting some bumps in the road with their marriage. Most of the problems centered on her two sons – Dean and Chris. Tom had never been a stepparent before, and he might have liked it had he liked the boys. "But everything I detested in a kid, they both were – they treated their mom badly, skipped school, smoked pot. Millie had a weakness for them, and she believed them to a fault. She wanted me to be the disciplinarian, because their real dad was out of their life. It wasn't a good situation."

Millie also went to work for another developer who was able to pay her twice as much. "When she changed jobs, it changed our relationship," Tom said. "Everything was built on our working together, and now that was gone." Worse was that Millie was now running with her own crowd, separate from her husband. "She was a drinker, and we had talked about that before we got married. She promised she wouldn't drink without me. But now she was. She was staying out late, drinking, and I didn't like the image she was setting. I finally told her that it was either me or the booze."

In 1980, they divorced.

Wasdin was ready to move on. He was also ready to find that one woman he could marry, and stay married to, for the rest of his life.

Chapter 16

ANOTHER BEND ALONG THE ROAD OF LIFE

"From the beginning we made a great pair. The coach and the cheerleader made a great team. Life was never the same again. It changed my life like it had never been changed before." – Tom Wasdin

After his divorce from Millie, Tom Wasdin dove straight into another development project. This one would be called Beach Woods, and once again Wasdin would be going in thirds with Rick Stottler and Charlie Moehle.

"We ran the project very similar to Ocean Woods," he said. "It ran from the river to the ocean in the south beaches. It sold very fast and we raised the prices just as we had done at Ocean Woods. The homeowners were watching the lawsuit at Ocean Woods and they were getting ready to sue us. We resolved the issue before it got to that. We weren't going to make the same mistake twice."

Wasdin was a fast learner. His mind was eager for information, like paper yearning for ink. At the same time, the teacher and coach in him often came through in that he'd be generous with his knowledge, skills and philosophies. In fact, people started referring to him by the title Coach again – only now it was because of the life lessons and what he called his wise Wasdinisms that he passed on to others.

"He taught me an awful lot," said Bill Starmer, who started as a young architect at Stottler Stagg & Associates, before working his way up. "Tom taught me a lot about people. He'd do most anything for anybody he respected and cared for. He was always going out of his way to make sure I felt comfortable in a situation. He was very kind and generous."

Like others, Starmer marveled at Wasdin's work ethic, but at the same time he saw a man who could also laugh and have a good time. One time, the two men were driving back to Brevard County after a business trip.

"Tom was driving a Cadillac and he was tired," Starmer said. "It was a long drive. He asked me if I would drive. I said, 'Sure.' So Tom put his seat back, slid out of his driving position and into the back seat, saying, 'It's yours.' That's when I slid over from the passenger seat into the driver's seat. We never pulled over."

The two men also started playing racquetball together. Wasdin had just had surgery to combat increasingly intolerable Trigeminal Neuralgia, where a brain surgeon permanently removed a golf ball-sized piece of bone from the back of his head, leaving an unprotected hole there.

"Sure enough, the first time we played I hit him right there where he'd had the surgery," Starmer said. "He went down to his knees. He kidded me, saying, 'You don't have to hit me so you could win.' The next time we played, wouldn't you know I hit him in the exact same spot. That was the last time we played. He still claims that I tried to kill him."

As he told the story, Starmer chuckled, adding, "As much as Tom could be a drillmaster and demand that things be done right, he was fun to be around."

Most of all, Starmer, who later broke off into his own business in Central Florida, learned a lot about work ethic and preparation from Wasdin.

"People like to do what they do as a business," Starmer said. "But a lot of people don't like to build a business, to market and do the things that get you the work that you enjoy doing. When I'd called the people I thought I needed to call, Tom would pick up the phone and call 10 more people. He would persistently tell me, 'You've got to talk to people.' I learned from him to go that extra mile; to learn a little more about my clients and my competition. That comes from Tom. He likes to learn as much as he can as quick as he can. And being the coach that he was, he doesn't leave anything to chance."

As Wasdin learned and settled in as a builder, he eventually began the third Brevard County Woods project – Harbor Woods. His divorce from Millie left him single again, and Tom wasn't looking to marry for a fourth time. But love came looking for him, although neither he nor the former Susie Thortsen knew it at the time. Tom had remembered Susie from his days coaching at Cocoa Beach High School, when Susie's brother Vern was one of his star players and Susie was the pretty cheerleader and homecoming queen whom he tried to keep away from his boys.

Susie had graduated from the University of Florida, married, became a mother to her son Andrew, or Drew as he was called, and was teaching school in Atlanta when she and her first husband decided to divorce. Returning home during the divorce proceedings, she didn't quite know what her next move was.

"I'd come home basically to regroup," she said. "I was a single mom now, and a teacher's salary wasn't going to be enough. I wanted to get into something that would allow me to raise my child."

She had worked for almost a year and a half for a prestigious real estate appraising company in Gainesville, running their office. She found that not only did she like real estate, but felt she could be just as successful, if not more so, than some of the top real estate agents she'd come in contact with. "I observed a lot," she said, "and at times I remember thinking, 'She's a top realtor? She can't even find the keys to her car. If she can become one of the top agents, then maybe I can, too.'"

Susie was a tough and tenacious young woman, with a lot of spunk and ambition, unafraid to take a chance. She paid her own way through school, and she had a desire to see and experience the world. Once, several years earlier, when she was a student at Brevard Junior College, Susie saw a flier advertising for international students. She applied and was accepted to be a governess in Stuttgart, Germany, working essentially as a nanny for a family that had five kids, primarily teaching them English.

Said Susie, "I had visions of being Julie Andrews in 'The Sound of Music'."

Her flight out of Florida to Germany connected in Nassau, Bahamas, where she was to fly on International Air Bahamas. To board her flight, Susie had to walk onto the tarmac and climb a set of stairs. When she got to the top step and handed the flight attendant her boarding pass, a nearby Qantas Airlines plane suddenly started its engines, the force of which literally blew the staircase away from the plane just as Susie was attempting to board.

"I took a step and there was nothing there," she said. "I fell about 15 feet to the ground."

As she fell, she tried to claw at the side of the plane, and it ripped her nails off her fingers. Bloodied and dazed, she was carted away on a stretcher while her luggage flew to Germany. For some reason, after taking her to the Princess Margaret Hospital, Bahamian officials took her to a hotel. After phone calls to her parents, which led to a phone call with an attorney back home, her phone was cut off.

"I had no phone, no clothes, no medical attention and I guess I started getting hysterical," she said. "It was scary. Finally, a doctor came and gave me a shot in my rear end that knocked me out. When I woke up the next morning my bed was all bloody. I was bleeding from where he'd given me a shot."

They finally arranged to get her home, taking her to the airport in a stretcher. A lawsuit reached a settlement that basically did nothing more than pay for her medical expenses and attorney fees.

The accident resulted in back problems later in life. But at the time, it ended Susie's adventure of living and working overseas. Instead, she took out a loan and headed to the University of Florida, eventually earning a bachelor's degree in education and becoming an elementary school teacher in Atlanta, where her brother Vern had also gone to school – playing football at Georgia Tech. But after returning to Cocoa Beach as a 27-year-old single mom who was going through a divorce, she was looking for a career change.

One day, Susie's mother told her: "You need to call Tom Wasdin. He's a successful businessman and maybe he can help you find a job."

She did call him, and Wasdin brought her in for an interview, taking her around to various construction sites and development projects.

"I was in awe," she said. "I'd never been on a construction site, but here he was taking me around in this big blue Cadillac to what they were building, showing me finished models, the Pier. Tom was wearing white jeans and a navy blue shirt. He looked fabulous."

Meanwhile, Susie was wearing a tropical-print blouse and skirt, a sort of casual suit, which her mother had to sew her into because she was so thin.

What Tom liked about Susie was what he had remembered about her from Cocoa Beach High; that she was "highly involved, in the band, a majorette, a cheerleader, the homecoming queen, and in student government. That told me something. It told me that she's a self-starter, that she's ambitious and that she's striving to do great things."

He had a couple of concerns, though.

Susie was a single mom, not yet divorced, and he didn't want to invest in training her and then have her move back to Atlanta to return to her husband. If she wanted to work on her marriage, that was fine. But for his purposes, he needed to know if she was committed to a new life or if there was a chance she was returning to her husband. Susie assured him that there was no chance. He also knew she loved Atlanta, and he didn't want to lose her to a big city after having her onboard for only a few months.

"I don't want to waste your time, and I don't want you to waste ours," he said.

As much as she loved the city life, Susie was looking for stability. If she was hired, she'd primarily be on the Harbor Woods project, behind the Merritt Square Mall, and she saw how it projected five to seven years out.

"I could see that if I grasped the project and worked hard, I could be there as long as I wanted to," she said.

She got the job with the title of Vice President of Marketing and Sales, and went right to work, selling. And sell she did.

Wasdin was President of the project, and immediately he could see that his new VP was someone unique and special.

"Even the lady who trained Susie was impressed with her right away," he said. "She also didn't think we'd be able to keep her very long. She made the comment that she was training Susie, but Susie was a better salesperson than she was. I was always worried that Susie was too big for Brevard County. She was too pretty, too young and really too good to be true."

He added, "Susie was unbelievable. She sold 100 condos in two days, before we could even raise the prices. A sewer moratorium stopped construction after 72 units. But even when interest rates went up to 18 percent, Susie was able to close all 72 units."

Tom quickly saw that what he had was "a natural-born salesperson."

In fact, those first couple of days people were lining up to buy Harbor Woods units from Susie. One man was on his way to get donuts when he saw the line of people. Stopping to see why, he ended up being sold a unit by Susie. Afterward, the man told her, "What am I going to tell my wife? I was supposed to get donuts, and now I'm coming back as the new owner of a condo."

By the end of the week, she'd sold all but three units. As it got close to 5 p.m. that Friday, and she needed to pick up her son Drew from daycare, she called Tom to tell him that all but three units were sold and that she was heading out. "If that's all you can do, then fine," Wasdin said. He'd been a coach, and he knew how to motivate people, pushing the right buttons. It was certainly the right button with Susie. "I called my mom to pick up Drew and I stayed there until I sold those last three units," she said. "I was going to show him."

In the meantime, word quickly got around that Tom Wasdin had an attractive, personable, high-energy young woman selling units for him at Harbor Woods. Wasdin's soon to be ex-wife Millie, who was now working for a competitor, came and posed as a prospective buyer, just to see who this dynamite new employee was.

Little did Millie or even Tom know at the time, but this new employee named Susie would eventually take on a much bigger role.

Years later, Wasdin would joke to friends that he couldn't afford to pay Susie all her commission fees, so he decided to marry her. In reality, it happened innocently enough. Over Labor Day weekend, there was a party both had been invited to in South Merritt Island.

"Are you going?" Tom asked Susie one day.

"I don't know," she replied. "I don't have a date."

"I don't have a date, either," Tom said. "How about I chaperone you there and then you can go your way and I'll go mine?"

They agreed. It was a BYOB party, so they had to bring something. Susie suggested that instead of bringing Chivas Regal blended Scotch whisky, they bring J&B instead, because it was just as good but at two-thirds the cost. "That impressed me," Tom said. "She was always thinking about saving money."

After the party a group was going to the Holiday Inn for drinks.

"I wouldn't mind getting a drink," Susie said, "but I don't really want to go there."

They ended up at the ABC Lounge on Merritt Island, where Susie experienced Tom's dry sense of humor and he experienced her ability to take a tease and dish it right back.

When the waitress came to their table and asked what they were drinking, Tom said: "My favorite drink is a White Russian, but I don't want one tonight because it makes me horny."

Without missing a beat, Susie told the waitress: "Bring us two double White Russians, and keep them coming."

It was a fun night, talking, laughing, dancing.

"We slow danced that night," Susie said, "and I found out that Tom is quite the dancer."

A social friendship developed. Nothing serious. At least, not at first.

"We started meeting after work," Tom said. "She was dating other people and so was I."

Said Susie, "We even set each other up with our friends."

There was something different and special about Tom, though. Susie appreciated that he was always a gentleman, polite, mannerly, and interesting.

"He was just such a nice person," she said. "All my life I'd been around jocks and dated jocks. Jocks are usually not nice. They're so into themselves. Tom was not like those guys. He was also the hardest-working person I've ever been around. I learned so much from him. I didn't just learn the real estate and development business."

Eventually, as the years progressed, other girlfriends and boyfriends faded away, until the two were seeing each other exclusively.

"Susie became my best friend," Tom said.

They were doing a lot together – at work and away from work.

"We worked hard, and we played hard," Susie said.

Tom not only continued to be impressed with Susie's work ethic – if needed she would mix concrete, pour concrete and paint – but also with the way she managed money. Once, as a Christmas gift, he gave Susie ten one-hundred dollar bills and told her that he didn't know what to get her, but to go spend the money on something for herself.

"I don't think I'd ever seen a hundred-dollar bill before," she said.

Susie bought a few things at the Merritt Square Mall, nothing special, and then gave Tom almost $800 back, along with the receipts from what she'd purchased.

"That impressed me," he said. "Most women would have spent all the money."

For a while, Susie kept the relationship secret from her parents. She knew they had a tremendous amount of respect for the man they always called Coach Wasdin. But the age difference was almost 14 years, and she feared they wouldn't approve.

Meanwhile, from time to time Tom invited Susie's parents to some of the functions they would go to together.

"One time, he had four tickets to the Citrus Bowl and he invited my parents to come with us," Susie said. "My dad was a big beer drinker, and he found a tap somewhere in that stadium, beneath the stands. The next thing I know, he's coming down the stairs toward us with his beer. Then he tripped and fell. My father was a big man, 6-foot-4 and about 230 pounds, and he was just rolling down the stairs. Eventually he landed on his feet, still holding his beer upright."

The family and Tom all got along well together, so perhaps it shouldn't have been a surprise when later that week Susie's mom turned to her and said, "I think Tom Wasdin is the man for you."

The comment struck Susie, and it also comforted her. From then on, she didn't keep the relationship secret.

A wedding proposal didn't happen the usual way. In fact, Susie isn't too sure that a proper proposal ever really happened.

Once, as Drew was getting bigger and Susie was struggling to carry him, Tom said to her, "If he gets too big to where you can't carry him yourself, then maybe we ought to get married."

Tom had grown to love the boy, but he was also wary, given his experience as a stepdad with Millie's two boys. Once, when Susie came to his condo for a barbecue, wearing a bikini, Tom admits to being "knocked out" by how attractive she was. "At the same time," he said, "I realized it wasn't just this glamorous woman in a bikini. There was a child involved, and I took that seriously."

So they continued to move slowly, with little hints here and there about getting married.

Another time, while playing in the Mixed Club Championship at the Suntree Country Club, Susie needed to sink a putt in order for them to win the tournament.

"Susie," Tom said, "if you make this putt we'll get married."

"I rammed it in," Susie recalled, smiling.

One thing Susie liked about Tom was that he was always so thoughtful, but in a creative way. "He always had little gifts for me; he was always cool with surprises. One night at my condo, after I'd put Drew to bed, he pulled out this little box and gave it to me."

Inside was a ring with five stunning, marquise-cut diamonds.

"What's this?" she asked.

"What do you mean?" Tom replied. "It's your Christmas gift."

"Yeah, but what does *that* mean?"

"I thought we should get married," he said.

"So this is an engagement ring?"

"Well, yeah."

That following summer, on August 21, 1985, Tom and Susie married, tying the knot at sunset in Key West, about 1,000 yards off of Mallory Square on a well-appointed racing schooner, with a crew of 17, which was once owned by the Pulitzer family.

To Our Family & Friends

We would formally like to announce that we were married in Key West, Florida, August 21, 1985 at 8:28 p.m. as we watched the sun disappear in to the water. As the day ended, we began our wonderful life together as husband and wife.

We are happily settled in our new home at Suntree with our son, Drew. Please feel free to visit us, as our friends and family are very much in our thoughts each day.

Tom and Susie Wasdin

The wedding announcement Susie mailed *before* she and Tom Wasdin married in Key West, Florida

"Susie was smart," Tom said, laughing. "She mailed the announcements that we were married *before* we got married. That way, there was no backing out. Not that I wanted to. From the beginning we made a great pair. The coach and the cheerleader made a great team. Life was never the same again. It changed my life like it had never been changed before."

The boat, once owned by the Pulitzer family, where Tom and Susie Wasdin married.

The two became a power couple – *the* power couple – along the Space Coast, throwing themselves into business ventures, politics and philanthropy.

Andy Barber, for one, was not surprised. Barber had worked for Rick Stottler before venturing on his own. Later, he partnered with Wasdin for several years, creating the Wasdin/Barber Development Corp. After his frustrating experiences with Rick Stottler, Barber appreciated so much more working with Wasdin.

"Tom is a game-changer and a natural-born leader," Barber said. "He is versatile on many subjects, and he always seems to find a way out of any problem. I don't know how anybody but Tom could have survived and accomplished as much as he did in those Stottler Stagg years. Tom is a gentleman, and it's a true pleasure when I get to see him. He can inspire more in people than just about anybody else I know."

Wasdin's ability to inspire others would serve him and others well as he moved into the next chapter of his life. As it did – as he entered with his life partner Susie into the prime and most productive years of his life – it was also a time to reflect on those who had inspired and shaped him.

Chapter 17

REMEMBERING OLD ROOTS WHILE ESTABLISHING NEW ONES

"He was the guy. Tom Wasdin was it along the Space Coast. But Tom's very humble. For what he's done and to stay as humble as he has says something. But that's Tom. He's just a great people person. He'd be fine with governors or just sitting around a campfire." – Robin Turner

Even at the height of his career, Tom Wasdin never forgot his humble roots. Auntie and Uncle were getting up in years, with his Auntie Estelle suffering from heart problems. Auntie was Tom's father's sister. She and her husband took in young Tom and Dorothy after their mother died. Tom was only three months old at the time, and Dorothy was less than two years old.

"She was a wonderful mother," Tom said. "I could not have had a better one. Dorothy and I were very fortunate to have her raise us after our mother died. Even though we had very little money to buy clothes, she always managed to dress us properly. Our clothes were always clean. She was a great cook. We had fresh biscuits every morning for breakfast. Strawberry shortcake was my favorite dessert she made for us. She cooked the best fried chicken I've ever had in my life."

Late in Auntie's life, Tom visited her when she was in Shands Hospital in Gainesville.

"I told her how much she meant to me and that she was the only mother I ever had. I called her mother that day. In retrospect, I should have always called her mother, because that day when I called her mother she broke down and cried tears of joy. That's when I knew I should have been calling her mother all the time, and not Auntie."

It was the last time Tom saw his mother. Jewell Estelle Wasdin Gunter died not long after that, on July 10, 1989.

"I was so thankful that I was able to have that talk with her before she passed away," Tom said. "I have nothing but wonderful memories about her. I loved her very much."

As he got older, Tom saw more clearly how the adult figures he had in his life while growing up truly shaped him. His father's work ethic and business sense. Auntie's kindness and selfless love. And then there was Uncle, the last survivor.

"Uncle had the most influence on me of anyone in my life. He was strong, loving, caring and he always showed his love for me. When I was young, every night before I went to sleep, he always kissed me good night and told me how much he loved me. He set a great example for me to follow as a Christian man. He was the most sin-free person I ever met. He built his life around the Waldo Baptist Church. We had a prayer before every meal."

Uncle, who had remarried to a wonderful woman named Ellie May, had a tremendous desire to live. He told Tom and Dorothy he wanted to have a heart operation to repair a badly damaged valve, with the hope that it would improve the quality of his life. It was a risky surgery.

"We all have to go sometime," he told Tom the night before the surgery, adding that "not waking up from surgery is a good way to go, if that's how God wants me to go."

Uncle never made it through the surgery, waking up only long enough to recognize Ellie May, Tom and Dorothy and then falling back asleep, never to awaken again. Eventually, Ellie May, Tom and Dorothy consented to have Uncle taken off life support. "He passed away shortly after that," Tom said. "He earlier told me he was ready to die and I think we did what we thought he would have wanted us to do. It was a very sad day for me. My best friend, my father and the most influential person in my life was gone."

Dorothy asked her brother to speak at Uncle's funeral. Tom did, but it was extremely difficult.

"I broke down a few times," he said. "The only thing that made it possible to speak was that I knew he was where he wanted to be. I told everyone that day that he was a Christian's Christian. I also thanked him for being the greatest father a son could have ever had."

Again Tom reflected, now as an adult, just exactly how much he'd been shaped and influenced.

"I learned so much from him. Even today, I think of him often. His high standards are hard for me to live up to. The way he treated others was a great example for me. I never heard him use profanity. He always went out of his way to help others. Probably the most important thing I learned from him was the way he treated others when they disappointed him. He still forgave them. I know I sometimes disappointed him, but he always forgave me. He once told me that one of the greatest blessings God gave him and Auntie was giving them Dorothy and me. Only as I get older do I realize what a blessing he was to me. He could not have loved us more. He and Auntie were one of the greatest blessings we have ever had."

The influence, of course, was real. Again and again, people who worked for and did business with Tom Wasdin were struck by how positive and encouraging and forgiving he always was.

Doc Kelley saw that early on, when he was brought in to run businesses and do things on the Pier that he never thought he could do, had it not been for Wasdin's encouragement and unfailing belief in him.

Robin Turner saw those traits early, as well.

"I never went to college, but I graduated from the University of Wasdin," he said. "He taught me a lot. We had a great relationship and I came to love and respect him. One of Tom's sayings was that when you walk in a room it's more important for people to know who you are than for you to know who they are."

That only happens if you've networked and gotten to know people *before* you need to know them.

"He'd also say that it was better for people to brag about you rather than you being the one who was talking about yourself."

Turner was one of those people who would brag about Wasdin, telling him that he was the most powerful person in the county. Wasdin had a hard time believing it, though.

"Oh, he was *the* guy," Turner insisted. "Tom Wasdin was *it* along the Space Coast. But Tom's very humble. For what he's done and to stay as humble as he has says something. But that's Tom. He's just a great people person. He'd be fine with governors or just sitting around a campfire."

One of the more ambitious projects that Wasdin, Stottler and Turner took on was the old Cocoa Stadium, which used to house the Houston Astros during spring training, as well as fielding a Class A minor league team. The facility had become rundown, but Wasdin and Stottler saw potential. In 1984, they paid the City of Cocoa a million dollars for the property. They put $200,000 down and paid $80,000 a year for 10 years, without interest.

It was a massive undertaking. The property was 50 acres, housing Cocoa Stadium and its 5,000 seats, four additional baseball fields, a 100-room dormitory, a cafeteria, meeting rooms and eventually four multipurpose athletic fields. It was, however, the one venture in all his years in business that made Wasdin feel like he was back in sports. But he quickly saw, too, that it was a business. First of all, they had to sue the Houston Astros to force them to honor their lease.

"Not only were they not meeting the terms of their lease, someone also broke into the facility in the middle of the night," Wasdin said. "We suspect it was them. There was missing equipment and evidence of vandalism. After that, we settled our lawsuit for $80,000."

It wasn't an easy lawsuit to litigate. The Astros had retained Philip F. Nohrr, a high-powered and well-respected Brevard County attorney, as their legal counsel. Meanwhile, Wasdin and his associates retained Joe D. Matheny, who was no legal slouch in his own right.

After the lawsuit was successfully litigated, they got down to the work of renovating and upgrading the facility. Wasdin renamed it Cocoa Expo. They brought in Joe Brinkman's Umpire School, Clint Hurdle's Big League baseball academy and various AAU and college sporting events. Eventually they also brought in the Brevard County Fair, which was Turner's brainstorm – a successful annual venture that routinely brought in big-name music acts like Willie Nelson, The Charlie Daniels Band, Carlos Santana, Bad Company, ZZ Top, The Judds, .38 Special, The Allman Brothers, Beach Boys, Mel Tillis and others.

It also was Cocoa Expo that an expansion MLB team – the Florida Marlins – targeted when they needed a short-term spring training facility. Stottler always marveled at Wasdin's marketing skills, as well as his ability to bring people together. Of all his manifold strengths, those were maybe the most impressive. Perhaps part of Stottler's admiration was because those were two areas where he struggled. It seemed a no-brainer to have the Marlins at Cocoa Expo for a year, while their new facility in Viera was built. But Stottler's stubbornness in working out an agreement grated on the new franchise until negotiations broke down. Desperate, County Commissioner Sue Schmitt came to Wasdin and asked if he would replace Stottler and resume negotiations with the Marlins and their representative, Richard Anderson. Wasdin did, and the two successfully negotiated a contract, with the Marlins playing their historic first spring training at the historic Cocoa Stadium.

Through the years, there were many other business ventures and developments. Some turned out well and were very successful. Among them were:

- The aforementioned Brevard County Fair. It was 1986 when Wasdin and his group received the charter for the fair from the Florida Department of Agriculture. At the time, Wasdin's cousin, Doyle Connor, was Florida's Commissioner of Agriculture.
- Kennedy Point Yacht Club & Marina. Located on the Indian River in south Titusville, it was a nice upscale community. The development, built in 1985, had 92 boat slips, a pool, clubhouse, and a pair of tennis and racquetball courts. When popular astronaut Deke Slayton retired, Wasdin hired him to be its spokesperson.

And some were not so successful. Among those were:

- Lake Harney Woods. The development, started in 1985 in South Volusia County, was a large rural subdivision with 10-acre lots. But lot sales were slow and the project was eventually taken over by American Bank.
- A joint venture with the Northwest Savings and Loan Association out of Spencer, Iowa proved to be another failure. The financial institution had a number of projects in 1985 that seemed promising, but they also had deep financial trouble, which eventually did everything in. "All of our projects failed because they ran out of funds to complete the projects," Wasdin said. "Also, sales were slow because of the Challenger shuttle disaster and a change in tax laws on second homes."

Looking back, 1985 was probably his busiest and most climactic year. There were a plate-load of projects and, of course, Tom's marriage to Susie. It was also the year the Wasdin Group, Inc., was established. It was a semi-break from Rick Stottler and it gave Susie and Tom, who was 50 at the time, their own company to build homes in the bustling new Suntree area of Brevard County, just north of Melbourne.

"Susie was selling homes for Fairfield, the owners of Suntree," Tom recalled. "She was highly successful and making a lot of money. But she was unhappy with a lot of the homes that were being built by the Suntree builders. In her opinion, most of them didn't suit the needs of a wife."

"They were nice homes, well-built, but they left a lot to be desired," Susie said. "They did things like put brown carpet next to gray carpet. There'd be no pantries, or not near enough closet space. I just saw how they could do things better."

Finally, after hearing Susie complain once more about how the houses were designed, Tom told her, "If you know so much and you think you can do better, why don't you build homes?"

So she did. Not only did her first few homes sell immediately, over the next few years, Susie designed, sold and built over 150 custom homes in Brevard County.

"I'd never built anything in my life, but before long I couldn't go out to eat without drawing floor plans on napkins," she said. "I had simple, basic concepts – one-story houses, open and airy, a kitchen pantry, a great room concept, beautiful bathrooms, his and her closets, and a pool option with a great view of the pool if you decided to have one."

Susie also had a knack for taking areas that were an afterthought, or perhaps had no thought attached to them, and devising ways to accentuate them, thereby creating a wow factor. She took bathroom mirrors and had TV sets built into them. Little nooks and crannies and different niches suddenly became areas with unique decorative touches and designs.

Toward the goal of becoming elite and unique home builders, Tom and Susie worked well together.

"Tom was a master at selecting lots, with at-site selection," Susie said. "He can see it before it's done. And I was doing the floor plans. We were building all over the county. People were coming into developments, specifically saying, 'We want a Wasdin model.' We were proud of what we built. We always lived where we built. A lot of

A brochure cover featuring a high-end custom home that Susie Wasdin designed and built.

builders won't do that. We did. We built very good homes. And back in the late '80s we were building houses as fast as we could put them up."

It was really a family affair, too.

Said Tom, "It was around that same time that my son, Steve Wasdin, graduated from BYU and joined the Wasdin Group to handle construction."

From his third marriage, Wasdin had learned some lessons on being a stepparent, and in 1993 he adopted Susie's son Drew. It was actually Drew's desire to have his stepdad become his adopted father. He was about 14 years old then, and their bond had become that close.

"I viewed him as my dad," Drew said. "He was my role model, my mentor, my coach, the one I looked up to as a father. My real dad, my biological dad, I only saw a couple of times a year. When I told him that I wanted Tom to adopt me, he didn't have a problem with that. In fact, he was receptive. He admired and respected Tom and how he'd raised me and what I'd become."

Drew sensed that Tom had latched onto him in ways that he had missed with his own biological children. One of those areas was sports – both playing them with Drew and teaching them. No matter where they lived, the Wasdin home had a basketball goal. "It wouldn't be one of those cheaper ones that you role up to your driveway," Drew said. "We always had a glass backboard with an in-ground pole where we'd dig a hole, pour the concrete mix and add water."

In addition, the Wasdin home was always the hub of youthful activity, a magnet for the neighborhood kids, playing sports. As always, there Tom would be, filling that familiar role as a coach again, all the while cajoling, encouraging, teaching ... and sometimes playing. Said Drew, "He was always there to fill in that gap if we needed an extra player."

Often, Drew and Tom played one-on-one basketball. "He'd never let me win," Drew said. "Finally, one time, and I'll never forget it, I beat him in one-on-one. I was in either the 6th or 7th grade. It was exhilarating." Even now, the memory makes Drew smile. "Dad won't admit that I was that young when I beat him for the first time," he said. "But I was."

Not letting Drew win was a good lesson early in life for the boy. Sometimes, that lesson also proved to be a painful one – literally.

"There was a time when I was about 14 years old," Drew recalled, "when I was begging him to get boxing gloves, and he kept asking me, 'Are you sure? Are you sure you want to do this?'"

Drew was sure. Or at least he thought he was.

"He got the boxing gloves and we put them on, just messing around," Drew said. "Dad got one or two punches in, and then I got one right on the nose. That's when I'd had enough. It was a pretty quick event. Once again, he wasn't going to let me win."

It was around that time that Drew began to realize that his father was not like the other fathers. His father knew sports, and not simply on a superficial level. He *really* knew sports.

"He knew so much more than the other fathers," Drew said. "He never coached me directly, but I could see that my coaches respected him and would listen to him if he offered advice. Because of him, I became passionate about sports, pursuing it to be good at it and not just for something to do. He was always making sure I went to camps, especially basketball camps. Over the course of a summer, I'd go from Brevard Community College to Stetson to Florida State and as far as Michigan for basketball camps."

But Drew could only play sports as long as he kept his grades up. Tom didn't expect him to be a straight-A student, but he did want him to maintain a 3.0 grade point average. Even when he was a student at the University of Florida, Drew maintained a 3.0 GPA or better.

And wherever Drew was playing, Tom and Susie were always there.

Sometimes that required juggling, and a clear sense of priorities. Drew recalled how he was supposed to be at a church camp one summer. During the week of the camp, he also had a soccer match and baseball game scheduled – both on the same day.

"I just assumed that I wouldn't do the church camp," Drew said. "But church was always important to my father. He arranged it so they could take me to the soccer match and the baseball game, while not having to miss the whole church camp because of it. It took a lot of logistics and several hours of driving, but he did it, and they had me back to church camp that night."

Tom often took Drew on trips with him and Susie to the NCAA Final Four in men's basketball, providing some special memories.

"I kind of sensed that because he missed so much with his own children when they were growing up, separated from him and living far away, that he got to do things with me as his son, especially sports, and that he enjoyed it."

Not that there weren't the rough spots that parents and children normally have, especially when it's a stepparent and a stepchild.

"When Drew was about 10," Tom recalled, "I'd come home from work and Susie would be crying because of things Drew was doing. I knew from my earlier experience that I couldn't be the main, or sole, disciplinarian. So the next time it happened, I called both Susie and Drew to me. I told Drew that the next time I came home and saw his mom crying I was going to give him a spanking that he would take to his grave. And then I told Susie she was going to have to watch me spank Drew. Well, he didn't want that spanking and Susie didn't want to see him get spanked. After that, it never happened again. They took care of it themselves. But the most important thing I learned from my earlier marriage is that you have to show them love."

And he did. In Drew, Tom now had a boy he could both mold and show him the kind of love that every boy needs, especially from a father.

"Dad had the greatest influence on my life," Drew Wasdin said, years later. "Not only was he my dad, he was also my coach, teacher and the best friend I have ever had. He has always been there for me, as I would be for him. I love you, Dad."

Even as they were raising children and stepchildren, Tom and Susie continued to work together on several new business projects. Most did very well, but there were some setbacks.

In 1988, they teamed with Andy Barber to build The Lakes of Ridge Manor on Merritt Island, and it was very successful. In 1996, they developed Bay Point along the Indian River in Titusville, purchasing the condominium project from the FDIC, and then closing on enough units to pay off the FDIC and pocket the profits from six units free and clear. Later, Tom's old friend Joe Williams purchased a unit and lived there with his family.

It was in 1996 when the Wasdin Group, Inc., at the urging of Tom's son Steve, opened an office in Dade County to rebuild homes destroyed by Hurricane Andrew. "It was a bad mistake," Tom recalled. "We lost $200,000, and that's when my son Steve left the Wasdin Group. I learned that it's hard to do business in Dade County if you're not Hispanic. The building officials were all of Hispanic descent. We even hired bilingual office staff to try and compete. But it didn't work. We left South Florida and changed the name to Wasdin Associates, Inc."

Because of his upbringing, and the summers he would spend with his father at construction sites, Steve grew up to love the construction and development business. But he was young and Susie was Tom's wife and the two strong personalities often clashed.

"In retrospect, I should have made Susie the boss," Tom said. "That was my fault."

Said Steve, "I had great ambitions as a young person, fresh out of college, and I probably had a lot of opinions."

He also had a lot of pressure.

"When you're Tom Wasdin's son it increases the pressure to do great things," he said. "For a lot of reasons, I was under a tremendous amount of pressure. It was my decision to leave. It was painful. I just about broke emotionally."

Steve later went on to become very successful in the construction and the development business. And the longer he's been in the business, the more he marvels at his father's success and how he achieved the things he has.

"My father is a very honest man," Steve said. "He taught me honesty early in life. I was about 5 or 6, and I had my dad's car keys, playing with them. He told me to be careful, that those keys were important. Well, I wound up throwing them onto a second story window sill. Later, when he asked me where the keys were, I lied to him."

For that, little Steve was disciplined.

"He did so very lovingly," Steve said. "He spanked me, but he was very much under control. Because of that little thing, it increased my sense of right and wrong, of being honest. Our industry brings out a lot of dishonest practices. Often you see the most dishonest people thriving, and it's frustrating to see. But I always saw in my dad that at no point did he ever entertain any thought of doing anything dishonest. That has always stuck with me. Other things, too. My father has been a walking example his entire life of discipline, work ethic, a very direct sense of integrity, thriftiness ... and I absolutely subscribe to all those traits in my life. I worship my father. He's still my hero."

As the years went on, Steve and Susie's relationship not only mended, but bonded.

"We get along very well now," Susie said.

As that relationship improved, Tom's relationship with Rick Stottler deteriorated. For various reasons, and not just because he was doing more projects on his own, Wasdin and Stottler drifted apart. Stottler was getting involved in more businesses, and with other people – both of which made Wasdin uncomfortable. There were times when there were projects that Wasdin, Stottler and Charlie Moehle all had a third ownership in, only to have Stottler buy out Moehle and thus leave Wasdin virtually voiceless regarding business decisions on those projects. The biggest rift that developed between the two old friends is that they didn't see eye-to-eye on an English soccer player named Giles Malone, whom Stottler housed when Malone was an exchange student at Cocoa Beach High School, and then later coached with him at

Florida Tech. Malone became a Stottler protégé, whom Rick eventually brought in to help run some of his business ventures.

"My relationship with Rick changed drastically after he brought in Giles Malone," Wasdin said. "It seemed that he and Giles were running most of our companies, and as a minority owner I had very little influence or say. Not just that, it was also becoming harder for me to know exactly what was going on financially with our companies. He was opening side businesses with other people that were hurting our business. I had a lot of assets with Rick, but as a minority owner I could do little about it. It was time to get out."

Robin Turner, Wasdin's old employee-turned-friend had recently separated from Stottler, starting a string of fairs in the Northeast along with other business ventures that made him a millionaire. Turner knew well what Wasdin was going through with Stottler, which was the reason why he had severed his relationship with him.

"Stottler was unethical and very sneaky," Turner said. "You could never trust him. There was no loyalty to anybody. He was always screwing people. Tom's not like that. In all the years I've known Tom, I've never met anyone who disliked him. With those leg irons that were his partnership with Rick Stottler, you'd have thought that there would have been some guilt by association. But none of Rick's reputation stuck with Tom. That tells you how strong he is."

Strong, yes. But Tom Wasdin wasn't getting any younger. It was 1998 and Wasdin was closing in on his 63rd birthday. The pain near his jaw that he thought was a toothache was diagnosed as Trigeminal Neuralgia, an excruciatingly painful disorder known as the suicide disease. It was affecting him and it wasn't getting better, even driving him to the brink of taking his life.

"I was having serious health issues and I knew that no one lives forever," he said. "I needed to plan long-term, and I needed to be debt free. It was time to do my financial planning for the rest of my life. I wanted to have my assets under my control. I also wanted to plan for my retirement, but Rick didn't see the need for financial planning. He'd tell me not to worry, that he'd take care of things and make sure I had no financial problems. But I had more confidence in me taking care of my financial planning than I did Rick. There were just too many of his actions at the time that made me question his intent."

The two old friends talked about parting ways and Stottler offered Wasdin $1 million – $100,000 a year over 10 years from the Cocoa Beach Pier profits – to make a clean break. Wasdin, however, knew it wasn't enough. He also knew, sadly, that this wasn't going to end amicably.

"I could see that we weren't going to work it out without a lawsuit. So Susie and I set aside $100,000 for attorney fees. We also made sure that we had built up enough of a nest egg so that whatever the outcome was with Rick, it wasn't going to interfere with our ability to financially be able to retire. Then we hired Jim Fallace, who was the best attorney I could find to handle a suit against Rick. It was time to do it. I wasn't getting any younger."

It was a sad end to their long relationship, one that went all the way back to 1963, when Rick Stottler was walking down the hallways at Cocoa Beach High School looking for this new guy, Tom Wasdin, to coach his adult league basketball team. All the late nights playing pinball and cards, talking about life; the years when Tom would return to manage the Pier; all the basketball games Stottler came to at Jacksonville University, cheering the Dolphins; the years playing softball together, with Rick often the pitcher and Tom the catcher; Wasdin's marriage to Millie at Rick's house; all their business ventures together.

And now this.

Talking to each other through lawyers.

Wasdin's attorney, Jim Fallace, recommended a settlement figure that he thought they could get, noting that Stottler was embroiled in another lawsuit and also highly leveraged. They met in Fallace's office, and the attorney wrote the Wasdins' offer on a chalkboard for Stottler and his attorney, Joe Miniclier, to see. Stottler's reaction was immediate and angry.

"No way! No way!" he said, as he stormed out of the office.

But two days later, Joe Miniclier called to say Stottler had accepted the offer.

"We received cash and the Kennedy Point Yacht Club & Marina, debt free, and Rick received everything else and all associated debt," Wasdin said. "I was happy with the settlement and I think he was, too. I could have gotten more, but it had debt associated with it."

In later years, the two men patched up their friendship. After a prolonged battle with Parkinson's Disease, Rick Stottler died on December 2, 2010.

"I have only good memories of what we accomplished, the good times and the many good things about Rick," Wasdin said. "I sometimes think, 'What if?'"

At the time, though, he had other things to think about. The Trigeminal Neuralgia was getting worse, and after exhausting all medical procedures and possible solutions, he could only see one thing that was left to do.

Possibly take his life.

Chapter 18

IN BATTLE WITH A BEAST

"I thought my life was over. In fact, I considered ending my life many times. But because of my faith in God and the support of my loving wife, Susie, as well as the support from my friends and family, I learned a valuable lesson of not ever giving up." – Tom Wasdin

It felt like a scratch, a slight crawl of pain across Tom Wasdin's cheek. Maybe it was a toothache, perhaps a cavity or a cracked tooth. At worse, he thought he might need a root canal. It wasn't *that* bad. But it was there. A scratch of pain. Little did Wasdin realize the magnitude of the horrific beast behind the claw that was causing the scratch.

It all began shortly after Wasdin began his new life, in 1975, when he was with Stottler Stagg & Associates and the firm won an award for design and construction management for their work on the United States Bicentennial Exhibition of Space and Technology at the Kennedy Space Center. The pain came and went, noticeable but hardly unmanageable. At a routine checkup with his dentist, Dr. L. Wayne Robben in Cocoa Beach, Wasdin explained to him the feeling, telling his dentist it was akin to an electrical shock on the left side of his mouth.

"It's like sparklers going off in my mouth," Wasdin told Dr. Robben. "Sparklers that are causing some pain."

Dr. Robben poked around, prodding into different areas of Wasdin's mouth, but found nothing wrong. But something *was* wrong. Over the next several months, the pain appeared more frequently and with increasing measures of intensity. Early in 1976, Wasdin went to Dr. Robben again. On a scale of 1 to 10, he estimated the pain at about a 2. Again, noticeable but still manageable. Dr. Robben sent him to a specialist who performed gum surgery, a painful and unpleasant experience that took three weeks from which to heal. It made Wasdin's gums healthier, but it didn't make the pain go away. In fact, it was getting worse – stronger in intensity and longer in duration.

"It would last for about a second or two," Wasdin said. "And it was getting strong enough to take my attention away from whatever I was doing. It was like mashing my finger two or three times a day."

By now, he had discerned that this unknown Beast was a trigger pain, and something that built up over time, exploding in a burst of pain, and then receding for a short while. The triggers were eating, coughing, yawning, swallowing ... basically any muscle movement that involved his mouth; including smiling.

But this was obviously nothing to smile about.

Dr. Robben sent Wasdin to another specialist, who did a root canal. But again it did nothing to stop the steady progression of pain.

Out of local options and ideas, Dr. Robben referred Wasdin to the University of Florida's Department of Dentistry. The doctors there suspected that it might be nerve damage at the roof of Wasdin's mouth, so they did surgery, cutting and peeling back the roof of his mouth to see if anything was wrong. Nothing was. Nothing, that is, except that when the Novocain wore off the Beast came back. The only thing the surgery accomplished was to fill Wasdin with a mouthful of stitches.

By now the pain on a scale to 10 was bouncing between 3 and 4. He saw a chiropractor, got acupuncture, was analyzed by a specialist in Orlando for a new condition that people were talking about – TMJ, which is a dysfunction of the temporomandibular joint. The specialist diagnosed Wasdin with a bite problem and fitted him with a mouth guard that Wasdin wore 24 hours a day, every day, for several weeks. The pain got worse. The Beast was starting to roar.

Nothing improved the situation. But even as the pain increased, Wasdin's hope didn't wane. He went on two different types of drugs, but instead of helping to manage the pain, they had a tranquilizing effect while also causing tremors. In fact, the tremors stayed with him, even years after he stopped taking the medication. His overall health started suffering. Even his normal exercise routine could cause problems. If Wasdin was jogging, he could trigger the pain; a pain so intense he'd have to stop and endure it until it subsided. Some people, when they're engaged in physical activity, experience a cramp in their calf or hamstring. Wasdin thought to himself that this is exactly what it felt like when the burst of pain visited the left side of his face. It was like a cramp, something you'd feel coming, try to stop, but couldn't. It would then grip his face as if it were on fire, or being electrocuted, while subsequently being hacked by an ice pick. It would shoot up into the side of his face, until his whole head felt as if it were in an unrelenting vice grip of unspeakable and unrelenting pain.

Wasdin got to where he could hide it. If he was making a presentation to the county commission, he'd divert attention by pretending to pick up a piece of paper. "I got good at covering it up," he said. "Only a few people knew about it. Millie, when we were married, then Susie, Rick Stottler, and a few friends. But that was about it. I didn't want people to worry about me."

It was in 1980 when Dr. Robben gave Wasdin an article written by Dr. Albert L. Rhoton, Jr., from the University of Florida Department of Neurological Surgery. The article explained a condition called Trigeminal Neuralgia, or TN. It also used the term tic douloureux. Dr. Robben suggested to Wasdin that he call Dr. Rhoton. He also added, "I hope it's not Trigeminal Neuralgia."

It was about this time when Wasdin began marketing services for Stottler Stagg & Associates, while also studying for his general contractor's license. He was building Beach Woods and Ocean Woods and preparing to begin construction on Harbor Woods. It was the same year that he and Millie got divorced and he hired a new VP of Marketing for Harbor Woods – Susie Thortsen, the former cheerleader from his days teaching at Cocoa Beach High who would later become his wife. Wasdin's children from his second marriage – Steve and Lori – were staying with him at Chateau By The Sea during the summer. He was 45, in his prime.

"Life was wonderful," Wasdin said, "except for the growing pain."

He called Dr. Rhoton in his Gainesville office and the doctor prescribed a drug called Tegretol, instructing Wasdin to call him back a few days after taking the medication. The effect was immediate. Within 24 hours, the Beast went away. For the first time in five years, Wasdin was completely pain-free. It was good news. And bad.

On the phone again with Dr. Rhoton, Wasdin excitedly told him the pain had stopped.

Dr. Rhoton replied with the words that would change Wasdin's life. "I think you have Trigeminal Neuralgia."

Later, Wasdin would learn that Trigeminal Neuralgia is called the "Suicide Disease." He would also understand why.

"Those spasms of pain are probably the most intense pain known to man," Dr. Rhoton said. "It's like a lightning strike. I've been with hundreds of patients when they've had an episode, and seen them screaming in agony."

Immediately, Dr. Rhoton scheduled Wasdin for an appointment in his office. The initial game plan was to manage TN with whatever effective dose of Tegretol was required.

Wasdin assumed the Tegretol would simply be something he'd take the rest of his life. End of pain. Bye bye Beast. No problem. But gradually, over months, the dose of Tegretol kept increasing to the point that it affected just about everything in Wasdin's life. He felt like a zombie, lethargic, groggy and foggy, his memory suddenly spotty and his concentration nowhere near what it used to be.

"I felt like a computer that was overloaded and took longer to process information," he said.

Always a workhorse who put in yeoman's days on the job, Wasdin found himself working even longer hours to compensate for Tegretol's side effects. If not for his acute organizational skills and ingrained habits of keeping action items, Wasdin would've failed. For sure. As it was, few people around him detected even a hint of a problem.

After starting at a low dose of Tegretol – about 100mg a day – Wasdin was soon up to a staggering 1,600mg a day. It particularly startled him when he read in a book about TN not to take more than 1,200mg of Tegretol a day.

"I didn't like taking all that medication," he said. "But I sure didn't like the pain, either."

By 1983, the pain was worse – much worse. The Beast was vicious, relentless. On a scale to 10, if he didn't take his medication, the pain was now at 7 or 8.

But Wasdin couldn't continue taking the medication, not at those enormous doses. He consulted with Dr. Rhoton, who was alarmed at how much Tegretol that Wasdin was taking. "An elephant couldn't be standing after taking that much Tegretol," he said. Dr. Rhoton explained what few options there were at the time. Wasdin decided on Microvascular Decompression – or MVD. If MVD was successful – and statistics at the time showed that it was in 80 percent of patients – Wasdin would not only be drug-free, but pain-free.

It was not risk-free, though. This was serious brain surgery, taking out a chunk of bone at the base of his cranium. But it seemed like the last resort, and the situation was getting desperate. In December of 1983, Wasdin checked into Shands Hospital at the University of Florida in Gainesville.

In the recovery room, Tom overheard one of the nurses say, "Don't worry about him. He isn't going to make it."

The nurse was talking about another patient, but Wasdin didn't know that.

"I thought she was talking about me," he said. "I thought I was going to die."

He spent 10 days post-operation in the hospital, eventually returning to work on a part-time basis three weeks after the surgery. Susie Thortsen, who was now in a serious relationship with Tom, helped him recover.

Weeks went by without any pain. A month. Two months. Wasdin could hardly believe it. The surgery was painful, as was the recovery process. But it was worth it. And then, one day, about three months down the road, Wasdin felt that sharp scratch of pain again, in all its raging intensity. The Beast was back.

"It was," he said, "one of the most disappointing days of my life."

He trudged forward with work. In 1984, Wasdin was part of a group that bought Cocoa Stadium from the City of Cocoa and per Wasdin's suggestion renamed it Cocoa Expo, Inc. A fair charter was secured and preparations moved forward to organize the Brevard County Fair at Cocoa Expo.

After consulting with Dr. Rhoton again, Wasdin decided to try another procedure – radiofrequency lesioning, or RFL. The benefits from such a surgery were temporary, lasting on average about a year. Basically, RFL numbed the nerve and thus the pain, creating the aftereffects of a Novocain shot that didn't wear off. If Wasdin couldn't live with the numbness, the nerve and its feeling would come back. But so would the pain. He reasoned that the procedure was worth going through, and it would take about a year to see how well it worked.

Susie knew he'd been in pain, but didn't appreciate just how much. "Tom is a master at hiding it," she said. "When we first started dating, he didn't speak about it. I had no idea how devastating it was."

Sure enough, the surgery stopped the pain while also leaving Wasdin with 24/7 numbness over much of the left side of his face. But he could live with that. If it drove the Beast away, he would welcome the tradeoff. About a year later, though, as the nerve regenerated, the numbness dissipated, and the Beast returned. So Dr. Rhoton did the same procedure again, only this time he went deeper into the nerve to create a longer benefit. And this time, he went into two branches of the trigeminal nerve. It worked, for a while. But eventually the numbness wore off, and the pain returned, worse than before.

Initially, they tried to control the pain with Tegretol. But when that stopped being as effective, causing Wasdin to increase the dosage to the point where there were severe side effects, he consulted again with Dr. Rhoton. They decided to perform another RFL procedure – only this time going deeper. Again, it rendered most of the left side of his face perpetually numb. But again, it chased the Beast away, lasting this time for about five years. As the pain crept back, Wasdin returned to Tegretol for some relief.

Life went on.

During that time, Tom and Susie married in 1985, and shortly afterward he adopted her son, Drew. Meanwhile, his own son from his second marriage, Steve, joined the Wasdin Group, Inc. Workwise, Wasdin was appointed to the Space Coast Tourist Development Council. He was busy, productive and enjoying life to the full again. The perpetual numbness on the left side of his face was a constant nuisance. He couldn't tell if food was dribbling out of the corner of his mouth, or if his left nostril was running. But he was pain-free and it was worth it, allowing him to fully throw himself into his life and work.

"I had no idea how heavily involved Tom was in leadership and community service and construction," Dr. Rhoton said. "All those years I was seeing him, I didn't realize all the work he was doing in the community. When I think about it, I'm just amazed, with all that he was going through, that he was able to manage business affairs and continue in civic activities, construction, and giving to others. It's a great tribute to him, and to Susie, who helped him manage his way through this."

But that was Tom Wasdin. He figured he could fight and find a way. But the Beast had other ideas.

In 1989, when the pain returned, intense and as excruciating as ever, Wasdin decided to try medication again, despite the side effects. But the side effects were just as bad, if not worse, than ever before. His quality of life and ability to work suffered. Again, he returned to Dr. Rhoton for another RFL procedure on the left side of his face, this time covering all three trigeminal branches. Again, he dealt with the constant numbness, only this time it was not on most of the left side of his face – it was on the *entire* left side; including the left side of gums and tongue.

Then, in 1993, a scratch clawed on the other side – the right side – of his face. It couldn't be, could it? Bilateral Trigeminal Neuralgia is an extremely rare condition. It's almost as if the pain is piling on, unmerciful and unforgiving. Wasdin again turned to Tegretol, gradually increasing the dosage to match the increasing severity of pain.

It affected him, but didn't stop him. During this time, Wasdin was President of Florida's Amateur Athletic Union, or AAU. He was involved in moving the AAU's national headquarters to Disney World in Orlando. He also received the national President's Award for the AAU. Closer to home, he was chairman of Keep Brevard Beautiful, and given the KBB's Pelly Award.

But the Tegretol was draining him, and in 1995, he submitted to another RFL procedure, this time on the right side of his face, targeting two branches of his trigeminal nerve. Though it stopped the pain, it now meant that two-thirds of the right side of his face was also perpetually numb, including his entire mouth and tongue.

The only feeling he had remaining was on the lower third of the right side of his face. Wasdin had to learn to talk again and also how to chew. Occasionally, in doing that, he'd bite the inside of his cheek and not know it until he could taste the blood. But even his taste wasn't what it once was. It was muted. He also lost some of his hearing. Any kind of feeling on his lips, gums and most of his face was gone. It wasn't uncommon, when Wasdin drank, to spill the liquid on himself. Since his nose was numb, something as simple as blowing his nose became a challenge. He had to constantly concentrate on chewing his food, hampered as he was now because of the inability to move his jaw from side to side.

Meanwhile, the Tegretol wasn't working and the pain was hitting a full 10.

Out of frustration, Tom told Susie, "I wish you could take some of this Tegretol, so you could know what it does to your body." Another time, he said, "I wish people could feel this pain one time, to know what it's like."

Not only was Wasdin living with inhumane pain – fully realizing why Trigeminal Neuralgia is also called the "Suicide Disease" – he was constantly battling with the side effects of the Tegretol. One time, so groggy and unsteady, he fell face forward, his head crashing into a coffee table. Susie lived in constant fear that another sudden fall like that might kill him.

What she didn't know is that her husband was considering a deliberate death.

In 1998, fearing that he was out of options, fighting despondency, he faced the prospect that if his one remaining trigeminal nerve, full of pain, was also numbed, it would effectively end his ability to eat solid food, talk or basically function. There was even a possibility that he could have total numbness all over his face *and* the hellish pain.

Wasdin visited his pastor, Dr. Gary Spencer, at the Suntree Methodist Church in Florida.

"What does the Bible say about suicide?" he asked.

Dr. Spencer couldn't help noticing how startlingly sad Wasdin was, dispirited. What he didn't know is that Wasdin had researched, and learned, that in 1994, Oregon had passed Ballot Measure 16, which for all intents legalized physician-assisted suicide. Like the old coach that he was, Wasdin was formulating a game plan.

"He was very somber," Dr. Spencer recalled. "The tone in his voice, the look in his eyes, everything about him was serious. It wasn't Tom. Not the Tom that I knew. This was a man who was always upbeat, positive, jovial. I'd never seen him down. And now he's asking me about suicide."

Dr. Spencer explained to Wasdin that the Bible didn't address suicide. He shared with him the sixth commandment, which was "thou shall not kill," knowing that he didn't need to spell out the scripture in that it also could be interpreted as forbidding someone to take their own life. At the same time, he also explained that God cares for each of us individually, and doesn't want us to suffer.

"This pain," Wasdin said, before pausing. "I'm telling you, this pain ... there are times if I had a gun I'd shoot myself. Sometimes it goes away for a couple of hours, sometimes a couple of minutes. Gary, I don't know if I can continue with this thing."

Wasdin's mouth barely moved when he spoke. It was part of what he had to learn to do when he learned to speak again. He was 23 years down the road from when this Trigeminal Neuralgia inflicted its first scratch of pain on him.

"Tom," Dr. Spencer said. "If you ever get close to doing what you're talking about, I want you to promise you'll give me a call."

Wasdin promised.

At the same time, he didn't fear death. He just feared displeasing God.

"I've always been a man of faith, and I don't think death is the worst thing that can happen to you," he said. "Being able to go to sleep and not wake up did not seem like a bad option."

Even physicians can understand that line of thinking.

"It's the most intense pain that a human being can experience," Dr. Rhoton said. "When you combine that with the inability to get it under control, you do see how people can consider that it's better off to be dead."

But Wasdin didn't want to check out. He loved life too much. Still, he knew he had to figure out a way to get his life back.

"I never came to terms with suicide," he said. "It was an option I considered. I knew that was an option in Oregon, to go to sleep one night and not wake up. It was on the table. But I knew I couldn't put my family through that."

Two years later, in 2000, Wasdin's worst concerns became a reality. The pain appeared in the third and final branch on the right side of his face. Through the years, he'd tried everything – from medical science to surgeries to various alternative methods to manage the pain. He'd been on something called a pain-free diet. In fact, it was while on this diet that the Wasdins were invited to Governor Jeb Bush's inauguration.

"Everything we did, we did together," Susie said. "So we were both on the diet, bringing our own food with us wherever we went.

When they were checking into the Double Tree Hotel in Tallahassee on a cold, January day, Susie was pulling in a cooler of food while wearing a mink coat and matching head band. The bellman noticed this.

"Mrs. Wasdin, we have nice restaurants here," he said.

"Oh, I think we're aware of that," Susie replied. "But we bring our own food."

"I could understand doing that if this were the Clintons," the bellman said. "But these are the Bushes."

It was a funny exchange. But there was nothing funny about how nothing was working for Tom. By now, the Beast was attacking the final quadrant of his face. He increased his dosage of drugs and forged on. In 2002, Governor Jeb Bush appointed him to the Florida Sports Foundation. By 2003, though, the serious side effects of taking 1,600mg of Tegretol had him desperate for other options.

"His was a very highly complex and difficult case of Trigeminal Neuralgia," Dr. Rhoton said. "Most people you see will only get Trigeminal Neuralgia in one side of their face and in only one or two branches. To get someone who gets it in all three branches, and then to have it skip to the other side and get it in one, two or three branches ... that's just not typical. That's a very severe case."

In fact, in the thousands of patients Dr. Rhoton has treated for TN, he can count on one hand the number who've had it on both sides of their face.

Dr. Rhoton referred Wasdin to another physician, Dr. Peter Jannetta.

The Microvascular Decompression surgery – or MVD – that Dr. Rhoton had already done on Wasdin had actually been developed by Dr. Jannetta. In fact, many of the physicians were now referring to it as the "Jannetta Procedure."

It had Wasdin's hopes up.

"Just the thought of having a pain-free life was overwhelming to me," he said. "To think that I could talk, smile and eat without pain for the first time in a very long time was exciting. I couldn't wait to get off the medication."

In May of 2003, Dr. Jannetta performed the surgery, meeting with Susie while Tom was in recovery.

"How did the surgery go?" Susie asked him.

"It was a Bo Derek," Dr. Jannetta replied.

In other words, a perfect 10.

The next two days in the hospital, Wasdin was pain-free.

On the third day, he was released, and he and Susie went to the hotel where Susie had been staying. Suddenly, a 10 struck. Only this time it wasn't a perfect 10. It was a full 10 on the pain scale.

"It was one of the worst pains I ever experienced," Wasdin said. "The pain was worse than from before the surgery."

Dr. Jannetta's partner, Dr. Ken Casey, told him it might be phantom pain. It wasn't. The Beast was back, and with a vengeance.

"The disappointments were so devastating," Susie said. "Sometimes it was really hard to be positive and move forward. It got to where we felt like we couldn't stand to hear another disappointment."

A year later, he was taking a cocktail of daily medications – 1,600mg of Tegretol and 2,500mg of Neurontin. It was helping, but not enough. It didn't stop the pain, and Wasdin could hardly chew just to eat. He eliminated Neurontin and upped his Tegretol to 2,400mg a day combined with 1,600mg of Depakote. Susie monitored what he was taking, because, heavily medicated, Tom had a hard time keeping track. There were times when he tried to back off on the drugs, only to experience the Beast in all its fury. In spite of years of ongoing medication, his liver tests were always normal, with one doctor telling him that he had what they call in the profession a "mountain liver" – a term for a hearty liver able to withstand a tremendous load of toxins.

There was a TNA National Conference in Orlando in the fall of 2004. During a breakout session, Susie heard Dr. Jeffrey A. Brown speak and liked him and what he had to say. She called his office in Great Neck, NY, on Long Island, and in November, 2004, set up an appointment. All they hoped for was that Dr. Brown could help them manage the medications before they totally poisoned Tom's body. Dr. Brown had other ideas, though. He wanted Wasdin to consider allowing him to perform a balloon compression procedure, and get him off the drugs. "The medication slows down the whole nervous system," he said. "It slows down brain function. It's like taking a shot of whiskey every four hours." Or in Tom Wasdin's case, with the amount of medication he was on, even more often.

"There were times when he was like a zombie, sleeping 12 to 14 hours a day, and taking naps," Susie said. "That was the only time he had relief, when he was in bed. It was awful. His eyes were so sad. And I was sad, too, because there was nothing I could do to help him."

But Susie was a help, a tremendous help, running the business and rentals while also taking care of her parents in their failing health.

The Wasdins had heard of the balloon procedure, and knew that Dr. Casey could perform it.

"If we do the balloon compression," Susie asked, "why should we choose you over Dr. Casey?"

"Because," Dr. Brown replied, "I taught him how to do it."

As they sat in Dr. Brown's office, on a Saturday, November 13, arrangements were discussed for surgery. Suddenly, Tom didn't feel well. He felt flush. They took his temperature and saw that it had soared to 103 degrees. Though they didn't know it then, he was suffering from an acute kidney infection. Immediately, Dr. Brown wanted to rush him to an emergency room.

"But what about the Gator-South Carolina game?" Wasdin asked, only half-joking, employing the dry wit that his friends had become accustomed to.

Dr. Brown looked at him, puzzled.

"What's a Gator-South Carolina game?" he asked.

What Dr. Brown lacked in knowledge of Southeastern Conference football he more than made up in knowledge of Trigeminal Neuralgia. In February of 2005, the Wasdins flew to New York for the balloon compression procedure ... or so they thought. Because of weather, their plane was forced to land in Baltimore, where the Wasdins spent the day at the airport. Finally, they were able to make reservations to get on a train to New York.

"Tom was in a wheelchair because he had not eaten in days, and he was weak due to that," Susie said. "He could hardly swallow. Could hardly speak. Even drinking water with a straw was difficult because of the pain."

There was a slight commotion on the train. A few guys were helping Susie with the wheelchair, with the luggage. "Stop it, we're fine," she said. But they wouldn't. Little did she know why, but Tom had seen why.

"They ... took ... my ... wallet," he said haltingly, barely moving his mouth to utter the words.

Susie screamed: "Pickpockets!"

The guys ran, throwing Tom's wallet to the floor.

It was a long day, but finally they got to Long Island at 11 p.m. Once again, Tom was running a fever.

Dr. Brown got Tom stabilized and performed a balloon compression procedure on the right side of his face. What that meant is that Dr. Brown positioned a balloon-tipped catheter next to Tom's trigeminal nerve just as it passed through a tight spot at the base of his skull. Then he inflated the balloon to a precisely measured pressure so that it squeezed the trigeminal nerve. That squeeze, which lasted about a minute, damaged only the fibers in the nerve that transmit touch sensations to the brain. In doing so, the operation selectively avoided injuring pain fibers. The trick is that it's the sensation of a cool breeze, a gentle kiss, or a toothbrush that triggers shocks of pain. Block these sensations and the pain is stopped in its tracks.

By now, Tom and Susie had learned not to get their hopes up too high. They also knew, though they didn't want to say it aloud to each other, that this was likely a last resort. Later that day, when he awoke from the procedure, the look on his face brought tears to Susie's eyes.

"He was smiling," she said. "It was the first time I'd seen him smile in years. I'd gone years without seeing his teeth, without seeing his smile, without seeing that sparkle in his eyes. He was sad, so sad. Sad all the time. To see him smile ..."

She knew. And Tom knew, too.

The pain was gone.

Well, it was gone on the right side of his face. But several weeks later, after all the medication wore off, the pain returned to the left side of his face. So a couple of months after that, Dr. Brown performed a balloon compression procedure there, too. Again, Wasdin awoke pain-free from the surgery – smiling.

He lives today with constant numbness all over his face. That's one of the aftereffects of all the various procedures he's had. "The pain comes from a short circuit, where an artery or vein pounds against the nerve and strips its insulation," Dr. Brown said. "The operation injures the nerve just enough so it turns down the voltage, and you don't get the fiery jabs from the bad wire downstream."

When Wasdin is out for a meal, friends know to touch a corner of their own mouth to alert Wasdin to food that might be clinging to his lips or face. He is never without a handkerchief, using it to periodically wipe his mouth and nose, just in case. Sometimes he eats with a small mirror in front of him.

In February of 2008, he made a decision to go public with the disease, agreeing to an interview with *Florida Today* newspaper.

Through 2013, Tom Wasdin was still pain-free. Numb, but without that knee-buckling, excruciating pain anymore. The longer he remains pain-free, the better his future prognosis is. "If there's going to be a reoccurrence, it usually happens in the first three to five years," Dr. Brown said. "At this point, the odds are against the pain coming back."

But that doesn't mean that Dr. Brown no longer wants to see Wasdin.

"He's not just my patient now, he's a friend and mentor," he said. "If I need advice, worldly advice, Tom is a guy I go to. He's not like any other patient I've had. He's a philosopher. He's got a lot of common sense. When I need to make a decision, Tom is a guy I talk with."

Others talk to him, too.

It's not uncommon for Wasdin to get a phone call, a letter, an email, from someone suffering from the horrendous disease. He always makes time for them. His advice is consistent:

- Take control of your pain.
- Join the Facial Pain Association (FPA).
- Educate yourself.
- Read the book "Striking Back!" from the FPA.
- Learn about all your options.
- See a doctor and prepare your questions.
- Don't leave your doctor until you're satisfied with all the answers.
- Keep records so as to help your doctor with their diagnosis.
- Know where, when and how the pain comes.
- Keep track of medications you're taking.
- Don't be afraid to ask your doctor for references and their experience.
- Take someone with you as a second set of eyes and ears.

Dale Craven was one of those people who contacted Wasdin, having been referred to him by George Scholz, one of Tom's former players at Jacksonville University. Like Wasdin, Craven suffered for years with pain, with nobody able to determine its cause. Eventually, he was diagnosed with Trigeminal Neuralgia, which was when Scholz told him about Wasdin, and how he had the condition on both sides of his face.

"I couldn't imagine how awful that had to be for him," Craven said.

Craven called Wasdin for help. "He was so nice to talk to," he said. "He gave me the information I needed to book an appointment with Dr. Jeffrey Brown."

Craven scheduled an appointment with Dr. Brown on May 27, 2010, had surgery the very next day, and has been pain-free since.

Another person who can't thank Wasdin enough is Sean Tabb.

"I woke up one morning, the second week of March in 2011, with the worst pain I've ever experienced in my life," Tabb said. "I was coaching basketball as an assistant at Brown University in Providence, Rhode Island. We had about a month left in the season and it took everything in me to make it through the rest of the year. I had no idea as to what or why I was experiencing this pain; sharp stabbing sensations that started next to my ear going down to the bottom of my jaw. As soon as the season concluded, I was forced to resign because the pain had become too intense. It may have been the lowest point of my life. At the age of 36, I had to move back in with my parents. At this point, I visited dentists, doctors, neurologists, and finally after two months I was diagnosed with Trigeminal Neuralgia. This diagnosis meant nothing to me. I had never heard of Trigeminal Neuralgia and truly didn't know where to go to get help. After visiting with a neurologist at Brown University, I was told the pain was something I may have to live with the rest of my life."

Or did he?

Tabb spent hours doing research on the Internet, eventually finding the national website for facial pain, where he came across the name of one of its board members – Tom Wasdin. When Tabb Googled Wasdin's name he learned that Wasdin was a former college basketball coach, like himself. "I felt that we might be able to make some sort of a connection," he said.

Did they ever.

"I called Mr. Wasdin and left a voicemail explaining my situation," Tabb said. "He called me back, having no idea who this strange person from Connecticut was who was calling him. Once we connected, I knew immediately I made contact with the right person. He calmed me down, explained exactly the situation, and told me things would get better. In fact, he told me the one thing I truly needed to hear; the pain would go away and he knew exactly who would be able to make this happen."

At that point, Wasdin didn't just put Tabb in touch with Dr. Brown; he called Dr. Brown personally for him.

"In addition, since by this point I had trouble talking because of the pain, both Tom and Susie Wasdin explained to my parents everything that was needed to know about the situation," Tabb said. "A month later, I had successful Microvascular Decompression surgery with Dr. Brown. I am currently one-hundred percent pain-free. I often wonder what would have happened had I not reached out to Tom Wasdin. I don't get too far along in my thoughts, however, as it scares me to even go back to that time in my life. Tom Wasdin is truly one of those rare special people we meet in our lives who is completely selfless. To say I am lucky to have met him is an incredible understatement. I will be forever grateful to Tom Wasdin, as I truly believe he saved my life."

In addition to helping people one-on-one, the Wasdins have also worked toward, and funded with their own money, research into Trigeminal Neuralgia. They once even hired a lobbyist, their friend Eddy Pauley, to help the cause. He flew to Washington, D.C. to talk with the chairman of the appropriations committee. But it was when Alaska's infamous "bridge to nowhere" surfaced in the news, angering constituents over earmarks and tag alongs. "It was bad timing," Susie said. "TN is still an 'orphan disease.' But we're hoping that will change and that more people will step forward to help. We've heard of some celebrities who have TN. We're hoping they can get involved."

That hasn't stopped the Wasdins. For years, Tom has been actively involved with the Trigeminal Neuralgia Association, now called TNA The Facial Pain Association and also serves on their board.

"Tom has always felt that the medical profession as a whole should learn about this and that more time, energy and resources should be devoted to this," said Dr. Michael Pasternak, the association's former president and now the Founding Trustee of the Facial Pain Research Foundation, which is a division of TNA The Facial Pain Association.

"Immediately after the approval of the foundation, the Wasdins got involved," Dr. Pasternak said. "They've been generous with their donations in the past, but on May 1, 2011 they made a matching grant for $120,000 to help with research, trying to find a cure. That grant was simply invaluable for getting our foundation going. It was the seed money. Two projects were started from that money. One with Dr. Lucia Notterpek, who is doing research in fixing myelin and nerve repair. The other is funding research for Dr. Andrew Ahn, who is a top neurologist and neuroscientist. Both are at the University of Florida."

Because of the Wasdins' generous grant, it's drawn attention to the TN cause and resulted in more funding from other donations.

Dr. Pasternak recalled that in the summer of 2013, he got a phone call from a woman who wanted to donate $50,000 for research. "Her brother had TN for two months. Two months! He took a gun and blew his brains out. This was an educated man, the head of a large company. He couldn't take it. Listen, there's a reason why this is called the suicide disease. If you Google worst pains, you'll see that Trigeminal Neuralgia is right there at the top."

During these pain-free years, Wasdin has remained active, trying to help others.

"The guy is a gem," Dr. Pasternak said. "He could've walked away from it, but instead he stepped up and encouraged a lot of people. And I didn't even have to ask him. Tom got all of it rolling, and I'll be forever grateful for his leadership."

There are other aftereffects Wasdin has from his decades-long battle with the Beast. However, some of these aftereffects are good ones.

Because he couldn't hardly speak during those intense times when he had TN, he learned to listen more, and saw the benefits in doing so. "I used to always carry conversations and be a leader in every group," he said. "Now I listen more. When I say something, I don't say a lot, but hopefully by saying less it can mean more."

He acquired other qualities, too.

"This ordeal taught me patience. It taught me to appreciate the things I have. It gave me empathy for other people who are having problems. It made me appreciate the people in my life. It made me commit more to giving back to the community; more than I probably would have. It taught me humility. Going through something like this humbles you. It also taught me not to sweat the small stuff. I remember that my uncle taught me that one of the toughest things in life is learning how to handle disappointments. I thought about that a lot when I was battling TN."

One other thing.

"Miracles happen every day, and I can truly attest to that," he said. "I thought my life was over. In fact, I considered ending my life many times. But because of my faith in God and the support of my loving wife, Susie, as well as the support from my friends and family, I learned a valuable lesson of not ever giving up."

Chapter 19

LEAVING FOOTPRINTS ALONG THE SPACE COAST

"What I did as a coach wasn't going to help establish credibility and a track record as a builder. Decades later, after I'd reached a certain amount of success; it was nice to be called 'Coach' again."
– Tom Wasdin

When Tom Wasdin arrived back in Brevard County in 1973, eager to embark on a new career, he was at first simply trying to find his footing on this fresh path he was taking. He never imagined that decades later he'd not only find that footing, but that he'd also leave indelible footprints along the Space Coast.

Indeed, the very fact that Brevard County also came to be known as the Space Coast is a part of Tom Wasdin's legacy.

Initially, part of Wasdin's drive was to distance himself from his accomplishments as a coach. Not that he wasn't proud of what he'd done. Hardly. "It was just that, in those early years back in Brevard County, all the articles written about me were about being a coach, and I wanted to move away from that part of my life and establish myself in other ways," he said. "What I did as a coach wasn't going to help establish credibility and a track record as a builder. Decades later, after I'd reached a certain amount of success: it was nice to be called 'Coach' again."

So yes, he was driven to establish himself in his new career. But the fact is, he was just plain driven. Soon, though, Wasdin also realized that the things he learned and employed as a successful coach also served him well in the business world.

Ultra prepared and organized, Wasdin soon devised ways to keep a hectic pace that left many people scratching their heads, wondering when the man found time to sleep. At one point, during the sweet spot of his career, he'd gotten involved in so many business and civic ventures that he sat on 22 different boards of directors.

Wasdin had a card system that kept his schedule organized. He kept a card for every project he was on, filling it with pertinent information and deadlines. He also kept a to-do card in his shirt pocket as he went about his day.

"I always set aside time in the early morning to organize my day," he said. "I'd have my calendar with what I needed to do, and I'd meditate and think about it. Then I'd try to start the day ahead of everyone else. Most people get to the office and get a cup of coffee. When I got to the office I was ready to go."

During the day, he'd cross off items and jot down new ones.

"It was my way of being organized," Wasdin said. "I thought the best way of doing things was to not rely on memory. Have it written down. This way, you can leave your mind open to think about new ways of doing things."

That doesn't mean he didn't keep mental notes. They were just different mental notes than people normally keep. He observed how people went about their business, and filed certain things away in his head.

"If I was in a meeting and I saw someone not writing down notes, not making a list, not noting what the action items were, I'd suspect they weren't going to be prepared for the next meeting. Usually they weren't."

Wasdin made sure that all the action items from meetings were typed and distributed to everyone immediately after the meeting adjourned. The first thing he'd do at the next meeting was go down the list of action items, one by one. It quickly gave him insight into who was reliable and who wasn't.

He read Dale Carnegie and other gurus in leadership and success. He began memorizing and then writing down on a legal pad various quotes, aphorisms and maxims – some that he heard or read; others that he coined.

They came to be known as "Wasdinisms."

"I tried to live by them and was pleased when I saw other people employing that into their routines," he said. "It was my common sense way to success – simple and easy to remember."

One phrase Wasdin coined, which probably became his most favorite, was the one that launched him into the middle of just about every important business matter going on in Brevard County. That favorite phrase was:

When you need a friend, it's too late to make one.

"You need to make friends every day," Wasdin explained. Toward that end, he became what he called a different kind of marketing guy. "I made a point of socializing with my clients. I became friends with all my clients, and some became very close friends. I found that most people like to do business with their friends, especially if their friends are credible, competitive and trustworthy."

It fed into another saying he often espoused:

A friend tells you what you need to hear, not what you want to hear.

"I tried to tell people the truth in a way they'd understand, while at the same time respecting their right to have their own opinion. From my standpoint, I tried to be trustworthy, reliable and consistent with my beliefs and personality. I tried to be what I thought a good friend to me was."

Part of being a good friend was listening. It was also a good business practice.

"Many people like to talk rather than listen," Wasdin said. "So I figured, I'll make people happy and let them talk and I'll listen. It was my way of finding out what the hot buttons were for them; what they liked and didn't like."

Clients appreciated that. They also appreciated a question Wasdin would ask them early on.

"I'd ask them, 'If you had the perfect consultant, what would they be like?' Whatever they said, then we'd try to be that. I also realized that anytime you have a project, you're going to have some problems, some conflicts. I always tried to diminish those conflicts. I never wanted to make my client look bad. I always tried to protect them. If something went wrong, I never came back to them and said, 'You said to do it this way.' If they made a decision and it blew up, I tried to take responsibility. If it worked out, they got the credit. It's the same philosophy I had with my players when I was coaching."

He developed his "4 Legs of a Stool" model for success:
1. Health
2. Finances
3. Family
4. Spiritual

He'd speak before groups and explain how important having those four legs was. "Three legs, and you're a little wobbly. Two legs, it's difficult. One leg, you're going to fail."

Tom Wasdin the businessman.

Whatever he espoused, Wasdin also put into practice. Every year, he looked at his own four legs of the stool and wrote down a list of goals beneath each leg. Goal-setting, and writing those goals down, was a part of his daily, weekly, monthly and yearly routine. In fact, at the end of the year, usually over Christmas vacation and often when he and Susie were on a skiing trip, he would review how he did with the goals from that year, and then make a fresh list for the upcoming year. Part of those goals was long-range, pointing toward a time when he wanted to retire.

"These were the action items for my life," he said. "Setting goals and writing them down was my device to bring happiness and success into my life, and also to aim toward retirement."

His goals were specific and his to-do list often long.

Wasdin soon found himself involved with various business organizations, like the Chamber of Commerce and several home builders associations. It was on the Chamber of Commerce that he got to know, and become friends with, Brevard Community College president Dr. Maxwell King. Dr. King was also a frequent diner at the Pier House restaurant, where he'd often run into Wasdin. They soon became golfing buddies, as well.

"I saw right away how positive Tom is with people, and how he helps people," Dr. King said. "He's a great citizen and a great community leader."

Rick Stottler and Tom Wasdin flanking Brevard Community College President, Dr. Maxwell C. King. Stottler and Wasdin are presenting Dr. King an endowment check for the Maxwell C. King Center for the Performing Arts.

Dr. King soon tapped into Wasdin for the BCC Foundation, which fed into Wasdin establishing – with his own money – an endowment for a faculty chair called the Wasdin Family Faculty Chair for Men's Basketball.

"I wanted to get people with name recognition in the community to help raise money," Dr. King said. "Tom didn't just fit that category; he was at the top of it."

Susie and Tom Wasdin flanked by Brevard Community College basketball coach Don Smith and Dr. Elena Flom, the Executive Director of BCC's foundation. The Wasdins established the Wasdin Family Faculty Chair for Men's Basketball. It was the college's first faculty chair.

In 1985, when BCC was searching for a new basketball coach, Wasdin got involved. He knew of Don Smith, who was an assistant at Georgia Southern when Wasdin was Jacksonville University's head coach. Smith had just spent 12 years at the University of New Orleans – six years as an assistant and another six as the head coach. Wasdin advised BCC to target Smith, and the school did, eventually hiring him.

Not only didn't Smith know about Wasdin's involvement with his hiring, he didn't even realize that Wasdin lived in Brevard County, much less that he was closely involved with BCC.

"When Tom got out of coaching, I lost track of him," Smith said. "But after I got to BCC, we became good friends. He helped me a great deal with my program. When we went to the NJCAA National Tournament in 2000, he sat with me on the bench that season as an unpaid assistant, and he was very instrumental to our success. He was always so calm and cool when I might be getting wild, getting on a referee or on one of my players. He'd give me advice, offer a suggestion, but never with an ego. He was invaluable. To have a man with that much knowledge, someone who is that wise, wanting to help you, you'd be silly not to tap into that."

Wasdin often helped Smith and BCC with recruiting, too.

"We'd take the players to the Pier House restaurant to eat," Smith said. "Tom gave us a great deal, great service and treated us like kings. It was a great environment to take a recruit, right there on the ocean."

Whenever Smith needed help, whether it was a Faculty Endowed Chair or the Marathon Golf fundraising event or anything else, he always found Tom Wasdin there, ready to do what he could. One time, Wasdin played 224 holes of golf in one day during a fundraiser, setting a Florida state senior record.

"Tom did more than anyone else to help BCC athletics; more than anyone else by giving his time and money," Smith said. "AAU sporting events would not have come to Brevard County without Tom's contacts and his involvement as the President of the AAU. He was always there when I needed him."

What Smith remembers most is how Wasdin rallied support from his influential friends and spearheaded the movement that saved not only basketball at BCC, but the entire athletic department. The community college had decided to do away with all its sports programs. Frantic, Smith appealed to the community for help while trying to convince the school to keep sports. But Smith was not only up against his own school, but also a statewide trend that had community colleges eliminating sports altogether. Valencia College and others had already taken those steps. The dominoes were falling ... and now it was BCC's turn.

"I got nowhere," Smith said. "I was just beaten."

Wasdin knew what was going on and he called Smith. The two men met for breakfast in Cocoa Village.

"Don, are you going to do anything about this?" Wasdin asked.

"I've tried, Tom," Smith replied. "They've beaten me down."

"Well, I'll help you," Wasdin sad. "But you've got to make up your mind that you want to do this. If you want to do this, if you want to save basketball and sports, then let's go get after it."

"Okay," Smith replied, energized by his friend's words. "Let's go. Let's do it."

In reality, it was Wasdin with the help of his influential friends who did it. Smith helped in whatever way he could. But he also couldn't help but think of one of Wasdin's favorite phrases – *when you need a friend, it's too late to make one* – and how he saw Tom put that maxim into action.

"Everyone knows Tom, and Tom knows everyone," Smith said. "He tapped into all his connections, organized committees and got people involved. I could not have done the things he did. He saved BCC sports."

Later, because of how Wasdin not only helped save sports at BCC, but also bucked the statewide trend of eliminating sports altogether, the Florida Community College Basketball Hall of Fame inducted him into their organization.

It was these types of things that, through the years, Dr. King watched and admired, marveling at how Wasdin kept giving back to the community.

"He has a real ability to get out and communicate with people," Dr. King said. "He's been a great community leader. Not only does he have name recognition, but he gets things done. The way he's involved himself, not only locally but statewide, has been a wonderful asset to our community. Tom Wasdin has made our community a much better place. I wish we had more citizens like him."

Chapter 20

PUBLIC SERVICE, POLITICS AND PEOPLE

"He was very effective and very powerful; a shaker and a mover. At the same time, he had a quiet approach. Low key. Very humble. People like Tom, and Tom knows a lot of people." – Marguerita Engel

Tom Wasdin's résumé reads like a narrative of several lives – not just one. If there was a cause or community endeavor, he wasn't just involved, he was intricately involved, immersing himself in whatever work needed to be done.

It was, perhaps, Wasdin's active participation and contribution with the Tourist Development Council where he had his greatest impact. From that platform, he was able to reach into many of the other boards and committees he sat on, facilitating positive change and progress in the community. Getting on the TDC was a process, though. It had nine seats, and it broke down this way:

- One seat to a county commissioner.
- One seat to the largest city in the county.
- One seat to another city in the county, which would be appointed by the board of county commissioners.
- One at-large seat.
- Five seats appointed individually by each of the five county commissioners.

Wasdin had helped Theo York get elected to a county commissioner seat, after which York appointed him to the TDC.

"It was a natural thing for me to be involved with the TDC," Wasdin said. "We had the Pier and we were promoting it as a tourist destination. I felt like it was important to do the best job we could do for the hoteliers. If your hotels are full, so are your stores and restaurants. Everyone wins."

It went beyond just good business sense. Sure, it was smart to get to know as many people and make as many connections as he could via various chambers and home builder associations. But Wasdin wanted to be involved because it was the right thing to do.

"My philosophy is that whatever you get involved in, be productive," he said. "Make a difference. Work. Work your way up to leadership positions. Be an important part of what you're involved in. Try to make it better. Don't be there just to have your name on a letterhead."

Prior to Wasdin's involvement, the TDC twice tried to pass the tourist tax ... and twice it failed.

So the first thing Wasdin recommended was something that tied into another one of his core beliefs, which was: *If you don't know how to do something, hire someone who does know.* So the TDC hired a consultant, and what they learned is why the tourist tax didn't pass.

"They told us that two-thirds of the people in the county don't want tourists. They clog up the streets, take their spot at restaurants, trash the beach. So we began marketing the tax and making sure we allocated money in ways that benefitted the community – like re-nourishing the beach, providing dune crossovers for beach access, improving waterfront areas, improving parks. We also made sure that some money would go to the Brevard Cultural Alliance. Kay Burk, President of the Brevard Cultural Alliance, and the board there threw a hundred percent of their support behind us. The environmentalists were behind it, too. There was something there for the whole community."

The next time the tourist tax came up for a vote, it passed; the aftereffect of which had a huge and long-lasting impact on the county, pumping tens of millions of dollars into the economy over the years.

Wasdin also did other things with the TDC that had a lasting impact on Brevard County. He knew words were important. It's why he spearheaded changing the name from the Canaveral Pier to the Cocoa Beach Pier. Similarly, he knew that Brevard County needed a better way to promote itself. Brevard sounded too much like Broward County in South Florida, and it was confusing to people.

Once a Coach, Always a Coach

Tom Wasdin was instrumental in changing the name of the Canaveral Pier to the Cocoa Beach Pier. It then took several years of hard work to transform it from a fishing pier to a Space Coast landmark known internationally.

The Florida Department of Commerce had devised names of Florida's coastal areas, rather than just the Atlantic Coast and Gulf Coast. They came up with names for different sections – First Coast, Palm Coast, Treasure Coast, Gold Coast, Emerald Coast, Forgotten Coast, Sun Coast; and for Brevard County the Space Coast.

Problem was, nobody was really using the moniker Space Coast, in spite of the fact that out of all the coastal names the Florida Department of Commerce had devised, Space Coast provided immediate geographic recognition. Mention the Sun Coast or Emerald Coast, and people scratch their heads and ask: Where's that? But mention Space Coast and there's no confusion. It's where the Kennedy Space Center is, where all the launches originate from. It is why, when a new area code was needed, Wasdin and other TDC members, along with various Space Coast leaders, asked for, and got, 321, as in 3-2-1 liftoff. It was the same with changing SR 528 from being called the Bee Line to the Beachline, which Larry Mullin from the Sterling Cruise Lines proposed, while simultaneously promoting the expressway as linking Orlando and Disney World to the closest of all the Florida beaches.

Wasdin saw the need to move away from nebulous name Brevard County and toward something more catchy and specific. He also knew that something was needed to pull together a diverse 72-mile long county that had no one area or city truly at the forefront.

One year, when Wasdin was the Chairman of the TDC, he and the TDC Executive Director, Ralph McMullen, went to the Travel Industry of America national convention, where they had a session on branding, eventually breaking off into smaller focus groups. Wasdin didn't want the TDC to be known as the Brevard County Tourist Development Council, again because Brevard sounded too much like Broward County in South Florida, which confused potential tourists.

"I asked them to help us come up with a new name," he said. "I explained to them that we were located on the East Coast of Florida where the Kennedy Space Center was. I also told them we had 72 miles of the nicest beaches in the state. After much discussion, they said we should brand our area Florida's Space Coast."

Of course, the moniker *Space Coast* was what the Florida Department of Commerce had already devised. It thus confirmed to Wasdin the importance of adopting and promoting the name, further branding the area as the Space Coast.

"I thought it was a great idea," he said. "A natural."

Emerging from that focus group, Wasdin went back to his fellow TDC members and told them they needed to be known as Florida's Space Coast. They then branded the name and heavily promoted it. The new name stuck – both locally and nationally. Wasdin believed that having both "Florida" and "Space Coast" in a title would be magic.

"He got us to change the name," said Marguerita Engel, who served both on the Titusville city council and the TDC. Later, Wasdin also convinced the Brevard County League of Cities to change their name to the Space Coast League of Cities.

Engel soon learned that such insight and leadership was the norm with Tom Wasdin.

"He was very much a community leader," she said. "He was an actual hands-on director, and that doesn't happen very often. I learned a lot from Tom – how to raise funds, promote organizations and give the sponsors their due credit. He was very effective and very powerful; a shaker and a mover. At the same time, he had a quiet approach. Low key. Very humble. People like Tom, and Tom knows a lot of people."

Wasdin knew so many people and was involved in so many things that Engel used to wonder: "Where does he find the time?"

She didn't contemplate the question too long. If she was involved in business activities with Tom Wasdin, Engel knew enough to hold on tight during the ride.

"A lot of times, people are caught in the past, always going back to the glory days and never able to see beyond that," Engel said. "That wasn't Tom. Tom was always moving forward. He was a famous coach, but he wasn't always harkening back to those days. He was always looking for the next project; the next successful project. He was very progressive."

Rusty Buchanan saw how progressive Wasdin was, and also how persistent. Buchanan had spent his career in amateur sports, working for adidas and with the AAU and Junior Olympics. He was working in Tallahassee, Florida, when Wasdin and Don Smith came to visit him. Because of the success Cocoa Expo had seen in developing and hosting amateur athletic events, such as college spring baseball, Wasdin had a vision that under the TDC there should be a Space Coast Sports Association, promoting sports in the county. He also knew they needed someone to run it. Wasdin had done his due diligence, and had called his friend, Bobby Dodd, who was President of the AAU. Dodd had recommended Buchanan. But when Wasdin and Smith met with Buchanan, he turned them down.

"I didn't see it," he said. "I didn't see how it would be successful."

A month or so later, Wasdin approached Buchanan again, this time with local politicos. Again, Buchanan turned them down.

A third time, Wasdin invited him to a meeting that included Wendy Ellis, who at the time was the chairperson of the Sports Committee. Ellis also worked for Cocoa Expo, and knew the importance of conducting amateur athletic events along the Space Coast. Ellis was capable, smart and forward thinking. In fact, she was the one who recommended that the Canaveral Pier's name be changed to the Cocoa Beach Pier. With Ellis' leadership they gave Buchanan an offer he couldn't refuse along with all the tools he needed to be successful.

"I took the job, but I still wasn't totally convinced it would work," he said. "My wife at the time was from Cocoa Beach and my in-laws were there. Meanwhile, my job was about to send me to Rochester, Minnesota. So it was either move to Rochester, or to Cocoa Beach."

Thirty-four years old at the time, Buchanan chose Cocoa Beach, as well as choosing to trust in Wasdin's vision for sports along the

Space Coast. Buchanan's title was Executive Director of the Sports Commission and his charge was to bring amateur sporting events to the Space Coast and make it profitable.

The year was 1991, and Buchanan had the Space Coast Sports Association bid on and eventually secure the AAU's 11-under national basketball championship. Since then, the Space Coast has won that annual bid every year ... and more. In those early years, groups simply met with the AAU and divvied up sports and their age groups. But through the years, realizing the economic impact, more and more, counties and communities joined the table, making it much more competitive.

"We were the first group in Florida to go after amateur sports," Buchanan said. "There was really nobody else doing what Tom's vision was. He had a vision I didn't see and I had been in the amateur athletic business my whole life. He saw a way to marry tourist tax money with youth sports, which nobody else was really doing. We went from 1991, where we were the first group to go after amateur sports, to now where there are about two dozen sports commissions around the state trying to get amateur sports, including Disney and its ESPN Wide World of Sports Complex. It's the thing to do now. But Tom saw that before anyone else did."

Soon, colleagues were calling Tom Wasdin "Mr. Tourism" in Brevard County.

"The man is a real go-getter, savvy, intelligent, a hard worker and very well-connected," Buchanan said. "When he gets something in his head that he wants, he perseveres."

Buchanan paused.

"I guess that's what happened with me," he said.

Meanwhile, on a national level with the AAU, the folks there could see the tireless work Wasdin was doing, and they appreciated it.

"Tom Wasdin is the epitome of what is good in volunteer members of the AAU," said AAU President Bobby Dodd, when he presented Wasdin with the annual President's Award for being the most outstanding AAU volunteer. "He gives unselfishly of himself to benefit young people of America and he sincerely wants to be a positive influence on their lives."

Susie and Tom Wasdin in a Space Coast Office of Tourism promotional photo that captured them walking along the Atlantic Ocean in Cocoa Beach, Florida

Susie and Tom Wasdin in a Space Coast Office of Tourism promotional photo at the Suntree Country Club in Melbourne, Florida

Tom Wasdin displaying his golf swing in a Space Coast Office of Tourism promotional photo at the Suntree Country Club.

Tom Jenkins remembers his first TDC meeting. Jenkins was an assistant Brevard County administrator at the time, and he really didn't know much about Tom Wasdin or his background in the community.

"Right away, he was one of those guys who just stands out," Jenkins said. "His leadership skills. His ability to lead a discussion and persuade. The TDC had an excellent collection of leaders, and he was one of them."

Wasdin and Jenkins became good friends, which fit into Wasdin's philosophy of *when you need a friend, it's too late to make one.* Some people might have seen it as playing politics, but Jenkins saw it differently.

"There were a lot of things that got done because of the personal commitment of his time and the personal commitment of money – often his own money," Jenkins said of Wasdin. People with self-interest often display a my-way-or-no-way attitude. But Jenkins didn't see that with Wasdin.

"He has this ability of bringing people together and forming a consensus," he said. "He's very good at listening and trying to understand everyone's point of view. He's not a guy who would go off saying, 'I know best. Do it my way.' Because he is a results-oriented guy and not just a talker, he'd go to all the different segments of the community and communicate with them. Regardless of the issue, even when there were political splits, he could bring it to a consensus. Yes, he had a lot of power in the community, but it was power in the sense that he was very good at getting things done. It wasn't power where he'd flaunt it. On the contrary, he is a very humble and very unassuming guy."

Tom and Susie Wasdin with Wayne Huizenga, who at the time was the Florida Marlins' owner. The photo was taken before the Marlins' first-ever spring training game, at Cocoa Expo.

Tom Wasdin with John Henry, who owned the Florida Marlins. Henry later became the owner of the Boston Red Sox.

Even still, when Wasdin talked, people listened. He wasn't the type of person who spoke just to hear the sound of his own voice. Wasdin picked his spots, and he always endeavored to establish a relationship with someone well before he might need to offer them a bit of advice or counsel. Once again, always the coach.

When Rob Varley became the TDC's president in 1994, he said Wasdin "was the first guy who walked into my office to welcome me. He immediately engaged me. Even years later, after he retired, he'd still drop by my office and give me advice."

The first time Wasdin gave Varley advice was shortly after Varley's first TDC meeting. "I'll never forget it," Varley recalled. "Two guys almost came to blows."

Wasdin reminded Varley that one of the reasons why he was hired was to bring people – and especially the two people who almost got into a fistfight – together. So Varley worked on it, dedicating a huge chunk of his time and energy on that effort. Wasdin noticed that. But he also noticed that Varley was spending so much time oiling a couple of squeaky wheels that he was neglecting a quiet, but important and influential TDC member – Rusty Fischer, who owned the iconic Bernard's Surf restaurant. So Wasdin pointed that out to Varley, doing it in an unassuming way. He first acknowledged all the TDC members Varley had been connecting with in the community. Then he got a list of the members and said, "I think there's one name you might've forgotten about."

"That's when Tom pointed to Rusty Fischer's name," Varley said. "And he was right. When I went to Rusty, I could see he was a little hurt, and that he felt ignored. I was screwing it up by forgetting an important person. From that point on, I built a great relationship with Rusty."

Through it all, whether it was a compliment or a critique, encouragement or a bit of enlightenment, Varley always appreciated Wasdin's approach.

"He never talked *down* to you," he said. "He always talked *with* you."

Given those people skills and his ability to bring sides together, it might've seemed natural for Wasdin to have gone into politics. But he never had the remotest interest in running for public office. That didn't mean, though, that he didn't involve himself with politics and politicians. In 1974, Wasdin went door-to-door with Mac McLouth, when McLouth was campaigning for Cape Canaveral's Port Commissioner. Early on, he also was involved with Lawton Chiles when Chiles ran for both the state senate and governorship; always housing Chiles' son, Bud Chiles, at Chateau By The Sea whenever Bud was in Brevard County campaigning.

There were others he helped. For county commissioner, there was Theo York, John Hurdle, Val Steele, Joe Wickham, Lee Wenner, Randy O'Brien, Gene Roberts, Charlie Roberts, Karen Andreas, Roger Dobson, Ron Pritchard, Mary Bolin, Chuck Nelson, Robin Fisher, Mark Cook, Andrea Deratany, Sue Carlson and Sue Schmitt.

He was actively involved with his old Paxon High student-athlete, Steve Pajcic, when Pajcic ran for governor. He assisted John Glenn in his presidential bid. John Vogt, Bud Gardner, Bill Posey, Tom Goodson, Thad Altman, Steve Crissafulli, Tim Deratany, Dave Weldon ... the list of campaigns that Wasdin got involved with at the local, state and national level was long and impressive.

Perhaps, though, the most unique campaign he got involved with was the one that started with a phone call that Susie Wasdin thought was a hoax.

"Is Tom Wasdin there?" the voice on the other end of the phone asked.

"He's not here," Susie replied. "May I take a message?"

"This is Jeb Bush," the voice said. "Would you please have Tom call me?"

Jeb Bush?

Surely, Jeb Bush hadn't just made a personal phone call reaching out to Tom Wasdin?

But he did.

Later, when Tom got on the phone with Jeb Bush, he broke some unfortunate news to the state's republican candidate for governor.

"I'm a democrat," Wasdin told him.

"I didn't know that," Bush said.

The two men talked, with Wasdin eventually convinced that Bush was the best man to govern Florida, and that Charles H. Bronson was the best man for Florida's Commissioner of Agriculture. Shortly thereafter, Wasdin started a campaign that he called: "Brevard County Democrats for Bush and Bronson."

After he got elected into office, Governor Bush appointed Wasdin to the Florida Sports Commission, with the charge of helping bring major sporting events like Super Bowls and NCAA National Championship Games to the state. In connection with that, Wasdin also became chairman of the grants committee for the Florida Sports Foundation. For four years, Wasdin was chairman of a committee that determined what grants were approved to help organizations conduct amateur sporting events. The FSF also assisted organizations in bringing major events like Super Bowls, BCS Bowls and an NCAA Final Four to Florida.

Susie and a bearded Tom Wasdin with Florida Governor Bob Graham. Because of his painful battle with Trigeminal Neuralgia, which could sometimes make even the act of shaving painful, Tom sported a beard for a short time.

Susie and Tom Wasdin flanking Attorney General Janet Reno, taken in Cocoa Beach, Florida, during President Bill Clinton's presidency.

At a fundraiser for Senator Bill Bradley during his first run for president. From left to right: Steve Pajcic, Bill Bradley, Susie Wasdin, Tom Wasdin. The photo was taken at the home of Steve Pajcic, who played college basketball with Bradley at Princeton University.

Susie and Tom Wasdin in Washington D.C., at President George W. Bush's first inauguration.

Susie and Tom Wasdin in Cocoa Beach, Florida, with Florida Governor Charlie Crist.

From left to right: Susie Wasdin, Tom Wasdin, Senator and former astronaut John Glenn, Sherrell Fischer, Rusty Fischer, Bonnie King.

Tom and Susie Wasdin with actor John Travolta.

Later, when Charlie Crist became the 44th Governor of Florida, he reappointed Wasdin, lengthening his time of service to more than seven years, which included serving two years as chairman of the Florida Sports Foundation.

Even while he was involved on a state level, Wasdin stayed heavily involved with local foundations and committees. One of them was the Brevard First task force, of which he became chairman. His goal was to encourage Brevardians to spend money in the county, rather than take it elsewhere. If tourists found the area enviable, then why not the locals? Their motto: "Spend Here, Eat Here, Vacation Here. We Have Everything Here."

It was around that time when Marguerita Engel, who served both on the city council and the TDC, told Wasdin: "Tom, you're one of the most powerful and influential persons in Brevard County."

The comment surprised him. Wasdin had never thought about it, and didn't believe it.

"I was just trying to help people and my community," he said. "Reflecting back on it, I was just doing what I thought I should be doing, and I was proud that I was able to make a difference. I never thought about being powerful. I just wanted to help."

Most people saw it as that. Sure there was a business interest. But people like local hotelier Dave Spain, who served on the TDC when

Wasdin was the chairman, were quick to defend any misconceptions that critics (usually borne out of jealousy) might have had.

"Tom is a guy who knows how to get things done," Spain said. "He's a worker, a guy who's not afraid to carry the water. When you look at the sum total of a person's life work, and you look at what Tom has accomplished, it's incredible the amount of things he's been able to do and the things he's been involved in. Just incredible. We wouldn't have things like a sports committee if it weren't for Tom Wasdin. Tom is the guy who made it happen. He did so much in so many areas. The man worked his ass off."

Even when there were disagreements and differences of opinion, Spain appreciated Wasdin's point of view and knew that there were no grudges. One of those disagreements came over building a stadium and baseball facility in Viera for the expansion Florida Marlins baseball team to spring train and house a Florida State League Class A minor league franchise. Wasdin was for it, while Spain and other hoteliers wanted the facility for amateur sports, believing that they had already lured the AAU and the United States Specialty Sports Association to relocate their national headquarters to Brevard County.

"Tom is the kind of guy who could be on the other side of an issue and not have you feel bad about it," Spain said. "He's very smooth, a very thoughtful guy, with an ability to mediate and discuss things while staying calm. He can build bridges and mend fences. I wish I was half as good as him. He's really been the biggest mentor to me, and not just from working with him, but from just observing and watching him. The coach in him never left. He was always coaching, always mentoring. If you were willing to listen and observe, you'd learn a lot. He certainly made me a better person and a better civic person."

Long after Tom retired and there no longer was a business interest, Spain noted that Wasdin still volunteered his time and expertise.

Bob Baugher has seen that through the years, while also relying on Wasdin's friendship and avuncular wisdom for the counsel he sometimes needed to hear. "I'm pretty damn strong-willed, very straightforward, and sometimes I need to temper some of that," said Baugher, who built Ron Jon Surf Shop into a Mecca before opening his own – bigger – retail store, calling it the Cocoa Beach Surf Company and housing it along with a Four Points By Sheraton hotel, the Shark Pit Bar & Grill and a Starbucks. Baugher also has various other business ventures along the Space Coast that cater to tourism.

Baugher always admired how Wasdin was able to "reach a consensus" with people. "When Tom was with Rick Stottler, he was always smoothing feathers while Rick was always ruffling feathers," Baugher said. "He could put people together, talk with everybody to reach a consensus, and get a deal done. That was his forte. He always had a good way with people."

As for Baugher, although he's been enormously successful in business, he admits that he sometimes comes across like a sledgehammer. One of those times was after Thomas Weinberg was elected Port Commissioner. Baugher wanted a word with Weinberg about the government's encroachment into private business. He got that word shortly after the 2011 election at a fundraiser for Bill Posey, who was running for a congressional seat.

"I probably pursued what was on my mind stronger than I should have," Baugher said. "There were some pretty heated words exchanged. He didn't think that was the time and place to have a discussion and I told him, 'Fine, then we'll discuss it when I sue everybody, and you are all deposed.'"

Within days, Baugher got a phone call from Wasdin, giving him basically the same counsel he'd given him through the years – the message you have might be the right one, but the delivery is often just as important, if not more so.

"You need to call Weinberg and apologize," Wasdin said.

Baugher did.

The two men met for a bite at Roberto's restaurant in Cocoa Beach, ironed out their disagreement, came to a consensus, "and since then we've become pretty good friends," Baugher said. "We've been able to find a common ground and work together."

Working with local politicians and getting involved with the TDC is what Wasdin had wanted to see Baugher do for many years. It wasn't until 9/11 when he finally connected with that message. After the terrorist attack, tourism along the Space Coast, as in other areas, came to a jarring halt. One day, angry, Baugher called to find out exactly what the TDC was going to do about the dearth of tourists. Wasdin encouraged him to get involved. Finally, Baugher did. Wasdin appointed him to the Marketing Committee, where Baugher impressed everyone with his tireless work ethic, productivity and ideas.

"He's a genius at marketing," Wasdin said of Baugher.

It was almost as if Wasdin were still coaching, putting people in positions where they could be successful.

"He's been a good friend," Baugher said.

And he's always been a good friend to the Space Coast.

Just the number of non-profits Tom and Susie Wasdin were involved in, some individually and others collectively, was staggering – the Brevard Cultural Alliance, BCC Foundation, Cocoa Village Playhouse, Junior Achievement, Maxwell C. King Center for the Performing Arts, Brevard Achievement Center/Very Special Arts, Wuesthoff Foundation, Central Brevard Humane Society, Cocoa Beach Area Chamber and the Cancer Society "Relay for Life."

Like Dave Spain and others, Tom Jenkins is also quick to point out that even when there wasn't a business interest for tourism, Wasdin still stayed involved in civic endeavors. Said Jenkins, "He was still one of those guys at the forefront of progress and making good things happen for the community."

Chapter 21

THE PERSONAL TOUCH

"He talks to you. He likes to help people, but he wants to make sure that you're doing the right thing. He helps you get straightened out. He gives you advice and good counsel. At the same time, he comes to the rescue right away." – Lorenzo Reddick

Tom Wasdin was simply ... involved. It didn't matter where the spotlight was or who was getting the credit. He was always pitching in, always helping, always working to make the Space Coast and the lives of the people who called it home better.

Brevard County administrator Tom Jenkins' stepson, Kenny, was close friends with Tom and Susie's son Drew. One day, Kenny came home from school, very disappointed. Kenny called his stepfather, who then called Wasdin. "Tom," Jenkins told his friend, "Kenny is devastated. He just got cut from his 8th grade basketball team. He's just destroyed."

Wasdin was also disappointed for Kenny. He'd already been working with him on his basketball skills with the goal of helping Kenny make that team. In spite of Tom's busy schedule, he immediately picked Kenny up and promptly enrolled him in Satellite Beach's Bitty Basketball program. Meanwhile, he continued to personally work with Kenny, Drew and another friend, Kevin Gillette, on their games. A few years later, Kenny made the Eau Gallie High varsity team.

"He always found time to work with the kids," Tom Jenkins said. "He'd coach them and play basketball with them. He spent a lot of time with them."

Linda South saw that personal interest. A career businesswoman who had done a lot of community work, South found herself, after spending some time as a volunteer board member, as the acting Executive Director of Brevard Workforce, which was then known as Space Coast Private Industry Council. It was to be a 90-day position while a permanent director was found. But South, 39 at the time, found that she had "a passion" for the position.

"I loved it, and I wanted it permanently," she said.

One problem. She didn't have a degree. She was hired anyway, but not without some controversy. Afterward Wasdin, who had pushed for her hiring, took her aside to offer her advice. He told South that she could go further in her career if she got a degree, and that doing so would also avoid the types of controversies that had just clouded her hiring.

"You're a smart woman, Linda," Wasdin told her. "But you're not going to achieve your full potential without that degree."

At first, South didn't fully appreciate that message.

"I thought I was the best person for the job, that I had come from owning and running businesses," she said. "But there was a perception that I wasn't educated, and that angered me. I took it as a personal challenge. It pushed me."

Over the next three years, taking night courses, South got her undergraduate degree. But she didn't stop there. She enrolled at Rollins College and got her MBA.

Did it help her career, as Wasdin had advised her it would?

"I got my MBA on a Saturday, and on Monday I showed up at Governor Jeb Bush's office to interview for a job," South said. She got the job, and was appointed the Director for the Agency of Workforce Innovation, or what many other states call the Secretary of Labor. Later, under Governor Charlie Crist, South served as the Secretary of the Department of Management Services.

"I can assure you," South said, reflecting back on those years, "that if I didn't have a degree none of that would have happened. It wouldn't have happened without Tom's encouragement, support and vision. He saw things in me that I didn't see."

Other people, like Bonnie King, also saw that personal interest from Wasdin. From its inception, King has worked on the TDC. But prior to that, she had known of Tom and met him and Susie several years earlier at an aerobics class, and liked him right away.

"He was funny, had a good sense of humor, and he was devoted to Susie and always talking about Drew," King said. "He was very nice, very friendly."

It was later, though, when they worked together on the TDC, that King's admiration really grew.

"I soon saw that this was a man who could work a challenge and create opportunities," she said. "He was so well-connected that he could always go to this person or that person to help us solve a problem or create an opportunity. He was a very powerful man and recognized as such. His sphere of influence was very broad. He always did things in a professional, non-challenging way. And he was always prepared, too. He always did his due diligence, got the facts, and had already looked at all sides. It was quite fascinating to watch the way he worked. It was very interesting to me. There were a lot of times when I'd see him in action, and I'd say to myself, 'I need to take notes.'"

Beyond that, King saw how Wasdin helped people, especially women, and particularly Tom's own wife, Susie. She also saw it with herself one day when Wasdin pulled her aside. There were some problems on the TDC, and King had said some things about her boss that Wasdin heard.

"Bonnie," he said, "you need to be loyal to your boss."

King tried to point out things that concerned her; things she felt weren't right.

"I know, I know," Wasdin said. "We know exactly what's going on and it's being handled. In the meantime, you need to be loyal to your boss."

Years later, King recalled the kind but firm way Wasdin handled the situation, and is still appreciative.

"It was a lesson learned, and it's a lesson I've taught my kids," she said.

Through the years, King again and again saw how well Tom treated Susie, helping her to succeed in her own ways, while also observing how Tom benefitted from Susie's growth and successes.

"Susie drew Tom into a lot of places he might not have gone," King said. "They were partners. It was something to see. Here you had Susie, a young lady struggling to raise a child, and she meets this wonderful man who sees her potential and helps her to reach it. Tom encouraged Susie and supported her to go out and achieve. Put them together and they were rocking and rolling. They were *the* power couple."

Not only were they the power couple, they were the couple you wanted at your social gatherings, and vice versa. And, if anything, the Wasdins could sure throw a party. Susie especially had a knack for making things fun and interesting.

When Robin Turner, whom Wasdin had hired years earlier to manage the Pier, got the Brevard County Fair going at the Cocoa Expo, with big acts like the Allman Brothers, Beach Boys, Willie Nelson and The Charlie Daniels Band appearing, the Wasdins converted the stadium's press box into a VIP viewing area, holding a party in it. Getting an invitation to that was coveted.

There was the time when the Wasdins hosted an offshore powerboat race and all five of the county commissioners attended a VIP party with the drivers. It was a rare sight to see all the county commissioners together, prompting the chairman to quip that maybe the next time they ought to just have their meetings at the Wasdin house, since everyone showed up there.

Their Christmas Party for clients, through Stottler Stagg and Associates, also became a go-to event. It drew a few hundred people, among them usually every elected official in the county. They didn't skimp, either. Great food, featuring fresh seafood, along with an open bar, was the norm.

Not to be forgotten, nor not invited to, was Tom and Susie's Super Bowl parties. It started as a group of Tom's golfing buddies, but eventually grew to become another go-to social gathering for the county's movers and shakers. By the early '90s the Wasdin Super Bowl Party had moved to the Rockledge Country Club, with more than a half dozen large-screen televisions accommodating a few hundred people – among them judges, politicians and business leaders. It was the place to be on Super Bowl Sunday. As always, it was Susie's touches that elevated the event into a stratosphere of fun.

Although he moved among Brevard County's powerbrokers, Wasdin never lost sight of the fact that he was just a guy who grew up on a farm in Waldo, Florida, and appreciated the help he'd gotten along the way. If he could help someone else, he would ... and often did. It was one of the reasons why people still referred to him as Coach Wasdin.

Lorenzo Reddick was one of those people who benefitted from Coach Wasdin's help. Wasdin had known Reddick back in the '60s, when he was a young maitre d' at a nice restaurant. As a young black man, and knowing what another young black man like Artis Gilmore would be looking for in a college, Reddick had offered advice on how to recruit the talented center and other black players that Joe Williams and Tom Wasdin were hoping to sign to letters-of-intent at Jacksonville University. Reddick had helped them back then. More than 35 years later, he contacted Wasdin, needing help. Reddick owned a little used car business in Orlando, when he ran into financial problems.

"Tom had called me earlier, to see how I was doing," Reddick said. "He was checking on me, because that's the way Tom is. He cares about people. He told me that if I had any problems, to give him a call. It wasn't too long after that when the economy took a downturn and I had a problem with my property taxes. That's when I called Tom up to see if he could help me. I needed two grand, or I was going to lose my house."

Not only did Wasdin help, but it staggered Reddick that "the very next day he was at my dealership. He took a check out of his pocket and gave it to me. He took care of my problem right away."

But Reddick would want people to know that it went beyond that; beyond just addressing a problem with money.

"If you've got a problem, he's concerned about it – about *you*. He doesn't give you grief if you've gotten into a bind. He talks to you. He likes to help people, but he wants to make sure that you're doing the right thing. He helps you get straightened out. He gives you advice and good counsel. At the same time, he comes to the rescue right away. He knows my problems and he's always been glad to help."

Another one of Reddick's problems came in the form of multiple back surgeries due to spinal stenosis. Again, when Reddick was in financial straits due to mounting medical bills, Wasdin was there for him.

"Tom's just a fantastic guy," he said. "For me, he's been a blessing."

It's one thing to help people you know, and another to help someone you just met.

Meir Shaked was one of those individuals.

Shaked had arrived in America from his native Israel, not knowing the language but looking for work and an opportunity. He learned about a job at the Ocean Woods development that Wasdin was building. It was there that he met Tom. Not only did he get a job, but "Tom took me into his home, and I stayed there a couple of months. We'd work out, jog together. He even co-signed on a car for me. The man hardly even knew me."

Shaked did various jobs around Ocean Woods, putting up fences and working as a night watchman.

"I never anticipated that people in America would be like this," he said. "To co-sign on a car for me was unbelievable. And Tom didn't do it because he's not smart. It wasn't because he was naive. He did it to help."

In those early years in America, Shaked didn't have much money. One day, he was at the Mousetrap in Cocoa Beach, having a few drinks. Tom came in, saw him, and pulled him aside.

"What are you doing here?" he asked Shaked.

The question was rhetorical.

"He was like a father," Shaked said. "Basically, what Tom was telling me is that I shouldn't be spending all my money on drinks. I didn't have money to waste. It was a very fatherly thing to do. He was looking out for me."

Years later, when Shaked became a successful businessman, owning his own car dealership, he found himself often giving back; primarily because of the example he was shown.

"Tom and Susie Wasdin are two of the most generous people you'll ever meet," he said. "And they do it quietly. Tom was there for me. He's like a father. The things he did for me, it's something you never forget."

Nor will they be forgotten.

Not by Meir Shaked, or by the myriads of people Tom Wasdin – or better yet, *Coach* Wasdin – touched along the Space Coast ... and beyond.

Chapter 22

THE LONG SUNSET

"I've had a wonderful life, and when it's over – it's over. I've been very blessed. I've had wonderful careers." – Tom Wasdin

Tom Wasdin stood on the balcony of his penthouse condominium, leaning on the banister, his sockless feet slipped into a pair of loafers with his right foot hooked around one of the guardrail posts. He wore shorts, an Hawaiian-print shirt and a satisfied smile as he peered across the undulating waters of the Indian River. Boats bobbed and pelicans peered from above. A jogger below ambled along Riverside Drive. It was early fall in 2013, and the sun had already skimmed across a late September sky, well into its descent, dragging the day's brilliant and bountiful colors with it.

"This doesn't look like Waldo," Wasdin mused, cutting the silence, his eyes focused into the distance, on something only he could see. "It's sometimes hard to believe how far I've come and the things I've done. It's like I've lived several lifetimes. Me. This country boy from Waldo."

He smiled again.

"I've had a wonderful life, and when it's over – it's over. I've been very blessed. I've had wonderful careers. Now I'm making a career out of retirement."

Semi-retirement, really.

Tom and Susie Wasdin still preside over multimillion-dollar real estate holdings, encompassing 80 pieces of property – apartments, condos, single-family homes, townhomes and commercial buildings. They work well together as a team, with Susie managing much of the rentals and Tom handling the bookwork. For the most part, it's low maintenance and fairly stress-free.

"We're still making money," he said. "And I don't owe a penny to anyone in this world."

Wasdin wanted it this way, free and clear, and he worked hard to get to this point, where he could fully enjoy his sunset years. He also made sure that the lessons he learned when his father died were not repeated – when 80 acres of land in his Waldo hometown had been promised to his sister Dorothy and him; only to be yanked away via a legal loophole. "I made sure I did my financial planning and established a living trust, so that there would be no confusion over my wishes."

Even with all his financial freedom and his financial planning in place, Wasdin hardly slipped into a sedentary retirement. He still stays involved and active in various areas. Earlier in the day, a local Brevard County politician, still recognizing Wasdin's clout and ability to get things done, even at 78, called him to spearhead a contingency plan to figure out what to do with the county's Space Coast Stadium and its surrounding facilities, should MLB's Washington Nationals decide to conduct their spring training elsewhere.

Wasdin still likes having a measure of power and influence, and he likes it for the same reasons that he did when he was younger. Brevard County – or the Space Coast, as he helped it to become known as – is not only his home. For him, it's also an ongoing obligation.

"You're judged by how you made your community better, and how you helped other people," he said. "You should leave this world a better place than when you came in."

Toward that end, and especially in his retirement, Wasdin continues to raise money for worthy causes and regularly gives a good chunk of cash to various charities. Obviously, promoting awareness and helping fund a cure for Trigeminal Neuralgia is something he remains passionately involved in. As has been their case throughout their lives, his wife Susie remains a partner not only in business but also in philanthropy, and in doing so has established her own name. It was only fitting that on November 7, 2013, Susie Wasdin was named Volunteer of the Year by *Florida Today* newspaper. Several years earlier, Tom had been honored by the same organization as Citizen of the Year.

Mostly, though, Tom continues to enjoy good health in his twilight years. When he's not involved in civic and charitable activities, he enjoys playing golf and working with a personal trainer – both about three times a week each. He and Susie travel often. Just a couple of months earlier, they took a trip to Hawaii, California and Nevada. They regularly attend University of Florida sporting events. And, oh, how Wasdin enjoys watching sports, either live or on television. Earlier in the week, he upgraded his TV to a 60-inch flat-panel set along with two smaller TV monitors so that he could watch multiple sporting events simultaneously. It was a long time in coming. To not have the latest and greatest almost seemed a sin for a man of his means.

"But we've always lived beneath our means," he said.

It's a philosophy that served him well. He is, after all, still the farm boy from Waldo. He's lived long enough to realize that it's the simpler things and the simpler lifestyle that is most often the happiest of times. He recalled his second marriage to Glenda. "We lived in a two-room house trailer, paycheck to paycheck, saving bottles to turn in so we could get enough cash to go to the drive-in movie, taking our own food with us. And we were as happy as we could be."

Still, the failed marriages are one of his sadnesses. Through the years, he's observed other couples, happily married to only each other, and wished that could've been the case for him and Susie. But you learn, and maybe because Wasdin did learn, it's why his life eventually led him to Susie; and Susie to him.

"With Sharon, I got married for all the wrong reasons," he said, referring to her unexpected pregnancy and how he felt tricked into marrying her. "Our social lives were so different, our ethics were so different, and what we wanted out of life was so different. She was a spoiled little rich girl from the city and I was just a country boy. I learned from that that you need to know who you can trust and who you can't trust. I learned that character, truthfulness and trustworthiness are important qualities."

He thought Glenda, a good woman, would be the one, and for sure she was the ultimate coach's wife. But that didn't last, either.

"What I learned from that marriage is that you have to work on relationships and keep them growing, or you'll grow apart. It didn't help that we had different interests and different religions. But still, the lesson I learned there is that no matter how good of a person you're married to, if you don't work on that relationship, you're going to grow apart."

The fallout from that were Steve and Lori, who grew up without having their father around all the time. "I feel like they suffered because of that, which I take responsibility for," he said. "It bothered me when Glenda and I broke up, because I love those kids. We have a good relationship now, but when they were growing up it was not nearly as close. I loved having them visit me, but it's not the same as being with them every day."

And then there was Millie, whom he married during that time when both were old enough to have figured out some of the ways of the world, and how to make a nice living in it, yet young enough to work hard and still have enough energy left over to play hard.

"With Millie, I learned that when you marry someone with kids, you're married to those kids, too," he said. "Her job was also more important to her than her marriage. But I think the most important thing I learned is what it meant to be a stepparent."

Tom and Susie Wasdin during his retirement years.

It served him well. When Susie came along, the love of his life, he was prepared not only to be a better husband, but to be a better stepparent. Several years after he and Susie married, Tom even adopted Susie's son – Drew.

As he stood on his balcony, with Susie inside getting ready to go out to dinner, which is also one of Tom's favorite things to do, he reflected on their 27-year marriage, ruminating at how he's been together with Susie longer than his other three marriages combined.

"As you mature, you should gain patience," he said. "I think I'm better at accepting people for who they are. Nobody's perfect. I wanted the perfect wife, and there's no such thing. It took me three marriages to find that out. Now I have a wife in Susie that I'm enjoying growing old with, someone who takes care of me, and someone who is there when I need her, and even when I don't. I couldn't be happier."

In addition to his personal ups and downs, there are the ones he

Tom Wasdin's grandchildren through his son, Steve. Standing in the back from left to right: Elizabeth Wasdin, Steven Wasdin II. Front row from left to right: Kelsey Wasdin, Christine Wasdin, Staisha Wasdin, and their mother, Stacey Swinney.

Once a Coach, Always a Coach

A family photo taken at Tom and Susie Wasdin's condominium in Cocoa, Florida. Seated on the couch from left to right: Steve Wasdin, Susie Wasdin, Tom Wasdin, Lori Wasdin Stroh. Surrounding them along the back, from left to right: Christine Wasdin, Isabella Stroh, Hayden Stroh, Elizabeth Wasdin, Steven Wasdin II, Delaney Stroh, Kelsey Wasdin.

A family photo taken at the Porcher House in Cocoa Village, Florida From left to right: Susie Wasdin, Lindsay Wasdin holding granddaughter Samantha, Drew Wasdin holding grandson Brayden, Tom Wasdin.

encountered in business – which can often be personal, too. One of the things Wasdin learned through the years is that it's best not to enter into business with family. "You have a tendency to go easy on them," he said, "and let them slide a bit."

Sometimes you can do that with close friends, too. There probably wasn't a closer friend Wasdin had, in business or otherwise, than Rick Stottler. That someone came between their relationship and wrecked it – and probably wrecked Stottler, too – still pains Wasdin. To think that a friendship that started in the hallways of Cocoa Beach High, playing on the same basketball and softball teams together, with their families so close that Stottler named his daughter the same as Wasdin's daughter – Lori – and that that daughter still calls Wasdin her uncle ... that it could all end in an ugly lawsuit is a great pain to his soul.

Sure, Tom and Rick somewhat patched things up before Stottler died.

But still.

"I could've been more assertive with Rick and expressed my opinion a lot stronger earlier in life, and I should have," Wasdin said. "For his benefit and mine, I should have done that."

Sometimes, sadly, it takes the end of someone's life before you realize that you shouldn't let things get too far. In his later years, Wasdin realized that he let too many busy decades go by without staying in touch with so many people who meant so much to him – his former players. So he rallied, reconnecting with those special people and those special times. It meant a lot to him recently when Pembrook Burrows III and his wife sent Tom and Susie a card that said: "Pembrook and I love you guys."

"Many of my former players are like family to me," he said.

As he reconnected with so many of those former players, Wasdin often wondered about the twists and turns his life took, and all the *what ifs*?

What if his good friend Joe Williams had not asked him to come to Jacksonville University as his assistant coach? What if he had stayed at Cocoa Beach High and continued on this trek to one day become a public school principal? What if he had not worked so hard on the recruiting trail, tag-teaming with Joe Williams to convince Artis Gilmore to come to Jacksonville. Gilmore not only became the greatest player in JU sports history, but also a Naismith National Basketball Hall of Fame inductee.

"Artis – that's a game-changer, a life changer," Wasdin said. "He opened a lot of doors for me."

Wasdin never wanted to bother Gilmore when he was playing in the ABA and NBA; never wanted to be perceived as just another guy trying to nibble away at his time. But after Gilmore's pro career ended, the two men reignited their friendship and became closer than ever.

"I still wish, though," Wasdin said, "that we had stayed in contact all those years he was playing."

And then there is the big *what if?*

What if he had stayed in coaching?

Wasdin doesn't think about it much, but people do remind him of it often. He mentioned recently seeing legendary college basketball coach Cliff Ellis, who had successful stints at South Alabama, Clemson, Auburn and Coastal Carolina. A Florida native who coached high school ball at Niceville and Ocala during JU's remarkable run in the late '60s and early '70s, Ellis quizzed Wasdin in the same manner that so many others have done through the years.

"Why'd you get out of coaching?" Ellis asked. "Nobody understands why you got out when you were at the top of your game. We were all trying to get where you were at. You were there, and you left."

"I couldn't handle the pressure," Wasdin told Ellis. "If we lost, I took it as my fault. I was giving more of my life to basketball than I was getting out of it. It never ended. I could never turn it off. There was always one more phone call to make, one more recruiting trip to take. It was so high profile. Everyone could see your failures. In the business world, only your accountant knows how good or bad you're doing."

So he got out, and he has no regrets.

And though Wasdin didn't continue as a basketball coach, he never stopped coaching, or being called Coach. It was just that he ended up doing some of his life's best work in various, different arenas.

"I never planned for this end destination," he said. "But I'm very happy with where I am in my life. I've been successful, much more than I ever dreamed I'd be. But I did have a plan that I wanted to be successful and that I wanted to work hard. I strived to be better every year. And I wanted one day to enjoy my retirement."

Wasdin's friends along the Space Coast, around the state and nationally are many and varied – from the famous to the fairly unknown.

"I'm proud of my reputation and the friends I have," he said. "The things I achieved, I tried to do it the right way. I've never stolen or taken advantage of somebody. As I look back on my life, I have good friends, a good family, and I've had some wonderful times. I've always kept my relationship with God, too. I never strayed far from my upbringing at the Waldo Baptist Church. There were a few times in my life, when I was busy and not selecting the right priorities and use of my time, that I didn't attend as much as I should. But for the most part, I've made time to go to church and not let anything interfere with that."

Even when they're traveling, Tom and Susie go to great lengths to find a place of worship to attend on Sundays. It doesn't even have to be their denomination.

And they do like to travel.

There are some trips still to take; some that will help Wasdin empty a few more items from his bucket list. A good golfer, who shot a 77 when he was 76, he has played some of the world's best golf courses, like Doral, Hilton Head, the TPC at Sawgrass, as well as St. Andrews and Carnoustie in Scotland. He'd still like to play Pebble Beach in California and the Bethpage Black course in Long Island, NY.

He'd like to cruise the Panama Canal and the waters of Alaska. He's been to Fenway Park and old Yankee Stadium, and now he'd like to attend a game at Wrigley Field and the new Yankee Stadium. He's been to the Super Bowl and the Masters, but he would like to eventually see a World Series game.

"Mostly, though, I just want to be happy," he said. "My goal is to stay happy. I've always believed that you are responsible for what you are and who you are. If you're not happy, you need to try and change that."

Along those lines, there are things he would change in his life. But who wouldn't?

He is satisfied, though.

He knows now that he has more yesterdays than tomorrows, and Tom Wasdin is okay with that.

"I know I'm playing the back nine," he said, using a golf analogy, still standing on his balcony as evening gathered. "Even though I'm not playing it as well as I used to play it, I can still play it well enough to have a good time. I intend to do that."

WASDINISMS

Tom Wasdin's list of inspired words to live by; some of which were coined and others quoted from various sources.

- When you need a friend it's too late to make one.
- A friend tells you what you need to hear, not what you want to hear.
- Don't burn bridges, because a bad bridge is better than no bridge at all.
- Today is the first day of the rest of your life.
- Do something every day to improve your quality of life.
- Listening is greater than talking. You learn more from listening than talking.
- It is better for other people to brag on you, than for you to brag on yourself.
- Unify your strengths and improve your weaknesses.
- The best achievements are derived from planned, written goals.
- It is not who you know, but who knows you.
- You are the only one responsible for your happiness.
- Happiness is a state of the mind.
- Always do more than people expect from you. Never do less.
- Under-promise and over-produce.
- Plan for the worst and strive for the best.
- If you don't like or respect yourself, no one else will.
- Don't blame others for your mistakes.
- If you don't like your boss, fire him. Get another job.
- You get only one time to make a first impression.
- It's not how much influence you have; it's how much people think you have.
- The more you give, the more you receive.
- Respect other people's right to have their own opinion.
- Agree to disagree without being disagreeable.

- You will never be happy unless you learn to successfully deal with disappointment.
- Lead, follow, or get out of the way. All good leaders must sometimes follow.
- The older you get, the more important your friends and family become.
- You are what you are because of what you have experienced.
- It is better for a person to remain quiet and thought a fool, than to open your mouth and remove all doubts.
- Surround yourself with positive people you enjoy, admire, trust and respect.
- One thing you cannot count on is life itself.
- Perception, many times, is reality.
- Utilize people's strengths. Downplay their weaknesses.
- It is easy to point out problems, but it is more important to solve them.
- If you can't change something, don't waste your time worrying about it.
- It is more beneficial to receive a business card than to give one out.
- The most important thing to an elected official is to get re-elected.
- Listen to others. Their knowledge becomes your own.
- Turn mistakes into a learning experience.
- Be one of a kind, not one of many.
- Loyalty cannot be purchased.
- Align yourself with winners.
- Spend less than you make.
- You do not go broke when you make a profit.
- Get involved in politics.
- Have faith and never, never give up.
- Charge for things you need, not for things you want.
- Know what you know and get help from an expert if you do not know something.

WHAT THEY SAY ABOUT TOM WASDIN

EARLY YEARS 1935-58

Hugh Noe, Waldo High School Principal, Teacher, Basketball and Football Coach
"Thomas Wasdin was captain and quarterback of the Waldo High six-man football team that was ranked No. 2 in the nation. He set two national records in six-man football. He was an outstanding basketball player and set a state record in basketball that stood for years. If he had not gotten injured, he would have played basketball at the University of Florida. In my opinion, he was better than most of the players at Florida at that time. He was the best all-around athlete to come out of Waldo. I never had a moment of trouble out of Thomas as a player or student. He was a natural leader. I have enjoyed following his career as a coach and businessman."

PAXON SCHOOL YEARS 1958-63

Welcome Shearer Sr., Principal at Paxon Senior High School
"Coach Wasdin built our basketball program from an all-time low to an all-time high. We have never again had the success that we had under Tom's coaching. When Coach Wasdin left for Cocoa Beach, our school lost a great coach and Jacksonville lost a fine gentleman."

Steve Pajcic, Paxon player, Attorney and Democratic Candidate for Governor of Florida
"Tom Wasdin was my first coach, and became my coach for life. Along the many lessons Coach Wasdin taught me are: you can't just assume

the game will be fair, you have to work the refs; you get to the championship one game at a time; you build a winning program by what you do outside the gym; there is nothing more important than the game ... until it's over."

Gary Pajcic, Paxon player, FSU All-American Quarterback and Attorney

"Tom Wasdin makes me think of the old saying that you can wake up each day and decide to either be excited about life or bored by it. Tom was always excited and enthusiastic and it rubbed off on everyone around him, particularly his players who loved playing for him."

Ronnie Sellers, Paxon player, FSU All-American and Insurance Agent

"'Never give in. Never give in. Never, never, never, never – in nothing great or small, large or petty – never give in.' That's from Winston Churchill's commencement speech in 1941. Tom Wasdin's presence in my life not only instilled a 'never give in, never give up' attitude in sports, but also in life. Coach Tom saw his players not as athletes winning games, but as individuals developing and becoming prepared for the future. All of us who were fortunate to play for Tom Wasdin had our lives made richer through our association with him."

Dennis Womack, Paxon player and Virginia Baseball Coach

"I have coached young men at all levels for more than 30 years and if I have had any success, it is because of men like Coach Tom Wasdin. Coach Wasdin has always been a winner and he instilled those traits in his athletes – discipline, work ethic, sense of fair play and a burning desire to succeed. As you can see, I still call him Coach Wasdin, which, for me, is the supreme compliment of respect."

James "Spunk" Bryant, Paxon player and St. John County Commissioner

"Without Coach Wasdin, I would not be where I am today. He was a great influence on everyone that played for him at Paxon."

Gary Harrington, Paxon player and Managing General Agent for American National Insurance
"Coach Wasdin has been a driving influence on my life since grade school. He taught me that with determination and work, I could achieve any goal. Coach is the correct title for him. Because of his coaching and encouragement, not only myself but for so many of my classmates, we are a lot further along in life than we would have been. The highest tribute I can think of is leaving a legacy of positively impacting so many people, and that is exactly what Tom Wasdin, my Coach, has done."

COCOA BEACH HIGH SCHOOL YEARS 1964-1966

Mike Henry, Guard on CBHS basketball team of 1964
"It is unbelievable the great influence Coach Wasdin has had on all of us players who played on the 1964 CBHS basketball team. When we get together, we spend most of our time talking about Coach Wasdin and how he influenced our lives. What great memories."

JACKSONVILLE UNIVERSITY YEARS 1966-1973

Joe Williams, Head Basketball Coach at JU, Furman and FSU and former General Manager of WBCC
"In the sixties Tom Wasdin was arguably the best high school coach in the state of Florida. When I had the opportunity at Jacksonville University, I persuaded Tom to help build that program and the result was going from NAIA to a nationally ranked NCAA basketball program. The most fun thing about working with Tom was that if things didn't go well, we never blamed each other. We just tried to solve the problem and move ahead. Those were heady days of Sports Illustrated and national television coverage. But what has remained is a lasting and loyal friendship that I treasure greatly."

Hugh Durham, Head Basketball Coach at JU, FSU and Georgia
"Tom was instrumental in recruiting the player that put JU basketball on the nation's basketball map – Artis Gilmore. Everyone knew

he could recruit. However, he also showed when he became the head coach in 1971, that he was also a great coach. I voted for him as national coach of the year in 1973. He was one of the few visiting coaches that had a winning record against FSU at Tully Gym. He has the best career winning percentage of any basketball coach at JU."

Don Rutledge, Supervisor of Officials for the NBA and WNBA and former Freshmen Coach at JU
"Tom Wasdin is a good and true friend. Working with Tom in the stressful occupation of coaching college basketball, I found out his true character. Tom is an imaginative, unrelenting and extremely hard worker that has always given his best to the task at hand, and the people who worked with him. His loyalty to his friends and fellow workers was the best. When he told you something was going to happen, it happened."

Tommy Hazouri, Jacksonville Mayor and JU Alumni Director from 1968-71
"Tom is special. He not only is a great leader – he develops other leaders along the way."

Cliff Ellis, 1999 Associated Press National Coach of the Year
"As a high school coach in Ocala, Fla., I met Tom Wasdin while he was Jacksonville University's head basketball coach. I attended his clinics and watched his teams play. He always found time to spend with me and share his thoughts and wisdom about the game. He also introduced me to the legendary John Wooden, whom I became friends with from that time until his death. Tom is a dear friend, and his life has been an exciting journey filled with many adventures. I have learned much from this man, and his life story reflects his ability to be a great teacher, an innovator, a great salesman, and a person who has made a tremendously positive impact on others."

Peter Kerasotis

BREVARD COUNTY YEARS 1973-2001

Dave Spain, Owner of Cocoa Beach Comfort Inn and former Tourist Development Council member
"Without Tom's vision there would not be a Space Coast Sports Association, and without his drive it would not have happened."

Don Smith, University of New Orleans Head Basketball Coach and Athletic Director and Head Basketball Coach at Brevard Community College
"Tom has done more to help BCC athletics by giving his time and money than anyone else while I was there. The Faculty Endowed Chair and the Marathon Golf event are just two examples of the many things he has done to help our program. He was always there when I needed him. AAU sporting events would not have come to Brevard County without Tom's contacts and involvement as President of Florida AAU."

Bobby Dodd, National AAU President
"Tom Wasdin is the epitome of what is good in volunteer members of the AAU. He gives unselfishly of himself to benefit the young people of America and sincerely wants to be a positive influence in their lives. I can't say enough good things about Tom. He is a fine human being."

Rob Varley, Executive Director, Space Coast Tourist Development Council
"Tom Wasdin was the first TDC member to pop into my office when I first arrived on the Space Coast in 1994. He has been a wonderful mentor, leader and volunteer. I learned early on that to get things done, if I had Tom in my corner, he was able to open doors for me. I consider us a good team."

Ralph McMullen, Executive Director, Space Coast Tourist Development Council
"I had the privilege of working with Tom Wasdin as the first executive director of the Tourist Development Council. As a new council, we needed a dynamic leader to pull the tourism industry together. Tom more than fulfilled this role. He provided great ideas and he was also a

good listener. He was fair and brought out the best in people. In return, they responded by providing him with not only great support but also with their trust and confidence in his ability to get the job done. Once again, Tom proved to be a great team leader at a crucial time, and we who have been associated with him have certainly benefited from his leadership."

Robin Turner, President, Fair Management, Inc. and co-owner of Wonderworks and Magical Midway
"I highly value my personal and business relationship with Mr. Wasdin."

Heidi Brandow, President of Cocoa Beach Area Chamber of Commerce
"Tom Wasdin is a champion for Brevard County and is a man of action. He has helped many people along the way succeed at each activity that they take on. I'm proud to call him my friend."

Joe Matheny, Chairman of Canaveral Port Authority
"As a successful businessman and civic leader, Tom Wasdin has been an inspiration to the business community of Brevard County and the Central Florida region."

Judge Frank Pound
"He was brilliant on a basketball court and brilliant in business. Anything Tom Wasdin touches becomes a slam-dunk!"

Mary Schwager, Former Teacher and Employee
"Tom altered the course of my life by giving me challenges that were not easy to reach. As a result, I had to stretch and try harder. I respect Tom's ability to motivate others."

Al Schwager, Former Employee, Surveyor and Truck Driver
"Tom Wasdin is a genuine Number One. My relationship with Tom goes back to 1975-76 at the 3rd Century America, the NASA Bicentennial celebration. It has continued through a number of projects, and a partnership in a charter boat operation. Through all these events, Tom

has demonstrated a quality of leadership which mysteriously enables others to perform at levels above previous norms."

Gregory Burgey, General Manager Kennedy Point Yacht Club & Marina
"Tom Wasdin is the true meaning of a great boss. I have had the privilege to work for Mr. Tom Wasdin for almost three years and it has been the best experience of my life. Tom has done some wonderful things for not only the marina, but the community. The inspiration to start the junior sailing program in Titusville is truly remarkable. The program encourages young kids to participate in an activity and learn responsibility and teamwork. The program is a huge success and well-received in the area. I could go through many hours talking about the many successes he has guided me through. The inspiration he gives me is most satisfying. I truly consider it a privilege to work with Tom. Tom has a way of dealing with people that is also remarkable. He is always there to help. I have never seen someone so dedicated to helping the community where he lives and works."

William E. Starmer, former SSA President; President Starmer Ranaldi Planning & Architecture, Inc.
"Tom Wasdin the Mentor. I have known Tom for 20 years and in thinking back there are three distinctive characteristics of his that stick in my mind, which identify Tom as a leader, mentor and friend. The first is a unique ability to read people, assess their hidden talents and strengths, and then lead them to understand and use those talents and strengths to better themselves. The second is an uninhibited style of constructive criticism that once again allows his 'victim' to understand a weakness and learn to overcome it or turn it into a strength. The third is his ability to analyze multiple sides of a given situation, helping you to look at things with a difference perspective and leading you to make informed decisions. I guess that is why so many affectionately still refer to him as Coach."

Marguerita Engel, former Executive Director of Keep Brevard Beautiful
"Any organization that is privileged to have Tom Wasdin as a volunteer

is most fortunate. Tom believes in being a 'working Chairman or Board Member.' He doesn't just lend his name to the roster and occasionally attend the meetings; he actively participates above and beyond expectations. With him, it's a 100% commitment regardless of the number of boards on which he sits. Tom takes his obligations seriously and never fails to deliver when he takes on a project."

Bill Taylor, President and CEO, Community Bank of the South
"Over the years it has been an esteemed pleasure of having Tom Wasdin on our Board of Directors. He has a tenacity to instill wisdom and knowledge in others around him. I will never forget a very valuable message I have learned from him, 'When you need a friend, it is too late to make a friend.' This is a lesson I pass on to others on a regular basis. This truth is undeniable, for Tom has been extremely successful with raising great funds for many of the community's civic and charitable organizations."

FAMILY

Steve Wasdin, Son
"My father has a unique gift for leadership and encompasses the ability to provide a vision to a group, the relationship skills to work through inter-group issues as they arise, and the tenacity to fight through external barriers that stand in the way. When the goal is accomplished, he then displays the maturity to reward and recognize the accomplishments of others in reaching the goal. On a personal note, I am grateful for the role model my father has provided for me and for his grandchildren. While it is often negatively said that you do not choose your family, I can think of no one else whom I would have chosen to be my father."

Drew Wasdin, Son, Commercial Underwriter State Farm Insurance
"Dad had the greatest influence on my life, not only was he my father, but a coach, teacher, and the best friend I have ever had. He has always been there for me, as I would be for him. I love you, Dad."

Vern Thortsen, CBHS player, Brother-In-Law, Partner, Cocoa Village Group, LLC
"In 1964-1966, Tom Wasdin was my PE teacher, my assistant football coach, and my basketball coach. I went on to play college football at Georgia Tech where I was coached by Bobby Dodd, Bud Carson, and former NFL coach and network analyst Jerry Glanville. They were all great leaders, but none of them were respected by their players more than Coach Wasdin was by his players. Now 35 years later, Coach Wasdin is my brother-in-law, a business partner, and a friend. There is no one that I respect more than Coach Tom Wasdin."

Susie Wasdin, Wife and Best Friend
"My life has been so enriched because of my wonderful relationship with my husband and Coach. He has encouraged me and allowed me to become the best that I can be. Only he was able to give me the confidence to succeed in my business endeavors. He is truly a remarkable individual and I am so blessed to have the privilege of being Mrs. Wasdin. He couldn't have been a better father for my son, Drew. His kindness and generosity and willingness to help others never cease to amaze me. I am so thankful that I will be able to grow old with the most wonderful man in the world. Being a part of the Wasdin family has made my life complete."

Acknowledgements

Special thanks go to special people, not only for their editing skills, but also for their valuable feedback. Thank you Bob Harvey, Lori Mangiaracina, Bonnie King, John Harrison and Shelley Kerasotis. Thank you especially to Nick Wynne, for his yeoman's work with editing and also with the photos that appear in this book. Thank you to the dozens of people who were interviewed for this tome, and for how they allowed me to press the rewind button on their memories and prod them for the kinds of anecdotes and details that bring a life story to life. Thank you Yvette Gioia of Gioia Photography for providing the author photo and book cover design. And finally, this book would not have been as rich with details on Jacksonville University's basketball seasons in the late 1960's and early 1970's if not for the exhaustive research of Dick Pruet, and his generosity in sharing that information.

Peter Kerasotis
Merritt Island, Florida
February 22, 2014

I appreciate my family and friends, who encouraged me to have my life story written. More than anything, this book is for them. Thank you, too, to the many people who offered their memories and input. I also could not have found a better writer to have told my life story. I've not only been amazed at the talent of Peter Kerasotis, but also his dedication, patience, hard work, energy and the many tireless hours he put into this book project. Without him, it would not have been as successful, or as enjoyable.

Thomas Errol Wasdin
Cocoa, Florida
February 22, 2014

www.ingramcontent.com/pod-product-compliance
Lightning Source LLC
Chambersburg PA
CBHW031313160426
43196CB00007B/513